T0304922

MY FAMILY
AND OTHER
SEEDLINGS

Also by Lalage Snow

War Gardens: A Journey Through Conflict in Search of Calm

MY FAMILY AND OTHER SEEDLINGS

A Year on a Dorset Allotment

LALAGE SNOW

QUERCUS

First published in Great Britain in 2024 by

QUERCUS

Quercus Editions Ltd
Carmelite House
50 Victoria Embankment
London EC4Y 0DZ

An Hachette UK company

Copyright © Lalage Snow 2024

The moral right of Lalage Snow to
be identified as the author of this work has been
asserted in accordance with the Copyright,
Designs and Patents Act, 1988.

Excerpts from 'Burnt Norton' by TS Eliot on pp. vii and 345 taken from
Four Quartets by kind permission of Faber & Faber Ltd

All rights reserved. No part of this publication
may be reproduced or transmitted in any form
or by any means, electronic or mechanical,
including photocopy, recording, or any
information storage and retrieval system,
without permission in writing from the publisher.

A CIP catalogue record for this book is available
from the British Library

HB ISBN 978 1 52942 887 2
TPB ISBN 978 1 52942 888 9
Ebook ISBN 978 1 52942 890 2

Every effort has been made to contact copyright holders.
However, the publishers will be glad to rectify in future
editions any inadvertent omissions brought to their attention.

Illustrations by Jonathan Rider

Quercus Editions Ltd hereby exclude all liability to the extent
permitted by law for any errors or omissions in this book and for any loss,
damage or expense (whether direct or indirect) suffered by a
third party relying on any information contained in this book.

10 9 8 7 6 5 4 3 2 1

Typeset by CC Book Production
Printed and bound in Great Britain by Clays Ltd, Elcograf S.p.A.

Papers used by Quercus are from well-managed forests and other responsible sources.

To my own sweet seedlings Harry, Ottilie and Kit,
may your roots delve deep and your branches touch the sky.
And to J, the dearest and the best.

'If all time is eternally present
All time is unredeemable'

TS Eliot, 'Burnt Norton'

Contents

Prologue

The story of Britain can be told through its allotments and their popularity and as events of the twenty-first century snowballed the demand for these small, at times unkempt, patches of land surged. A pandemic, war on the fringes of Europe, rising fuel and food prices, a housing shortage and a climate crisis are just some of the issues and it is clear that the story of Britain and its allotments is far from over. But I didn't know any of this when I first made inquiries about the overgrown allotment plots on the edge of my village in Dorset.

To be honest I had never thought much about growing vegetables or allotments until 2014 when I photographed and interviewed people living on the fringes and frontlines of the then nascent war in eastern Ukraine as a photojournalist. In the besieged city of Donetsk food imports had dwindled and supermarket shelves were empty. With nowhere to flee to and no end to the conflict in sight, people turned to their gardens for help. Out came the rudbeckia and roses, in went the lettuces and cabbages. Up came the ornamental borders and down went the potatoes, beets and carrots. Begonias were gone while soldier-straight leeks and garlic punched through the ground.

So when I heard that there were a few plots free on the allotment site in our village it seemed like as good a time as any to try my hand at self-sufficiency, stave off the effects of soaring food prices and lack of supermarket varieties, all while occupying my children's tiny minds with something a bit different. We would be helping to reduce our overall carbon footprint, filling our lungs with fresh air and be out of our small and increasingly cramped cottage as much as possible.

The elephant in the room being that I had never attempted to grow much beyond spinach before and am notoriously cavalier with regards to tending plants.

This would have to change and while I planted and propagated and learned 'on the grow', I researched the provenance of the vegetables themselves and how they came to be domesticated, discovering two origins: the Fertile Crescent and Mesoamerica. I discovered that the way in which the wild seeds and subsequent fruits and vegetables tens of thousands of years ago came to be as ordinary a part of our lives as soap and water and oft found shrivelled in the bottom of a fridge drawer is a history of global trade and exploration. The corroborating historical source texts, I was delighted to find, lead to the acquaintance of one or two old friends including Pliny the Elder whose writings on the natural world sent me down a few rabbit holes of research.

I also made some new friends along the way delving into taxonomy and the history of botanical illustrations and experimenting with vegetables I had never grown before. The other plot holders I met gradually over the course of the year confirmed my suspicion that gardeners – in this case vegetable gardeners – are generally very nice people with generous spirits, can-do attitudes and strong arms. While the conflict rumbled on in the east and I heard its siren call, my children Harry, Ottilie and Kit, with their own unique ways of observing the world, kept me grounded on our allotment on the fringes of the village and far from the fringes of war. They taught me to look closely at the ground beneath our feet – for there is life there so long as you give it time.

Dorset, 2023

March

New beginnings, old endings – Planning – The allotment
image – Why grow your own – A history of enclosures –
Ground preparation – The kitchen as a garden – A history
of spinach – OS allotments – The birth of the allotment –
Poo, pox and a gift of strawberries – Reflections on
Ukraine – First germinations

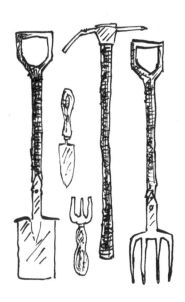

'It's yours if you want it.' The gamekeeper's wife was frowning at the patch of overgrown grass and dandelions. Last year's beans, all dried and shrivelled, still hung from some canes but another row of bamboo stakes, overwhelmed with the weight of an unpicked harvest, lay entangled in the long grass. Beyond them was a weedy mound of garden detritus including, as far as I could tell, a rusting fireguard, a reel of steel wire, some rotted-down wood and a tyre. A small area enclosed by net was behind me but was so covered with dandelions neither she nor I could hazard a guess as to what might have once grown there. And next to that, almost entirely obscured by the long couch grass, were the remains of a cold frame; panes of glass greening rapidly with algae and slime.

The gamekeeper's wife went on to say that the allotment had until last year been worked by the landlord and proprietor of the pub at the end of the village. 'So it won't be as hard as some of the others to make right.' She glanced at the remaining allotments which up until that moment had been doing a pretty good job of masquerading as scrubland. 'I mean,' she said, 'with all this space you'll have no need to buy any fruit or veg again.'

An image of balmy afternoons spent here with Harry and Ottilie, two of my three children then aged three and two, flashed before me. We would harvest carrots and radishes, pick lettuce leaves and water beans and sweet peas amid clouds of butterflies while six-month-old baby Kit gurgled contentedly in his pram marvelling at the sights, sounds and smells of nature's cinema.

There was another image hovering close by. That of the failed attempts at 'growing our own' since we first moved here four years ago: scorched and parched greens, crops gone to seed, leaves beset by bugs or blight or mice or slugs or all of the above, during one tragic summer. The rampaging, delinquent blackbird, bean supports toppled by storms, peas eaten by the dog not to mention the dead rat I found in the greenhouse or the annual parade of seedlings trampled by staggering toddler feet. I was not exactly a natural gardener.

But I have an inherited interest in gardening and growing thanks to a green-fingered mother and an award-winning garden designer brother and, despite not having the necessary skills or knowledge, was determined to make good this time. Besides, with an allotment everything would be different; we would make meals from this patch of land and preserve anything surplus for the winter. We would have rosy cheeks and skin made golden by the sun. We would wear dungarees and straw hats and be so very happy and at one with nature. Maybe the children would even like eating vegetables if they grew their own and perhaps we'd even get a beehive! J, my husband, would LOVE that.

The cold March wind blew and I shivered. The gamekeeper's wife was saying something about the parish council having a meeting about digging up the whole lot and starting again. 'But they say that every time we meet.' She rolled her eyes. 'So? Twenty quid for the year?'

A buzzard hovered overhead and the bruised clouds threatened rain. An army helicopter shuddered somewhere. The gamekeeper's wife coughed and tried not to look cold.

All over the world doom and gloom pervaded, I thought, staring at the frozen earth: war in eastern Europe, totalitarian regimes in power, refugees, climate change, pandemics, fire, famine, flood. The daily clutter which seeps into every waking moment of our lives thanks to rolling, scrolling news. But in this small piece of land perhaps there would be a stillness and a quietness which would turn the other cheek to the whirling chaos all around us. This slice of the planet beneath my feet would be indifferent to it all and committed to the future.

'All right,' I said with the sort of spontaneity usually reserved for the duty-free luxury beauty counter in airports or bijoux shops in bijoux countries where the currency exchange feels abstract. 'I'll bloody take it.'

'Great,' the gamekeeper's wife said and turned quickly on her heel. 'Put the cash in the letter box when you can.'

When she left I picked my way over the Somme-scape of the allotment and allowed my mind to drift into those honey-coloured afternoons of the forthcoming summer. As I walked, the ground beneath me felt even more solid and stubborn than it looked.

Shit.

Who was I kidding? I barely had enough time to shower these days, let alone engage in anything other than crowd controlling

9

various small children and making sure everyone was alive at the end of the day.

But at least the bean canes looked pretty sturdy. I nudged one with my foot and it collapsed.

What have I done, I thought to myself as the first spots of ice-cold rain began wetting my hair. And what am I even doing here?

Not so long ago Afghanistan had been my home. Working there largely as a freelance photojournalist and correspondent I lived in a villa-style house in a middle-class neighbourhood of Kabul with a garden tended to by a guard.

Life was not, for the expats living there, much of a daily struggle. Despite the attacks and security threats, we lived pretty hedonistically. There were tennis matches at the International Club, dinners in the expat restaurants followed by parties, after-parties and after-after-parties that flowed into the next day. There were film screenings and craft classes, Kabul-opoly (Monopoly) tournaments and Boggle nights, and an endless quest to sweet-talk embassy, United Nations or World Bank contacts into giving us access to cheap alcohol.

The friendships forged there remain some of the strongest to date. I even met J, an Englishman with an aversion to London and a deep love of the countryside. Although it was many years of friendship before we became a couple, amid the dust of Kabul we shared a nostalgia for something green and pleasant which we – along with other homesick expatriates – used to watch on box sets including *Jeeves and Wooster*, *Brideshead Revisited* and *Downton Abbey*.

This was a fetishised England of rolling hills and drystone walls, of open spaces and a green and pleasant land. Not a housing development, shopping mall or trading estate in sight and although we all knew it was a fantasy it was the place we called home and it was the home we idealised and lusted for.

In the darker days of life in Kabul (there were some – it wasn't all boozy parties and an adult adolescence) I used to read and reread 'The Lake Isle of Innisfree' which William Butler Yeats composed when homesick for Ireland in London. He conjures up a bucolic arcadia of 'nine-bean rows' and 'bee-loud glades' where the linnets thrived and where he was at peace. When things became difficult I yearned for a slice of that peace; those nine-bean rows and bee-loud glades seemed to call me home.

When J, Pullo (a rescue dog he had taken in as a puppy in Kabul) and I moved to a tiny cottage in the middle of a hamstone village with a summer fete of sheep racing and hay bales, a church roof appeal, a red telephone box, an old-fashioned pub, and a stream trickling through one end of it which hosted the annual duck race, we thought we had found a slice of old England. Friends visiting often remarked on how 'old England' it felt, how different the place we chose to be home seemed from the rest of the country. That Dorset still doesn't have a motorway is testimony to the pace of life here.

But when the novelty had worn thin it was hard not to miss the majesty and other-worldliness of Kabul. Or rather, it was hard not to miss the nether-worldliness of the Kabul we inhabited as young, free and independent adventurers. In a cruel twist, the nostalgia which induced a yearning for England turned on its head and instead produced a yearning for the freedom, the thrill, the chaos and the hedonism of that other life.

And now, four years and three children later, and despite Afghanistan having fallen to the Taliban, occasionally, just very occasionally, when the children are being difficult or I am stuck behind a tractor and late, or I am fatigued beyond comprehension or simply bored out of my tiny mind, I miss the place we used to call home.

Refugees returning to Afghanistan after the fall of the Taliban in the early 2000s would often plant a tree as a symbol of putting down roots and a fruitful future. Maybe an allotment would reignite a sense of rootedness and instil a love for rural England while giving me a purpose beyond the day-to-day; with rising living costs, climate change and food miles and worries over pesticides it felt continuously frivolous to be buying vegetables in supermarkets which would be just as cheap and easy to grow. And more organic. Perhaps through my own growing and nurturing I too would feel more connected to this new home of ours.

'I give it two weeks,' J said when I told him what I'd done.

'Why? Shhhhhhh.' Kit was mewling in my arms.

J looked at him and raised an eyebrow. He shook his head and sighed. 'Well don't come crying to me when you "Lally" yourself with exhaustion. I love you but this is on you. Besides, we already have a garden. If you're looking for some peace and quiet wouldn't that suffice? Anyway, aren't allotments for people with no gardens?'

Kit wailed.

'Shhhhh,' I said to Kit, 'he doesn't mean it.' To J I said, 'Shhhhh. It will be fun. You'll see.'

He rolled his eyes, grabbed a handful of chocolate digestives and retreated to his office on the other side of the garage. 'Just don't do anything stupid like getting a beehive.'

J was right, however. We *did* have a garden, and one that was already threatening to overwhelm us. In the warm summer months it was an extension of the house and we practically lived outside. But the problem is that in a garden you can mooch around changing things whenever you feel like it or whenever fashion dictates. A herbaceous border here, a box hedge there, an apple tree over in the corner. A garden is a thing of aestheticism and I wasn't very good at it. I didn't then understand how things grew and why and nor did I understand how to make things work together, above and below ground.

An allotment is the opposite of a garden, if you like. It is practical, no-frills and functional. With an allotment you don't need to worry about whether the peony and the rose will agree with the lavender, whether the nepeta will be overcrowded by spring tête-à-tête leaf dieback. Nor need you worry about the rampant ivy or the rapacious buddleia which appear from nowhere. An allotment is there for one reason and one reason only: for growing your own veg. At least, that was my understanding of it in those early days.

It didn't have to look pretty or elegant. Indeed, think of allotments and the very opposite of pretty usually comes into your mind; edgeland sites which tend to be home to run-down corrugated iron sheds, makeshift planters and a make-do-and-mend aesthetic. This pragmatism appealed to me. I could garden, feed my family and save money, I could try growing veg I'd never grown before and teach my children about where food comes from without worrying about how it looked. Anything else would be a bonus.

But there was another reason why I popped a twenty-pound note in the gamekeeper's wife's letter box a few days later. Since we moved here I had walked past the plots almost daily and wondered about them. Sometimes I would see a figure hunched over weeding or watering but in recent years I hardly saw anyone. It seemed to me that no one else in the village was making use of the plots bar the barrister and the vet. The allotments looked dejected, wasted and forgotten, grasses overwhelming what was once a productive site. In those cold March days when winter seemed reluctant to let go and I was searching and scanning for signs of renewal, they cried out to be used again.

'Are you sure it's wise, darling?' my mother said. I had popped over to my parents' house, a fifteen-minute drive away, to borrow my father's mattock and a spade. Having located both in a pile of garden tools in the shed, and having failed to squeeze them into the boot with the folded-up pushchair, I was now trying unsuccessfully to wedge them between two car seats in my very small and dented car. Harry and Ottilie were already strapped in and I was trying my hardest not to wake up Kit who was asleep in his chair on the front seat.

'Of course it is,' I said. 'It makes perfect sense, if you think about it. Something to do with the children over the summer. Isn't that right, Harry? Ott?'

'Lotment's very muddy,' Harry said earnestly.

'Lotment,' Ottilie said. 'Mud. Yucky yuck.' Harry giggled.

I swore at the mattock and then again at the spade when a splinter sliced into my finger.

'It's just that,' my mother said and then stopped to choose her words carefully. 'You have a lot on your plate right now, and this might be . . .'

'I'm hungry, Mummy,' Harry yelled. 'Is it time for lunch?'

'Yes, darling,' I said and tried to remember if we had anything in the fridge or if I'd have to stop at the petrol station for emergency sausage rolls.

'Here, take this.' My mother handed me the latest Royal Horticultural Society (RHS) magazine *The Garden* with advice for vegetable gardeners. 'And just don't take on too much . . .'

'I'm fine. I'm absolutely fine,' and I crunched into gear, spade wedged between my legs, mattock head sticking out of the window.

My mother-in-law is typing . . .

'Of course you'll need to plan the whole thing.' A keen and knowledgeable gardener, I had asked enthusiastically for some top tips.

I wrote:

'Yes of course,' and scratched my head.

My mother-in-law is typing . . .

'Would you like some raspberry bushes? They tend to do very well on allotments.'

This was news to me. But before I could reply . . .

My mother-in-law is typing . . .

'Just go for it! You've got your work cut out, but don't forget to plan, plan, plan!'

I don't think I've ever planned anything in my life; I've always just sort of winged it and hoped that no one ever found out. And anyway, I thought. You can't plan nature; you've got to let it happen.

Which of course is entirely the wrong approach to take because what is gardening – vegetable, flower or otherwise – if not an attempt to tame nature? To garden is to make something do what you want it to do: a bulb to flower here, a rose to climb there, a tree to shade that patch of grass over there. To garden vegetables is to make the plant do exactly what it is supposed to do at your bidding and according to your schedule.

I thought about this as I pottered around the garden at home picking up the detritus of the day and noticing the tulips punching through the ground. Since writing, photographing and interviewing hundreds of civilians who used gardening as a means of surviving conflict for my photojournalistic project and first book, *War Gardens*, I had learned that no matter how big or little or humble or grand a garden is, gardening is about committing to the future no matter what the present is. Our present when I'd planted those tulip bulbs with Harry was me, heavily pregnant with Kit and aghast at the continued unfurling of horror in Afghanistan, J on a work trip in Central Asia and Ottilie run into the ground with a fever. But here we were four and a half months later with the leaves spearing their way to spring from the depths of winter.

I waved at J who was in his wood workshop nursing a whisky with a thousand-yard stare after a family trip to the allotment which I had promised would be a wholesome and lovely thing. As our weekends seemed to be mostly comprised of divvying up childcare and trying to remember that WEEKENDS WITH THREE CHILDREN UNDER FOUR ARE FUN AND NOT AT ALL HELLISH AND HARD WORK we had set off after lunch with a spring in our step, spades in hand.

'So what is your vision, Lal?' J had asked once Harry and Ottilie had been neutralised on tufts of grass with rice cakes and he had taken in the sheer size of the hundred square metres or so of scrubby couch grass pretending to be an allotment.

'Ummmm, I'm not really sure. It's a blank canvas. I think some beds here and here. I'd waved my hand. 'And the bean canes, obviously,' I said. 'I'll grow beans on those.'

'You and your nine-bean rows,' he said.

I'd picked up one of the broken bean canes from the grass, snapped it into four pieces and staked out a long, thin bed of five-ish by two-ish metres. 'And maybe another there. And there. And maybe one more there.' I pointed. 'And a fruit cage. And maybe a bit of meadow there. For wildlife. What do you think?'

J had sucked his teeth. 'I think you've got your work cut out. And what exactly are you going to plant?'

I hadn't thought about that yet but tried to sound blasé. 'You know. The usual. Spinach. Chard. Some flowers. Some other sort of vegetables. Maybe some courgettes. That sort of thing.'

While I had paced up and down, J took the children to the swings. I'd tried to imagine what it could look like. But I could not. Monty Don makes it look effortless on *Gardeners' World*. Effortless it is not. My muscles already ached with exertion, my head spun with decisions.

Time, it appears, expands and contracts quite differently depending on the task in hand. Twenty minutes in a plant's growth is barely visible, in a garden it is hardly enough time to pull one's gloves on and set to work. But when it comes to childcare, twenty minutes can be interminable and before I had staked out a second bed, J returned to the plot looking haggard with the children snotty-nosed at his heels.

When we had put them all to bed he poured himself a whisky and me a glass of whatever was in the fridge. He retreated to his workshop in the garage, ostensibly to make yet another longbow, while I pottered before sitting down to draw up my plan. It was simple. Three horizontal rectangles denoting the soon-to-be dug beds labelled as follows; raspberries, beans, veg and flowers. So simple.

I sent it to my mother-in-law and awaited praise. 'Plan, plan, plan,' she had said.

She replied immediately with a '🫠'.

Oh.

Think of an allotment and an image will come to mind: a scraggly rectangular plot of land surrounded by similarly unkempt swatches of vegetation, homemade huts and broken fences or bonfires and compost heaps next to rows of overgrown beans, cabbages and carrots. These are the communal places which sit at the edges of cities and towns on the scraps of land so derelict that nobody else wants them or on the spaces too awkward or small to be of any real agricultural, commercial or building development use. These houseless gardens have existed at the edges of our world on the fringes of the slightly dodgy areas between car parks and railways, next to motorways, power stations and factories or in the floodplains of rivers to be glimpsed from the comfort of a car or a window seat on the 7.36 to Paddington or King's Cross.

Think of an allotment and a vision of a solitary, scruffy man of a certain age sporting a cloth cap tying beans to poles or bent over a row of produce might come to mind. With hands as worn as the hobnailed boots on his feet his world is one of thriftiness and tools, seed trays and prized vegetables and making do and mending while unwinding from the day or escaping a nagging wife. In this age of hyper-connectivity and fast food, fast news, fast delivery, fast everything all at the touch of a screen such a figure is a dying breed for if allotments sit on the edge of the unwanted space, the allotmenter, with one foot in the past and one in the present, does too.

But, having been part of our landscape for over two hundred years, allotments and by default allotmenters tell the story of Britain, as I was to find out. And as events of the twenty-first century spiralled, the demand for allotments surged. The story was far from over.

It was only when my garden designer brother paid a visit from London that I realised how lucky I had been to snap up a plot.

After I had picked his brains about a particularly dead-looking tree in the garden J was convinced was still alive, and after Ottilie had shown him her soggy rice cake, and after Kit had gurgled and Harry had shown him his new pirate ship ad nauseam, we all trotted down to the allotment.

'So which one is it?' He gazed at the scrubland.

I pointed at the bean canes. 'Oh,' he said. 'A nice little plot.'

Realising he had been looking at a third of the whole area I shook my head. 'No.' I pointed. 'It's from that fence to that fence. All of it.'

His eyes bulged with a combined look of envy, pity and awe. 'All of that? For twenty quid a month?'

I grinned. 'A year.'

He was silent and surveyed the surroundings. The village was looking particularly lovely and very much the idyll of the quintessential countryside with pretty hamstone cottages sitting contentedly in a pale sun. In the distance cows idled their way between fields, moos catching on a breeze. The church bells rang the hour and a cockerel crowed loudly nearby.

'God you're lucky living here,' my brother said. 'No police sirens or pollution. And all this.'

We *were* lucky and I would often pinch myself just to check it was all real. In London, my brother explained as we paced up and down challenging the children to find the longest worm and the smallest snail, he had been trying to get an allotment for years and was on several waiting lists – some as lengthy as fourteen years – for a fraction of the size of my plot. 'And these are all going begging?'

'Most of them.' I had yet to see anyone else down there.

'It's ridiculous,' my brother said. 'Here we are with food prices going berserk. We should all be growing our own.' Finding a few dried beans on the ground he gave me one. 'Start Harry off with this,' he said before absent-mindedly dropping the rest of the pod in the long grass.

Pocketing the bean, I told him about the dacha gardens I had visited in Ukraine when I went to Donetsk in search of the guns and roses of a war in its infancy. As a jaded photojournalist covering conflict some ten years ago I had begun a personal project looking at renarrating current conflicts through the eyes of those living them, and gardening as a means of escape or survival. As the antithesis of war, photographing gardening and gardeners was my way of turning the traditional idea of war photography on its head.

And when I heard that the eastern Ukrainian city of Donetsk was famed for its roses – in the 1970s one rose bush was planted for each member of the population – I simply had to go and see for myself what was going on.

What I found was a country of nascent gardeners. As inhabitants of a former breadbasket of the Soviet Union, Ukrainians have always had a strong relationship with the earth and many families used to have their own dacha. Originally small countryside second homes primarily used as weekend retreats, dachas came into their own when the centrally administered Soviet government failed to supply enough fresh food for the population. The country saw an increase of subsistence gardening with surplus produce sold at the sides of roads, further supplementing household incomes. With the collapse of the Soviet Union in the 1990s this way of living off the land became superfluous. Supermarkets and markets were stocked with cheap imported goods and dacha life became more of a hobby than a necessity and many families sold off their dachas and committed to modern urban living.

In 2014, when the air, rail and road routes in and out of Donetsk became choked up with conflict between Russian-backed separatists and the Ukrainian army, these foreign imports dried up. Shelves were empty, shops were boarded up, and those who could, left the city for places like Odessa or Mariupol.

Those who had nowhere to which they could escape returned to the old ways of living and subsistence growing and the garden regained popularity and usefulness.

'Maybe the same will happen to us,' I said hopefully.

My brother shook his head, bewildered. 'We are far too reliant on supermarket conveniences.'

He was right. The United Kingdom is heavily dependent on imports for its fruit and veg. It is estimated we import over 43 per cent of our vegetables and a whopping 85 per cent of our fruit. We are so reliant on these imports now that we even import over 60 per cent of the apples we eat despite having the perfect climate for growing them. There are some things like bananas that we can't grow easily here but beans, peas and carrots, well, they do well here and have been gracing the pages of cookery books since cookery books began. Worse still, the majority of our imports hail from increasingly climate-vulnerable countries including those in southern Europe and Morocco and Kenya, all of which are on the brink of their own food crisis – be it drought, flood or blight. I wouldn't mind SO much if the fruit and vegetables were seasonal but they aren't. Strawberries in November and apples in July are so commonplace that we are disgruntled if we can't find what we want, when we want it.

And then we throw it away. According to the climate action charity WRAP, daily we bin 20 million slices of bread, 4.4 million spuds, 1.2 million tomatoes and just under a million bananas. This equates to around 26 million quid straight in the bin – or £60 a month for an average family with children.[1] It is estimated that over a third of us don't even remember what we buy in the weekly shop.

Somehow we have lost touch with where food comes from and, worse, we don't seem to care. The food system is no longer simply a means of sustenance. It is one of the most successful, most innovative and most destructive industries on earth and diet-related disease is now the biggest cause of preventable illness and death in the developed world, which makes it worse than smoking.[2]

We in Britain had a glimmer of what life would be like with little imported produce during the strict Covid lockdowns of 2020–21. Not only did we have to queue outside shops, once inside fresh produce was often strictly rationed or not available at all. And post pandemic we saw similar supply chain disruption due to poor crops, inclement weather conditions and the soaring cost of fertiliser, energy and seeds in part due to the ongoing war in Ukraine and the economic effects of Brexit. The headline-grabbing tomato shortage of early 2023 goes to show how vulnerable this food supply chain really is.

And how ludicrous it is too. Why do we even have tomatoes in February? Because we can. If we import them.

'We should be rationed and made to grow,' my brother said only half joking. 'Might sort out the obesity crisis too.'

I said that perhaps no one has the time any more to tend to their vegetables and with eagerness showed him my plan. As a designer I was sure he would understand my vision.

He paused, commented politely on the number of raspberries I'd planned to cultivate and handed it back to me. 'Well. You've certainly got your work cut out.'

'I do wish people would stop saying that,' I said. It seemed to be the only thing anyone had to say about the idea of me taking this allotment on.

Even the pub landlord, and former holder of this plot, was surprised when I popped my head around the door a few days later and told him not to bother taking away the bean frames. 'There's no bindweed,' he said kindly, 'but you'd best make a start before the weeds set in properly. It was too much for me to do every day and I didn't have young children. You've got your work cut out!' he added.

My brother said now, 'Look. It's possible. But just make sure you prepare the ground properly. Manure, manure, manure.' I nodded and pretended I knew what he was talking about. Gardeners always bang on about manure but surely the ground is the ground. Dig it, plant some seeds, water it. End of. It took me a long time to understand the importance of manure. To really, really understand it.

Later that afternoon, when Harry and Ottilie were at nursery and I had tidied away the pirate ship and flower pot full of earthworms which had magically found itself into their bedroom, I strapped Kit to me and wandered back down to the allotment to do some gentle hard labour with the mattock. Inevitably, Kit did not want to be put down on the ground – even the softest grassy tufts proved to be too cold and miserable for him – and so, unable to labour, I sat on an upturned bucket bouncing him on my knee and thinking about those gardeners in Ukraine who had turned their flower beds into veg beds in a bid to survive.

I cooed to Kit, 'And what will things look like when you are grown up? What will be the anxiety of your age? What will you hope for?'

Kit smiled and gurgled.

And then he vomited.

There is a painting hanging in London's National Gallery by Sir Thomas Gainsborough completed in around 1750. It depicts Mr and Mrs Andrews, a young country couple positioned to the left of the canvas, he with a shotgun slung over one arm and dog at his heels, she poised and elegant in blue on a bench beneath an old oak tree on the edge of parkland overlooking their estate. In the distance there are church spires and the suggestion of quiet villages but for the most part it is the landscape spread out under a bruised sky which dominates the rest of the canvas, so much so that many scholars suggest it is a portrait of land as much as of the couple. Mr Andrews, a man dedicated to farming, owned nearly three thousand acres. And here it is: a vast swathe of fields and oak trees young and old. There are horses grazing on the left-hand side and on the right, just next to the couple, there is a newly harvested strip of corn that feels so real you can almost smell the sweet, dusty straw and damp grasses. It is sun-kissed and light, green and soft. So far, so Gainsborough (one of the leading portrait painters of his time, he is well known for his inclination for landscapes and rustic arcadia). It is England entirely. It is also the past, present and future of England for in the middle distance of the landscape and to the left of the couple there are two enclosed areas.

The year 1750 saw the beginning of a seismic change in England.

It was growing. Or rather, its population was; between 1500 and 1700 it had more than doubled from 2 million to 5 million. By 1800 it would be 16.5 million. With this swelling population, mass starvation was forecast and suddenly land and how it was used became a commodity.

Most of the country was operating on an open field system of farming which allowed access to villagers for grazing animals and growing a selection of crops in fields several hundred acres in size which were divided into cultivated or farmed strips – as seen in Gainsborough's landscape. The key benefit to open field farming on common land was that it was a collective activity – everyone had to agree on when and how things were done from sowing seeds to putting cattle out to pasture. Harvests and produce were also shared and often traded. Even a man with just one cow or a few geese was unlikely to starve. When it worked well, most people had enough to subsist and families could keep themselves afloat with a mixture of common land farming, collecting wood (they were allowed to take any branches they could reach with a billhook or shepherd's crook, giving us today's saying of 'by hook or by crook') and wool and basket weaving.

Enclosing land had been taking place since the Tudors (who did so for sheep – wool being a valuable commodity worldwide) but by the eighteenth century demand for land to feed the population – and lots of it – outstripped supply. With arable farming now lucrative (the price of wool had increased sixfold and demand from urban centres for meat and dairy products had also increased), there were fortunes to be made. The inclusion of two such enclosures in the painting of

Mr and Mrs Andrews is a nod to their resultant acquired wealth. They were not alone. Between 1750 and 1850 around four thousand Enclosure Acts were passed in parliament forcing common land up and down the country to be parcelled off for exclusive use.

We have these Acts to thank for the way most of the country looks today. That is, hawthorn and hazel hedges fencing in fields. It is hard to find an image of what pre-enclosure England looked like but Gainsborough's works give a pretty good indication of the effect the Parliamentary Enclosure Acts were having on the landscape.

Enclosures remain a thorny issue. For some, they underpinned the ecological and agricultural progression of modern Britain. This was, after all, an age of enlightenment and this new style of land management was seen as progressive. Boggy wastelands were drastically improved and thanks to regeneration and crop rotation, soil was made more fertile. For others, it was land theft which impoverished the many for the sake of the few. Either way, the change the reforms had on the landscape is undeniable. Those strips of farmed land in the open fields were sealed off and made private. A patchwork of neat squares and rectangles – like Mr Andrews' sheep field – replaced the open fields and its 'green and pleasant' wilds. And the effect on the rural poor was devastating.

A pretty grim version of England emerges. Villagers became waged agricultural workers solely dependent on their labour for income with no social protection and vulnerable to economic fluctuations. Combined with the advent of mechanised farming further eroding the need for labourers at all and mass unemployment, it is an England which marches straight towards the Victorian workhouses.

The Northamptonshire poet John Clare took a long look at this new countryside and was deeply disturbed.

Fence now meets fence in owners' little bounds
Of field and meadow large as garden grounds
In little parcels little minds to please
With men and flocks imprisoned ill at ease

'The Mores', written 1812–1831

What hope did the rural poor have?

I was desperate to make a start on the digging on the plot one morning. My method was a simple one. Using the mattock, scalp off the first few inches of grass and weeds, discard said scalp onto other bit of plot, loosen up the soil beneath and then spread some manure.

The wind was cold and Ottie who, without Harry (he was at nursery) and to whom she was devoted, was lost. 'Haaaaaiiii,' she kept calling before falling on her bottom and crying which prompted Kit, hungry or cold or both, to follow suit. When the church bell ringers started their weekly cacophonous practice the children's cries were even more anguished and I had no choice but to abandon the plot, carrying one child on my hip, one in the sling and pulling the mattock behind me, concrete scraping on metal.

This was to be the first of countless aborted digging missions. Indeed, after a week of not being able to get to work it dawned on me that maybe this whole endeavour was foolish. There was simply no time.

Double digging, which is what I thought I had been doing but in hindsight was really not, is a traditional labour-intensive way of turning soil over. You dig a trench one spade deep and then another and another and another and fill each trench with the soil from the previous trench.

There are of course other methods of working the land. I could have made raised beds, for example, with treated timber and sacks of compost and manure, the advantages here being weed management and drainage and the disadvantages being the huge cost.

Others don't dig at all. A no-dig veg bed involves spreading compost or well-rotted manure onto a weed-free soil surface. This is supposed to emulate the natural process of decomposition allowing the plants, fungi and organisms to bring the organic matter into the soil itself and not the spade. The reported benefits are that the soil's ecosystem is untouched which in turn yields more and bigger vegetables. The major benefit is obvious. Not having to dig.

But I didn't know any of this when I started out. So I stuck to the idea of digging like a true allotmenter as wet soil clods to a boot. And anyway it would have felt like cheating not to dig.

Having ordered twelve bags of manure from a farmer bloke my father knew, I managed to snatch a ten-minute session of digging – or rather, scalping one afternoon. I was delighted and invigorated to have broken the seal, so to speak. But my joy was short-lived: children and chickenpox. Cooped up with no respite and with rain lashing at the window for days I could do nothing but nurse, comfort, administer creams and antibiotics and just hope that spring would be late this year.

When, four or five days later, Harry was at last marginally less contagious I took everyone to the garden centre to buy seeds and to delight in the perma-spring of its shelves of plants already in flower and ready to bed in. In those displays there was the future and, beneath a leaden sky, there was colour. I got rather carried away. So much so that in addition to spinach, chard and tomato seeds, I splashed out on poppy, cosmos and ammi, envisaging our house full of these blousy bloomers all summer long.

The result of this sent J into a mild rampage. I was just minding my own business having that particular day finished digging ten square metres on the plot and frowning down at my allotment plan (which had progressed little beyond its first incarnation) and the RHS magazine my mother had given me, when I heard from the kitchen a clattering of pots and pans and then some swearing.

'How long till we get our kitchen back, Lals?' he asked when I appeared at the door.

'What do you mean?'

He pointed at the windowsill where I'd left trays of seeds Harry and I had planted that afternoon to germinate in fine compost balanced on numerous roasting tins. Six in total and their presence had resulted in a shifting of clutter to the worktops until they started sprouting and could be put outside. 'This is a rather literal interpretation of kitchen gardening, don't you think?'

I shrugged and said that he'd be seeing the benefits of it all in a few weeks. 'We'll be harvesting our own vegetables before you can say Land Army.'

'I don't see how,' he said leafing through the empty packets. 'I don't

even like spinach. Or chard. And these don't look much like vegetables,' he said waving the flower seed packets at me, eyes positively
bulging. 'And how am I meant to roast potatoes for supper?'

At which point my phone rang. Actually it didn't at all but I pretended it did, pointed and mouthed, 'My mother,' and retreated out of
earshot, immediately returning to the allotment plan and magazine.

Spinach is one of the easiest, most hassle-free and high-yielding leafy
vegetables to grow and as such had been my go-to for years. The
fast and reliable germination appealed to my impatience and their
abundance appealed to my stomach.

It is so easy to grow I once took a packet of seeds back to Kabul
with me after a period of leave and propagated them on a windowsill
one autumn. Sadly, they did not survive beyond the seedling stage
as I was sent on a two-week assignment and the poor things never
got watered.

But I need not have bothered; it was an abundant crop in Afghanistan and while lettuces were hard to come by, spinach could be
bought by the sack at a relatively low price. Native to Persia (Iran) and
the surrounding countries, spinach – or aspanakh, as it was known –
arrived in Europe with the Moorish conquest of Spain. Writing in
the twelfth century, Ibn al-Awwam, a landowner in Seville, southern
Spain, and author of the *kitab al filaha* (the book of agriculture),
described spinach as the 'prince of vegetables'.

The leafy green first came to France and England in the fourteenth
century and was quickly popular owing to its swift growth at a time
when most other vegetables were dormant. Eggs Florentine (eggs

baked on a bed of spinach) is a dish attributed to the leaf-loving Catherine de' Medici, the Florentine Queen of France, who loved spinach so much that she insisted on it at every meal.

I tricked J into digging a few days later. It came about like so.

Having dropped both Harry and Ott at nursery with no shoes (I had absolutely no idea where they were) and having met every muck-spreading tractor along the way I was anxious; if they're spreading muck, so should I be. I raced to the allotment for twenty minutes.

Half an hour later and at home, J yawned out of his office and suggested a walk. 'Orrrrr,' I said coyly, 'how about a saunter down to the allotments? It's very . . . warm down there. Got its own microclimate. Come and see what's what? You could even bring the dog!'

His dog, Pullo, had faithfully guarded the house we shared in Kabul. J had brought him back to the UK five years ago, only for him to develop what dog lovers refer to as 'a keen sense of territorial propriety' . . . He was trained and actively encouraged to bark in Kabul so as to keep out the ne'er-do-wells. And you really can't train an old dog new tricks. At any given time of the day the village reverberated with his low, deep bark. As a result, Pullo and I had not bonded this side of Afghanistan. When I said he could come with us J looked immediately suspicious but then glanced at his stuffy office and shuddered.

'Sure,' he said. 'Why not?'

When we arrived, spade and mattock already on-site, I started to remove a few sods here and there haphazardly and badly enough to guilt him into taking the mattock from me. It took him half an hour to do what would have taken me three days.

With digging firmly 'in operation' thanks to milder weather as the month progressed Harry and I ate lunch on the allotment almost daily. To be honest, he didn't do a great deal of digging but was fascinated by the life found beneath the surface of each sod and, while I dug and scraped and hauled the weeds away, he was happy squatting on his haunches, ham sandwich in hand, watching the centipedes and woodlice scuttle through the earth.

I happened upon a few potatoes the pub landlord must have forgotten about. I had never seen potatoes like that, just sitting there in the mud, casually waiting to be found. I gave a shriek of excitement at each discovery and gave them to Harry who lined them up in size order and named them.

We sat on upturned buckets and ate the remaining sandwiches wondering how long they'd been in the mud. We talked about what we could make with the potatoes and both got terribly excited at the thought of chips until it was time to take him to nursery. He named each spud after a member of the family and stubbornly refused to relinquish them from his pockets even when we arrived at nursery a while later.

Volunteer potatoes is the correct term for the sorts of spuds we found. Left over from a previous crop, in arable circles they are considered a weed but, as a novice, to me they were a gift. But I pitied them, those potatoes. The thought of anyone volunteering for a role on this plot was laughable. 'Right, lads,' a spud sergeant major would say. 'Got a plot on the east which needs occupying. Any takers?'

Only conscripts would be so unfortunate to be sent to my plot.

*

I was early to collect the children from nursery and with Kit in arms popped into a nearby junk shop masquerading, like so many do these days, as an antiques shop. It was mostly a collection of chipped enamelware, Victorian pine furniture, a few stained etchings and some bone-handled knives but in a corner was a pile of old Ordnance Survey maps of the outskirts of Yeovil from 1962.

It struck me, looking at them spread over the table in front of me, how much of the town was given over to allotments. In the 1800s Yeovil was known for its gloves – that's right: gloves. Three million were made there each year. By the twentieth century gloves had given way to defence, with huge munitions and aircraft-manufacturing sites scattered through the town. This of course made it a target for German bombers in the Second World War and the town was badly damaged. When looking at photographs taken pre- and post-war, what struck me most was how close the town centre was to open expanses of the Somerset and Dorset countryside. Very different to the sprawling concrete jungle now famed for its high crime rates, traffic, Albanian mafia-run county lines and Monday morning drunks roaming the streets. By those who don't live there it is known, rather uncharitably, as 'Yeovile' or 'Yobby Yeovil' but as a perennial supporter of the underdog I have always had a soft spot for it as an unfairly underfunded, unloved and rather abandoned market town.

The allotments depicted on the OS maps, I checked later, no longer existeded. Instead, there were red-brick housing developments, an industrial retail park and car parks and it started to make me wonder if in fifty years our own village, sandwiched between Sherborne and Yeovil, two towns which expand daily thanks to the numerous housing developments gnawing at the surrounding countryside, would even exist in isolation.

For those newly disenfranchised labourers of the eighteenth century, help was at hand. Their plight was being noticed and discussed in political circles and among the more philanthropic landowners and agriculturalists. Enclosures were seen as progressive forms of agriculture which regenerated boggy wasteland and, thanks to the introduction of crop rotation, guaranteed the quality of the soil. But the effect of denying access to common land meant that many were forced to leave the countryside in droves for the cities where living conditions were often worse due to overcrowding and poor sanitation but where employment was more plentiful thanks to the Industrial Revolution. Indeed, by the end of the century, London had swelled to a population of one million.

Those who stayed put to labour often relied on poor relief. Without land, survival was not a given.

The idea of giving land back to the poor was trialled in Tewkesbury by the lord of the manor in 1770. He noticed that people who had land attached to their cottages tended to look after them more than those without and so set aside five acres of land to be used by the poor. The result was that the poor rate was drastically reduced. Notable philanthropic members of the aristocracy, in part inspired by the successes in Tewkesbury, made other parcels of land available to the poor.

With the Industrial Revolution well underway the country was going through a seismic evolution. In addition, intellectual and cultural movements were shifting the social fabric. It was a time of great change.

Meanwhile over in France, and thanks in part to crop failure and famine among the labourers, revolution simmered. Arthur Young was a writer, traveller and close friend of Gainsborough's Mr Andrews; although unsuccessful as a farmer himself, he travelled to France just before the outbreak of the French Revolution and, seeing angry and dispossessed agricultural workers, began to think about land reform. He was convinced that the way to help struggling labourers was to re-enfranchise them, give them back a right to land and put forward a series of revolutionary ideas on land distribution allowing families with eight or more children free use of parcels – or 'lots' – of land.

The Board of Agriculture came up with more moderate suggestions, all of which were blocked in parliament, but the seed of rights to land was sown. 'Poor Plots' started appearing up and down the country.

Supporters of the idea of allotting land to the poor cited an improved diet, a source of hope and independence, and believed that access to land would train up the next generation in agricultural skills. Labourers, they said, would be more likely to stay than seek work in towns and cities. Another very real reason for providing labourers with land was to keep them sober. Bored, drunk, dispossessed and disenfranchised people were liable to revolt and protest, after all. And no one wanted a revolution on their hands.

There was huge opposition from landowners and farmers who feared that they would lose land and that labourers would be too exhausted after a day's work to do much cultivation of their own.

They feared the poor would prioritise their own land or that it would lead to an indolent, swaggering workforce.

Nonetheless, in 1806 King George III himself allotted five to eight acres in perpetuity to a village in Wiltshire in exchange for areas of common land elsewhere. A field of around six acres just south of Great Somerford became the first free gardens for use by the farm labourers.

The rural allotment was born.

'Where can I put the shit?' my father said standing at the gate.

It was an odd choice of a birthday present for a two-year-old and I looked blankly at him. Behind me Ottilie's birthday party was in full swing complete with bunting, pass the parcel, Marmite sandwiches and a hedgehog-shaped cake.

'Well?' he said. 'Where do you want the shit?'

I had forgotten about the manure entirely so, while six children charged around with wooden swords and balloons and, inexplicably, half a hosepipe, and while six adults drank enough wine as was appropriate for parents of very small children, he and J unloaded the manure.

Later, when the bunting had been put away and the children safely tucked up in bed, I stole a look at the bags of poo and shuddered. There was a hell of a lot of digging in to do. On the plus side, if the early warmth was anything to go by, we were in for a scorcher of a summer and my vision of golden afternoons harvesting the fruits of our labours wearing dungarees and straw hats was not so far off.

At least it wouldn't have been had the weather not turned the following day and become so anaemic in both light and warmth; snow was predicted and sub-zero temperatures falling at night which, combined with chickenpox now raging over dear Ottilie, did not a happy allotmenter maketh. In the quiet of a cold spring twilight, I wondered again whether this allotment endeavour wasn't just a lot more hassle than it was worth.

Two of our village friends Nico and Crystal, on hearing that I had taken on an allotment and themselves keen gardeners, had brought over six strawberry plants and I had not moved them from the paving stones by the front door. They would surely die if it froze. But they had so quickly become part of the detritus of toy/garden shrapnel, which also included the manure my father brought over, a half-dug-up buddleia plus all the tools needed to dig it up as well as Harry's green motorised tractor which seemed to have lost its bumper. Again.

Daily I stumbled over this visual to-do list whenever I loaded the car but was continuously distracted by various children, their car seats, the dog and so all thoughts of manuring the plot or strawberries or missing bumpers took a back seat.

In the end, unable to look at the chaos any more, a few days later I used the pram to transport the poo to the plot. With its seat detached it was sizeable and solid; a lot more so than the wobbly wheelbarrow. But I had underestimated the cold and overestimated Ottie's recovery. A vicious wind whipped us into a cold frenzy and when sleet sliced nastily, and when Ott tripped over an electric fence (mercifully, off), I admitted defeat and bundled everyone home for toast and jam. I tried not to feel frustrated. I tried really, really hard.

News about war in Ukraine was being read on the radio as I waited for the toaster to pop and I thought briefly of Alexi who I'd met on the outskirts of Donetsk.

Then a twenty-eight-year-old factory worker with no work to go to – all factories having been closed on account of the conflict – Alexi focused his attention on the garden of his grandmother's house in which he was living ahead of his forthcoming marriage. He had fond memories of playing in the garden as a child and wanted to revive it for his own children to come. In the end he had so much time on his hands that he had nothing left to do in the garden and its perfection was a perverse reminder of the war, the shelling of which was growing closer. Even as we talked on his veranda the ground shuddered. The photograph I have is of him standing amid a riot of colour with a spade in one hand and a green toy scoot-about tractor in the other, on which he used to play as a toddler.

Harry and I watched schizophrenic snow flurries blur the window and he asked earnestly if it was Christmas.

'No,' I said. 'Spring, silly. Or will be soon. Look!' I lifted him up to the windowsill to show the roasting tins of germinated seeds. Little shoots of green pushing out of their cocoon, searching for light and thirsty for water.

A slow smile beamed across Harry's face when I showed him and he whispered, 'Is that magic, Mumma?'

'It is,' I said.

Before I bundled him into the car for nursery we moved the germinating seedlings from the kitchen windowsill to the greenhouse to harden off – mindful of the two broken panes of glass – and I suddenly felt heavy: it was all very well having seeds germinating and doing what they were meant to do but much like a family they now needed to be nurtured.

My heart sank as moments later I reversed over something which sounded very much like a missing toy tractor bumper.

April

Better than the gym – Seed domestication – A new flag –
Beating the cost of living – Rotavator v spade – The fetish of
the countryside – Kenyan comparisons – More pox – Books
and tools – Guinea Gardens – Allotments abroad – Potting
on a child – Garden centre backup – Parenting and
cultivating – Comfort in the plot

Burning four hundred calories an hour – depending on the task in hand – they say that gardening is better than the gym. That may be but I'll warrant that a trip to the gym does not induce the level of aches experienced by the muscles we rarely use nor the industrial quantities of hand cream needed after an afternoon wielding a mattock, a fork and bags of well-rotted manure.

The pressure was on. I needed the ground prepared and I needed it prepared now. If not, I explained to J from my supine position on a foam roller, I'd miss the planting window.

He asked when exactly this window was. In truth I didn't actually know but assumed it was around about now owing to the gradual greening of the world outside and the busy tractors around the village. I muttered something vague and hoisted myself to standing to show him the contents of the greenhouse which I'd just cleaned and which sparkled brightly in the spring light.

It was brimming with life inside. The small staging area was crammed with little pots and trays of seeds poking through the fine compost like babies' teeth. It smelled humusy and damp in the greenhouse and J, forced to crouch beneath the sub-six-foot apex of the roof, inhaled deeply. It reminded him, he said, of his grandfather's greenhouse. 'Such a happy place,' he said. 'What on earth are you growing *here*?'

I had bought the peas as tiny seedlings from the garden centre and another lot from a supermarket and had potted them on to larger containers using pencils and forks as their support when I'd run out of sticks.

I explained as much and he shook his head, bewildered. 'I have a workshop of sticks you could have used.'

'Oh,' I said. 'Next time. These are squash, spinach and chard seedlings and this is the corn. Or will be soon,' I added. 'Only just sown them.'

With a blank canvas I had unlimited choice, a problem many first-time allotment holders find themselves faced with. What to plant and where? I was opting for plants that were resilient, abundant, low maintenance and had an appeal to children. All in all quite a big Venn diagram of requirements. But it was all a huge experiment because until then all I had ever grown to eat – with varying degrees of success – was spinach, chard, tomatoes, broad and runner beans and once, by accident, an onion.

'It's crazy to think that these are tame, domesticated plants,' he said. 'They literally can't survive without us.'

The history of human civilisation is really a history of seeds.

Some twelve hundred years ago, and there is much debate as to why, humans stopped running after food and instead started growing it. The advent of agrarian culture in an area spanning the edges of the Mediterranean and the Middle East, known as the Fertile Crescent,

rooted our ancestors to one place and enabled them to feed themselves with what they grew. Across the Atlantic in Mesoamerica, an
area covering south Mexico, Central America and the northern parts
of Peru, Ecuador and Bolivia, a similar change in human behaviour
was happening as people began to favour farming over hunting and
gathering.

East and west, farmers grew carbohydrates and protein. In the
Middle East it was wheat and chickpeas on the menu while in the
Americas it was maize and beans lining people's stomachs.

The tooth-like kernel of corn that I had so easily sown in fine
and nutrient-rich seed compost, for example, had its genetic roots
in the grasslands of Mesoamerica. Its genetic wild ancestor teosinte
is a large grass with kernels so hard they'd break your teeth. There is
much debate but it is thought that over time teosinte was sown and
grown and those with the longest ears and fattest kernels selected for
the following year and so on. This ultimately resulted in maize, the
most productive crop in the world and one which ironically enough
would not survive in the wild.

That is the thing about domesticated crops. They are a feat of
genetic engineering which has enabled us to have more reliable and
high-yielding crops year in, year out. A result of thousands of years
of seed selection, selective breeding, exploration and trade, they rely
on us for their continued existence. They need us to propagate, prick
out, space out, pot on, water and harvest, save and sow again. Leave
a vegetable garden to go to seed and unlike their wild ancestors
growing on the plains of our ancestors' homelands the fruits would
not survive.

Strange then, I thought in the greenhouse when J had left and I was watering and moving pots around, that the seeds were doing a pretty good job of domesticating *me*.

The planting window, as it quickly transpired when I went to the plot later, was also wide open for the weeds, the seeds of which had had a chance to leave their dormancy thanks to my digging and were already running amok.

I had bought a number of tarpaulins which when laid were to starve the weeds of light. A cruel April wind made this task somewhat challenging and every time I returned to the plot, I would find them half strewn over the ground like a stage curtain revealing a disastrous amateur production.

The village we had chosen to be our home was nestled in the folds of the countryside and although we could often hear the hum of tyre rubber on tarmac from the busy A-road a few miles away, it was easy enough to forget the rest of the world and the whirring chaos which rumbled through it.

A change of flag over the church was a reminder of global events. One morning, the Union flag that usually fluttered over the hamstone bell tower was replaced with the simple strip of blue and yellow.

The bells were chiming as we walked past on the way to the allotment and play park and Harry asked what the colours meant.

'Well,' I said. 'The blue is meant to be the sky.'

He looked up at the grey sky above us and frowned.

'On a sunny day,' I added. 'When there are no clouds. And the yellow is supposed to be a flower called a sunflower.'

'What's a sunflower?' His eyes widened.

'They are tall flowers about this high.' I raised my hand to my chest. 'Huge whoppers. And they have lovely big yellow heads which follow the sun throughout the day. Like a magnet, I suppose.'

'A magnet flower? What's a magnet flower?'

'No, a sunflower.'

Harry was quiet for a few moments as he thought about this. 'When it's sunny I'm going to wear my sunglasses,' he said earnestly. 'But not on Saturday or yesterday.'

And so ended the lesson on flag symbolism but, shivering in the play park moments later, I felt the memory of a war-ravaged landscape arch. In 2014, having spoken to and photographed civilians living in the line of war's sight somewhere between the rebel-held areas and the newly liberated towns, I'd been trying to find a safe passage back to my hotel in Donetsk, which was not easy given the beetling Ukrainian army tanks and the mortar shells falling not so far away. The ground shuddered when they fell. A whole village was evacuating in front of my eyes, inhabitants running for safety carrying whatever they could. But perhaps even sadder than the thought of what they left behind were the fields of un-harvested sunflowers. Weary browning heads sinking with rot beneath an infinite blue sky.

I thought about this with crystal clarity as I pushed Ottilie as high as I could on the swing or chased Harry up and down the slide, the Ukrainian flag flapping violently in the distance. I wondered if any sunflowers would be planted at all that year.

*

'Oh, you've got one of those, have you?' my friend's uncle said. 'Good for you.' The uncle ran a local and much-loved food and wine shop. His family had lived in the village for generations and I wanted to know a little bit more about the history of the allotment sites. Was I working ground that for centuries had been feeding the villagers?

Allotments are so much a part of the landscape that we cease to really notice them now. My friend's uncle sucked his teeth when I asked as if to wrack his brain. He had a vague memory of there being an orchard on the site.

I was surprised when instead of warning me about biting off more than I could chew he said, 'The soil is pretty good there but you'd better make a start on the rotavating before the weeds set in.'

I had no idea what rotavating was but did not want to admit as much.

'Been hard at it,' I replied.

'I tell you what. We'll sell your surplus.'

'Really?'

He peered through his spectacles and said, 'If you have a glut, why not?' I imagined myself in a few months, muscular and bronzed with equally healthy-looking children, loading wooden crates of muddy but succulent vegetables into the shop.

I looked up 'rotavating' a little later. It turned out that I need not have worried myself with digging at all. For as little as £50 I could have hired a machine to turn and chop and plough and furrow the whole plot churning it all into lovely topsoil. The argument *for* them was obvious. Back. Ache.

The argument against was just as relevant, however. In chopping up roots and weeds and turning hitherto dormant soil over, the rotavator leaves you thousands of weed root cuttings, each one ready to strike forth and grow into a nice big weed. By the dozen. The long-term problem far outweighed the short-term reprieve.

As the weather warmed, we made a day trip to the beach. In 1943 the coastal village of Tyneham (and around seven and a half thousand acres of heathland around the Purbeck Hills) was requisitioned by the War Office. The villagers were evacuated and the land used as firing ranges for the army and the place has remained in use by the MOD ever since. Free from farming and housing developments it is a beautiful spot; a haven for wildlife and nature and an outstanding stretch of pebbled beach leading into cool (it is England, after all) but crystal-clear water. Being a twenty-five-minute walk from the abandoned village that still stands, the beach was almost always empty and as we nearly always found ourselves alone there we used to pretend that we inhabited an England where there were still wild and isolated places.

Having not been there for a few years we were excited for the crisp blue chilly water and this secret part of England. I'd packed a picnic of sandwiches, quiche, cake, water for the children and brown bottled ale for J and I to share, along with an old tartan rug which was big enough to pull over our legs if it got too windy.

But as we pulled off the road to the abandoned stone houses we found our secret shared; we would not be alone. Indeed, with row upon row of cars, we were far from being alone. You almost couldn't see the grass for so much shining metal. We ate our picnic amid a cloud of vape smoke from a neighbouring group of twenty-somethings dunking crisps and pre-chopped carrot batons into plastic tubs of sauce. Two cars away someone was lighting a disposable barbeque. People were playing music from their phones and someone kicked a football onto our patch. Other people were enjoying themselves but we, sadly, were not. In the end we were so dispirited we didn't have the heart to join the snaking line of people making their way to the beach and drove away in silence.

With less than 20 per cent of the population living in rural England, the countryside proper – that of agriculture, arable fields and limitless skies – is a rare thing. Generation after generation we have moved further away from the land and the countryside has been all but domesticated. Take agricultural buildings, for example. 'The Granary' or 'Dairy House' or even 'Farmhouse'. Rare it is to find these used for their original purpose. Now they are more likely to be family homes I doubt most farmers today could afford. You are more likely to see a glossy 4x4 parked outside a gentrified farm building than a tractor. In our village there were originally eight farms. At the time of writing just two remain.

We don't need the land any more – not in the way we used to.

Across the board, we have become a nation of consumers not producers and I'll hazard a guess that all those pre-chopped carrot batons of our neighbouring car-park picnickers were not grown in the UK. It is not our fault, I thought, as we trailed home in heavy bank holiday traffic. Few of us have rural family ties and having access to a garden or land is considered a luxury. Furthermore, the world seems hell-bent on artificial intelligence and technology as the future but if we see land only as a playground and not as part of the bigger picture of life, we are pretty far down the rabbit hole of failing to understanding that relationship between land and food.

I hoped that my allotment would be the antidote for a fast-moving world and a nod to the old one which is fast disappearing.

When AJ, a New Yorker friend I'd made in Kabul who was now living in Kenya, was visiting for a few days, it occurred to me that we in Britain weren't the only ones facing rising food prices. She and I were re-securing the wayward tarpaulins on the plot when she told me about the vegetables growing in her garden in Nairobi. There were banana and mango trees growing wild and roses too with ancient roots profiting from the rich, red African soil. But since moving there she had started to grow a few tomatoes and lettuces.

Fresh produce is expensive in Nairobi. On the few times I'd visited I had baulked at the prices of lettuces, apples and beans which were largely grown for export.

Kenya's arable land and produce constitute about 70 per cent of its national commercial agricultural output. But while it feeds the world, parts of the population are set to starve. The rising cost of living has doubled the price of basic food items like rice, maize and cooking oil, making them beyond the reach of the most in need.

But, AJ explained, the two-season climate was ideal for growing your own vegetables. 'Especially tomatoes,' she said. 'We're growing a ton and have them, like, all the time.' Knowing I wasn't the only one turning my hand to vegetable growing gave me a boost.

As the days passed I began noticing the other plots and how things had started to emerge there. The other plot holders had started to sow and plant – when, I didn't know as I had yet to encounter anyone else down there – and the results were already visible. I felt like a swimmer in a race who hadn't heard the starting gun. But that was the problem. I didn't know what the race was; I didn't know where to plant or when or how. I just had a load of seedlings. Oh, and now a *baby* with chickenpox which put a stop to any activity on the allotment.

It was all I could do to stare out of the children's bedroom window from where I could see the greenhouse and the verdure of seedlings. I pressed my head against the cold glass and watched the peas yearning upwards. They seemed to be growing right in front of me, which boded well for their future on the plot if I ever had the chance to plant them out down there.

A truly global food are peas. Found the world over from China to the Indian subcontinent to Russia, from America to Australia to Europe, they are so popular in this country that they can be bought by the frozen kilo in service stations up and down the country and handily double up as a domestic ice pack for minor bruises and sprains.

But peas have been around for a very, very long time. Cultivated as a source of protein, easily dried and stored, they proved to be an excellent buffer against bad harvests[1] and for thousands of years they were grown in settlements across the Fertile Crescent.

The Romans, to whom we owe much of the provenance of what we now consider to be British dietary staples (although thankfully not the edible dormouse), brought the pea to Britain perhaps reluctantly as they did not hold it in much culinary esteem and reportedly cooked it for hours at a time.

Not until the seventeenth century were peas grown to be eaten fresh, but it was during the nineteenth-century breeding frenzy that swept much of western Europe and America that peas became an obsession – along with many other vegetables, as we shall see. Enthusiasts and farmers, rich and poor, everyone was at it. Hundreds of new varieties of pea were developed; the United States Department for Agriculture recorded four hundred and eight varieties. Their popularity has waned for today there are just over twenty.

In the short time since becoming a plot holder, I had started amassing a small library of books. There was the Royal Horticultural Society's *Half-Hour Allotment*, which promised to do what it said on the tin. The RHS had another allotment 'bible' which I added to Susan Campbell's *A History of Kitchen Gardening* and *Your Garden Week by Week* by A. Hellyer, another 'bible' first published in 1936. Over the year I would quadruple this number but it was to these tomes and the World Wide Web I turned for advice. Not that it made the blindest bit of difference to the way I gardened or propagated because nothing took into account my really very limited knowledge and understanding of the science of growth or soil or techniques. Pricking out, pinching out and earthing up were not yet part of my lexicon. Neither did any of the books take into account my time constraints nor my inability to remember and apply anything short-term.

What I did learn was about the importance of tools.

For a successful allotment the following were needed: a spade with a handle length suitable for your height, a decent fork (handle similarly sized), a trowel, a hoe, a rake, string. That was the basic foundation. Add to this a sieve, shears, secateurs, scissors, gloves.

I had a spade, I had a fork I'd picked up from the council tip for a pound which only had three prongs, I had a trowel and I had half a rake (the wooden handle having been snapped when driven over a year or two ago), my father's mattock, two rusting fork heads I'd found in the long grasses and somewhere in the house there was a ball of twine although that may have been squirrelled away by a child. I also had a weeding knife which was one up on the advice.

The knife was a basic thing with a wooden handle and a hooked metal blade which I had bought from the old city in Kabul. The trade bazaar of Murad Khani was a gardener's dream for while the black-smiths and forgers banged and hammered red-hot metal into shape for passing customers, above them hung their wares. Rows of spade heads and pitchforks, trowel ends and dibbers, weed knives and hoes neatly hanging and ready for action. All that was needed were handles which the woodworkers over the road could knock up in moments.

My last assignment in the country had been directing and filming a documentary about the gardeners of Kabul for the BBC and I'd bought the weed knife as a souvenir more than anything. I never imagined that one day I'd be using it in the weed-strewn ground of a Dorset allotment.

While Great Somerford in Wiltshire gave birth to the first rural allot-ment, for the movement to really thrive it needed a period of political and social upheaval. The early nineteenth century was fertile ground for discontentment. Rural England was not a happy or a fair place. The Enclosure Acts had already upset the status quo by depriving people of access to land and food. In 1815 unemployment was rife owing to the return of a quarter of a million demobilised soldiers from the Napoleonic Wars. Added to this was the technological advancement of mechanised machinery – particularly the threshing machine – which did away with many work opportunities through the winter. What little work existed was poorly paid with long hours. After two bad harvests in 1829 and 1830 labourers had had enough.

The Swing Riots flamed across the south of England beginning in Orpington, Kent, with the setting alight of a haystack. Over the following months, *The Times* said that barely a night passed 'without some farmer having a corn stack or barn set fire to.'[2] In August of that year, the first threshing machine was destroyed. This started a trend and by the end of September over one hundred more had been targeted. Farmers and landowners were left threatening notes by a mythical 'Captain Swing'.

Armed forces were needed to curb resistance and, while land-owners and farmers assembled their own armies of old soldiers and servants, the government recommissioned the yeomanry cavalry, pulled scarlet-coated Chelsea Pensioners out of retirement and deployed contingents of the Dragoon Guards in the south of England to squash rebellion.

Punishment for rioters was harsh; nineteen were executed, over five hundred were exported to Australia but there was huge public outcry and the riots, while not altogether successful in achieving employment and wage rises, did at least shake things up.

On the back of the riots and upheaval The Labourer's Friend Society (founded in 1830 by Benjamin Wills, a surgeon from London who wanted to improve working-class conditions) concluded that the allocation of land to individuals was a 'powerful means of bettering the condition of those classes who depend for their livelihood upon their manual labour'. In other words, people needed land to live.

The hope was also that by giving the 'bread of Independence', good morals would naturally follow. The society published a magazine which offered philanthropic landowners advice on setting up allotments and sent travelling agents around the country to find out where allotments were most needed. The then Prime Minister, Robert Peel, took notice and liked what he saw and the 1845 General Enclosure Act demanded that any future enclosure should include an allowance of allotments for the poor.

Uptake, however, slowed right down in the late 1840s due to the potato famine but by the 1850s allotments had bounced back and were fast becoming an established feature of country life in Britain. The government quickly realised that these small plots of land could be hugely beneficial to the poor at relatively little cost. By 1856 there were an estimated hundred thousand plots in existence.

In the towns something else was happening. As they were increasingly populated by people leaving the countryside, landlords, having worked out that there was an additional income to be made by providing gardens to tenants did just that. For a while, parts of Birmingham and Nottingham where the gardens were most plentiful became oases of calm. The Guinea Gardens, as they were then known, were more about the delights of leafy retreat than self-sufficiency, with summer houses and pretty borders instead of cabbages and turnips. However, owing to rapid industrial expansion and the need for land to build on, most of the gardens had disappeared by the late nineteenth century.

The utilitarian allotment, however, lived on and local councils were obliged to provide allotments if there was demand. And there was. Tracts of wasteland, bogs and disused fields not fit for building on were all put to better use and by 1873 there were 245,000 allotments across Britain; by 1890 there were nearly half a million.

Publications began springing up to cater to this new green-fingered population. An annual magazine, *One and All Gardening* ('a popular annual aimed for amateurs, allotment holders and working gardeners'), would have set the reader back two pence and informed them on a wide range of subjects from flowers to lawns to cabbages. The front cover was a charming pen-and-ink drawing depicting a lady watering tulips next to two beehives, another bringing milk in a bucket yoke held across her shoulders and a man in a cloth cap and shirtsleeves digging at the roots of his enormous cabbages.

Britain was not the only country to have an allotment movement. The rapid expansion of cities across Europe led to concerns around physical health and the need for tuberculosis-alleviating fresh air.

The first '*armengartens*' or 'poor gardens' were set up in Kiel, north-eastern Germany, in 1830. Their success was copied. Leipzig established family plots equipped with sheds and chalets, which became known as *schrebergartens*,* while in Berlin they were *Laubenkolonien*

---

* In Leipzig lived Dr Daniel Schreber, an advocate of exercise and outdoor recreation for the young. He had no interest in allotments per se but, on his death, a Schreber association was established and created an area of recreation and gardens for children to maintain. The idea did not fly – children apparently and perhaps understandably 'lacking the necessary endurance to garden' – but the plots were taken over by their parents. For more information see David Crouch and Colin Ward, *The Allotment: Its Landscape and Culture* (Five Leaves Publications, 1997).

summer-house colonies catering for families seeking refuge from overcrowding. The *Kleingartens* were provided by workers' organisations, or by factories for their employees, or by local authorities, and perhaps best mimic the social underpinning of the British allotment movement.

Allotment gardening spread from Germany to Poland as a result of a trend for a natural way of life and then to Holland where allotments were considered to be a vital preventative tool against alcoholism and depression. In Denmark allotments were more of a pleasure garden for those cooped up in cities than a means of alleviating poverty, but when visiting Copenhagen in 1904 a young Swedish social activist, Anna Lindhagen, saw a group of allotment gardeners digging and became interested. What then followed was tireless work back in her native Stockholm obtaining sites and involving the state, the city and private institutions to establish the Association of Allotments to alleviate conditions for the working classes. The association was the first of its kind in Europe to be headed up by women.

But not the only one.

Jardins ouvriers or workers' gardens were plots of land given out by municipalities at the end of the nineteenth century in France. Mirroring the allotment movement elsewhere in Europe, these parcels of allotted land were intended to improve the living conditions of workers through self-sufficiency and were initiated by Félicie Hervieu in the Ardennes region. She brought together one hundred and forty-five people from twenty-seven families and was so successful that in just five years the organisation involved one hundred and twenty-five families.

In Britain living conditions were slowly improving in the early 1900s and there was a wave of new reforms that anticipated the welfare state and the clearance of workhouses. Children could no longer buy tobacco, alcohol or fireworks and nor could they be involved in dangerous work or sent out to beg. Life for all was looking a little rosier and without the absolute critical need for food, labourers weren't quite so keen to spend hours on an allotment.

The Garden Museum in London has a number of photographs of early-twentieth-century allotments. They are pretty places with sizeable greenhouses or sheds, clouds of flowers foaming onto footpaths, all nestled among the urban skylines of chimneys, brick walls, roofs and, occasionally, telegraph poles. In one image taken in around 1905, a young man poses in front of a large greenhouse and cold frame. The border of the bed before him is lined with bricks and contains a number of roses and peonies, staked for support and doing pretty well. In another, taken in 1907, in Elland, now a suburb of Leeds, a mother and daughter pose hand in hand. The daughter looks like she has been chasing butterflies. The mother appears a little tired but not unhappy. The flowers of both are so abundant you can almost smell them. A sweet, fragrant summer of halcyon days gone by.

Once the essential means of survival, tending these plots of land was fast becoming a leisure activity similar to those enjoyed in the pleasure gardens of Europe. But unbeknownst to the subjects, at around that time Britain was signing alliances and treaties which would cement its involvement in the consequences of a Serbian student shooting an Austrian Archduke one late June morning of 1914.

*

There is an intensity to gardening and growing mimicked in that of parenting. The pressure of growing young children, civilising them, showing them right and wrong and how to be kind, how to dress themselves or how to use cutlery, is immense and the responsibility can be crushing.

I had recently received confirmation that Harry had a place at a local primary school nearby in the autumn and although this marked the beginning of boyhood and a whole new and exciting path, in truth, it filled me with melancholy. Just four years ago, we watched my belly grow with mounting anticipation – each of his kicks a step towards birth and a step away from the old life (a life that now felt so alien and far away that I could not really remember it wholly) but soon we would be trying on uniforms, organising book bags and committed to the regimen of school. Four years is not long. I wondered if he was ready.

Meanwhile the plot was ready and waiting and there were whole trays of seedlings squished in their pots and gagging to be planted out but I was stalling, nervous about committing to the next phase of the allotment. The daily watering, weeding, the extra work and the added responsibility of keeping everything alive. Once planted out there was no going back.

Later, after waging war on the couch grass with a strimmer borrowed from Crystal, Harry and I were pottering in the greenhouse sowing seeds and taking stock. 'Look!' he gasped, pointing at a flower pot where the runner bean my brother had given him was breaking through the surface of the soil. It was hunched over with the effort, improbably large leaves crossed across its chest like arms. Harry thought it would be bigger than Jack's beanstalk in the fairy tale. Watching him standing next to me, shoes on the wrong feet, muddy little fingers poking at the bean, he was an infant breaking through to boyhood.

Having recently developed an insatiable appetite for information – any information, be it about plants and how they grow, or clouds and why they move, or tractors and the size of their wheels, or words and how they make stories, or labels on food, or animals and why they make noises, and bees and why they buzz – he was more than ready.

It was me who wasn't ready. I wanted us all to stay static in the spring-green enchantment of childhood.

'Forget allotments or fledgling businesses or war reporting or aspirations of self-improvement or home improvement,' J said later when I voiced my woes. 'Watching them grow will be the finest achievement of our lives.'

A few days or so later J took the children to see his grandmother for the weekend, leaving me alone with orders to take it easy.

Which of course I ignored, driving straight away to the garden centre as soon as I had bid them goodbye and was sure they weren't coming back for forgotten shoes, bunnies, blankets or chocolate digestives. Thus unencumbered I enjoyed the simple act of browsing in silence. I lost myself in the aisles of trellising imagining what would soon trail over it. Amid the espaliered fruit trees I fantasised about a walled garden that I would one day have and among the climbers I lingered by a young wisteria the fragrance of which would one day be so intoxicating that passers-by would look up and smile.

Finding myself among the vegetable seedlings I was easily per-suaded to add to my trolley some strips of beetroots and carrots. It is always more economical to grow from seed but back then, as a novice vegetable grower, I did not back myself to succeed.

I made my way to the tills passing bundles of long twigs which were advertised as pea sticks for £17. While beans such as Harry's monster runner bean could easily clamber up a bamboo cane or otherwise, peas needed something a little bit more substantial over which to clamber. Hazel twigs and sticks offered the perfect frame. But £17?

Who on earth pays that much for sticks?

When I arrived back home the afternoon vigour and seedling-buying excitement from the garden centre quickly vanished. I tried to fathom where I'd plant everything (my initial scribbled plan having proven to be less than illuminating) and how far apart. Plants might not ask inane questions, throw food on the floor or need a nappy change but when you don't know what you are doing they can be burdensome. It felt like trying to complete a jigsaw without a picture.

The radio was on low in the kitchen and news about the war in Ukraine came in fits and starts. Someone had recently asked if I would go with them on assignment as their photographer was on leave and they needed someone to illustrate the bloody mess of that war. I had toyed with the idea briefly and then pushed it firmly away. Before having children I would have gone because before I had children I had no real responsibilities. I was just a journalist drifting between countries, searching for stories, asking questions and not minding if there were no concrete answers.

But now I had responsibilities. I had a family and a home and there was too much to lose. I was a mother, a nurturer, a cook, a cleaner, expected to have patience and always be ready with answers, wet wipes and Calpol and I was to be grounded. There was no question of going to war.

As the news rumbled from the radio I listened deep inside myself to see if I could hear the familiar siren call to war, which had been my driver for so long, and I heard it very faintly. That other me was there, somewhere hurtling towards war on a night train.

May

Plant supports – Weeds – The tomato dilemma – History of
tomatoes – Shopping locally (ish) – Bean theft and the war
on slugs – Cosmos and Kabul – Another bloody chore –
Allotment community – Allotment presents – History of the
fava – Plague – A vision of the future

Of course I bought them, those £17 sticks. I also bought more bean and courgette seedlings, which made me wonder if I was developing a problem. I'd lost track of what I had on the grow because the thing about garden centres is that they do a pretty good job of convincing you that you need more than whatever small trifling thing you went in for. What I was doing was 'not very allotment' in the old-fashioned sense of the word, not very thrifty. Not least because my reason for taking on an allotment was to cut the food bill not treble it with the addition of sticks and pre-propagated seedlings. And J quickly pointed out that we live next to woodland full of free pea sticks and that I was indeed a mug for parting with such precious cash.

Inspired one year by a friend's mother's kitchen garden in Devon which was an immaculate, organised and happy place for climbers like peas and beans, I'd looked into getting myself an array of beautifully designed metal supports for some peas I had bought from a discount supermarket in one of the gloomy pandemic lockdowns. Online I was quickly sucked into a part of the horticultural world I'd never known existed. Trumpet supports, lobster pot frames, girdle plant supports, border restrains, wrap-arounds, arches, grow-throughs and obelisks. In the garden centre it was no better. Bamboo, plastic, metal, wooden, and of every size and shape, they all promised to boost my blooms and produce in ways I could only imagine and I could easily and happily have parted with all my savings. In the end, I had played it safe with bamboo and buddleia canes. Which was just as well as, that year, the pea seedlings died within days of being planted out. You can support a plant all you like but if you can't garden, all you're left with is, well, supports.

Not so this year, I thought, manhandling the hazel pea sticks on the plot. There was just one problem: I had no idea how to use them. Running to higher ground in order to get a bar of phone reception I googled the solution – slightly counter the low-tech-no-tech nature of an allotment, but needs must. Judging by the minuscule images on my screen I could see there was no magic to planting the sticks; put them in the ground at an angle and facing each other. So I did.

Next, the seedlings themselves. I'd left it so long that the roots were compacted in their plugs and spiralled around each other. They seemed improbably tender to be supporting the luscious half-foot-tall leaves shooting above them. Many of them broke in my hands and I began to wonder if this whole exercise was a horticultural red herring. Especially when a bag of peas in the petrol station was just £2.50 and none of my children had yet to eat a pea without spitting it out. So far, when it came to growing my own peas, I was over £20 poorer which would make the overall cost per pea around 14p, which was rather more than I could have bought them for. But this was all a learning curve, I kept telling myself as I bedded the roots in.

I watered generously before setting to work on the pre-grown runner bean seedlings, planting each one at the foot of the canes left behind by the pub landlord. The seedling compost was fine and garden-centre-y, quite a contrast to the heavy loam of the ground into which I planted them. As there were still a number of canes to use I direct sowed a few beans into the ground. It was, so I'd been told, good soil down there.

It wasn't the first time I'd grown beans – maybe not quite as many at one time – but I fancied myself as a pretty good bean grower, nonetheless. But that night I lay awake with a feeling something akin to mother's guilt, wondering about the peas and beans on their first night, alone in the Big Wide World without shelter.

The weeds had, almost overnight, gone berserk. New tufts were appearing at an alarming pace as the planting window steadily closed.

'What's a weed?' Harry asked as we knelt down to begin removing them a day later.

I'd never given the subject of weed provenance much thought. A better person than me might say that a weed is just a plant in the wrong place but as that wrong place seemed always to be wherever I wanted to plant something, I happily admitted to not being a better person. We pulled the young weedlings from the ground and having soon cleared enough we set about planting the root crops of carrot, beetroot and celeriac seedlings.

In terms of finicky, fiddly detail it was up there with, I don't know, making your own graph paper. The needly roots needed disentangling and gentle handling and the whole process required patience and time and delicate hands, none of which I had. A valuable lesson learned: sow direct in the ground next time.

When you look at images of an allotment there are mostly ordered and neat rows and columns of produce, a battalion on parade of all that nature offers. We tried, Harry and I, to be neat and orderly but the columns of carrots were rather less than soldier straight and instead looked increasingly like a ramshackle rebel army.

Next up, the celeriac. Much more straightforward owing to their larger size and smaller number. 'By Christmas,' I grinned at Harry, 'we'll have twelve celeriac to gorge on.' Absolutely nothing could go wrong.

The annual tomato dilemma: how and where to grow them. For a few years I had put all my faith into a ready-made growbag in the greenhouse, watering daily and feeding weekly with a seaweed-based mixture. The results were never outstanding: a lot of leaf and some pretty small yellow fruits which bore no resemblance whatsoever to the seedling label photograph.

The best crop of tommies I had ever yielded came quite by accident from a self-seeder next to a climbing rose when Ottilie was born. With a newborn baby, I was not exactly consistent with watering anything, let alone a plant I didn't know existed. I didn't feed it, I didn't pick out the leaves, I did nothing. But the plant thrived; the more neglectful I was, the stronger it grew, and while the rose never flowered, it provided the best possible support for the tomato which bushed up and out and gave us months and months of delightful cherry fruits and, later, vats of green tomato chutney. This 'treat 'em mean, keep 'em growing' method of tomato maintenance is exactly what I should have been doing all along, I later read. Overwatering and overfeeding, especially in the early days, leads to more leaf and less fruit.

The following year, having watched an episode of *Gardeners' World* in which Monty Don trained his tomatoes to climb and clamber to the dizzy heights of his greenhouse roof, I planted three tomato seedlings in pots next to a sheltered suntrap of a wall and fixed strings from a trellis. Which they ignored. Perhaps they weren't climbers (I wasn't very discerning or understanding of the difference between bush tomatoes and cordon tomatoes) or was I too attentive with my watering and feeding? Or was it just a bad year for tommies? Either way, I cut the string and my losses early in the season.

This year would be different. I would be methodical. Ish. I had bought two seedlings from the garden centre and had grown a third quite by mistake – there must have been a stray seed lurking when Harry and I sowed them a few days ago. Recalling the accidental plant of two years ago, I had high hopes for the accidental seedling but was too much of a novice to the allotment to plant them down there. Instead a reversion to the growbag system. Harry and I laid it lengthways in the greenhouse, cut squares from the red plastic and scooped out the rich black earth with our hands to make space for the seedling roots and then we ignored them.

Today there are in excess of ten thousand varieties of tomatoes – it is the most popular vegetable grown in the world. We are so reliant on them for our sarnies, salads, stews and soups that when poor weather affected a crop, and then a supply route to supermarkets in early 2023, it was headline news.

But tomatoes haven't always been so popular.

*

Originating in their first wild incarnations in Peru, parts of Bolivia and Ecuador, tomatoes grew well on poor, dry ground. Considering the size of peas and that back then they were sour and not particularly tasty, it was a wonder they were ever domesticated at all especially given the proliferation of other more tasty plants.

Thankfully for us the Mayans took a shine to the fruit and became great breeders of tomatoes, creating a variety of colours and sizes. Even today, Mexico continues to be home to the greatest number of varieties of the tomato in the world.

Hernán Cortés, one of the first Spanish conquistadors exploring the Americas in the sixteenth century, is widely believed to be the man who introduced the tomato to Europe in 1524.*

The earliest varieties to arrive from the New World were often yellow. While the Spanish named the fruit 'tomate', a bastardisation of it local name, 'tomatl', in Italy they called it the golden apple – 'pomo d'oro' – which became 'pomme d'amour' in France. (This incorrectly gave it the reputation as an aphrodisiac, one which stuck in Britain until well into the seventeenth century.) 'Pomo d'oro' was by then cemented into the Italian language; 'pomodoro' today being the Italian for 'tomato', despite being thought of as a dangerous fruit likely to make the eater ill. This was not the poor tommie's fault.

At the time pewter was the material of choice for plates of the wealthy but tomato acid reacts so strongly with pewter that it causes lead to leach. For a long time tomatoes remained relegated

---

* He laid siege to what is now known as Mexico but as later conquistadors took Peruvian tomatoes home with them there is often some debate as to which country is the true homeland of the modern tomato.

to 'look don't eat'. It didn't help that the cold, damp British climate was not naturally kind to those earlier varieties that often failed to reach full maturity and tommies were often grown as an ornamental climber.[1]

The global popularity of the tomato now far outweighs supply and farmers and producers have concentrated on high-yielding, fast-growing hybrids. This is not such a bad thing as the improved flavour and disease resistance mean that more people are eating them. Indeed, tomatoes account for 16 per cent of all cultivation.

And all from a scraggly but determined little plant with not very delicious fruits.

So I had high hopes for the accidental seedling.

I had high hopes too for shopping 'local', one week, shunning the year-round produce of supermarkets and sticking to the season.

The local greengrocer in town was one of those wooden-fronted shops which looked like it had changed little over the years. Or perhaps that was its intention. Inside it smelled strongly of vegetable skins and waxy paper and wooden crates and I scoured the shelves for locally grown, seasonal inspiration.

Being at the end of those lean months, there was little by which to be inspired: a few ropey-looking root vegetables, a bag of lettuce for a fiver, potatoes and fruit imported from Spain or Israel. I'd always thought of myself as being a seasonal sort of consumer but standing on the cold stone floor and staring at the empty crates I realised I'd become seasonally spoilt.

I left with some button onions to add to a stew, some carrots, potatoes and, in a panic, a bunch of bananas and a bag of grapes for the children. I would hazard a guess that only the potatoes and carrots were grown locally. Twenty-eight pounds the poorer, I then hotfooted it to a supermarket to make up the deficit.

In Victorian Britain the average family was two adults and four children and the weekly household income varied from 11s 6d (£35 in today's money) for rural labouring, two and a half times that for mining families and three times as much for manufacturing families. Three quarters of a labouring family's income was spent on food – and three quarters of that alone would have been spent solely on bread.[2] People were almost always hungry.

According to the Office for National Statistics in the UK we spend just 16 per cent of our household budgets on food and non-alcoholic drinks at the time of writing. To a certain extent this is great; food is cheaper than it was and more readily available. There are supermarkets catering to all tastes and budgets and the wide-spread hunger experienced by our great-great-grandparents is no longer a threat.

Or so I thought. Ultra-processed food (UPFs) and ultra-high-processed food (UHPFs) have slowly been seeping into every corner of our diets. Originally designed by food engineers rather than cooked by cooks, these highly processed foods were conceived as a convenient, cheap, highly flavoured means to fill many bellies quickly and now account for more than half the calories eaten in the UK and US.[3] They bear little resemblance to food in its original state and are now considered to be as dangerous to our health as smoking, vaping or excessive drinking. The rub is in the ingredients

Or lack thereof. UHPFs are engineered from already refined foods such as cheap oils (including palm oil, the use of which is having disastrous effects on the world's rainforests), refined sugars, whey proteins and emulsifiers which are whizzed up into something flavoursome and easy on the wallet.

The trouble is that UPFs and UHPFs include everything from cereals to crisps to hot dogs to biscuits to sliced bread to non-dairy milk to chocolate bars to soft drinks to doughnuts and everything in between. Consumed in moderation these can bring joy and a quick energy boost when the afternoon lags or a drive from here to there seems endless. But they are not designed to be eaten in moderation and neither are they intended to be filling.

Do not be fooled by the marketing claims or the wholesome-looking packaging. What these engineers really want you to do is to return for seconds and thirds, run out and then buy some more. Cheerios might be high in fibre but they are off the scale when it comes to sugar. There is a giant leap between a carrot or cucumber stick and the packets of 'veggie puffs' aggressively marketed for toddlers embarking on their own food journey.

Don't get me wrong, I'm partial to salt and vinegar Pringles and pre-made meals from time to time. Haribo Tangfastics have always been my Achilles heel closely followed by jelly babies and my children have survived for days in a row on a staple of peanut butter sandwiches, frozen pizza or pasta-pesto. But if it costs more to buy a bag of apples than it does a pot of instant noodles or indeed a bag of sour jelly sweets then this convenience is a false economy and little wonder that obesity levels have doubled in a quarter of a century. In developing countries, emaciation is traditionally linked to poverty. In developed countries the opposite is true. This huge divergence between those who can afford to eat well and healthily and those who cannot is surely an indicator that something is terribly wrong.*

This twenty-first-century hunger conundrum is hardcore malnutrition and it's hardly surprising then that 10 per cent of four-to five-year-olds arrive at primary schools obese and a further 12 per cent are 'clinically overweight' and that Type 2 diabetes affects over 5 per cent.

This food is almost inescapable. Because it is assumed that we must always be starving. Think about it. From filling up a car with petrol to a trip to a museum, to a ride on a train to a walk in a national park to a meander down a high street, UPFs and UHPFs are everywhere. Even the pram we bought while still pregnant with Harry had a plastic cupholder attached to the handlebar.

I get it; many of us work two jobs and juggle family life. We don't have any time – or even the basic skills – to cook properly any more and we don't have enough cash for so many of the fresh ingredients.

But food is NOT convenient; at least, it shouldn't be. Having an allotment was teaching me that. It was hard labour just to prepare the ground let alone the tireless weeding or collecting the gallons of water needed to keep things alive. And I was only just starting.

---

* It should be noted that in the developing world where once malnutrition was the result of a dearth of calories, now the excess calories provided by UHPFs are leading to rising obesity, increased cases of bowel cancers and Type 2 diabetes, mirroring the problems we have here.

Standing in a supermarket staring at two long shelves with an A–Z of any type of food I could possibly want, I couldn't help feeling like Alice just trying to get out of Wonderland.

On cool, flat days redolent of February no one wanted to be outside. But the pressure was on to water daily and to water well when no rain was forecast. And so was the pressure to entertain the children.

Enticed by a Thermos of weak hot chocolate Ott and I (and a pram-confined Kit) sauntered down to the allotments. There had been a surge in growth despite the slate-white skies and cool temperatures and with the grasses now as high as her shoulders she became disorientated and entangled quickly when we filled our cans. We stopped to sit on my coat as a picnic rug and sipped from the Thermos and then started afresh with our watering cans.

First the beans. Only, the beans weren't there; someone had taken them.

'Why on earth would anyone steal bean seedlings?' I said aloud.

I knelt at the base of the canes to examine more closely. Ottie joined me, squatting on her haunches, and started pointing out the woodlice. Nothing. The more I looked, the less I saw. Every bean had mysteriously disappeared. I imagined a black-clothed gardener, utility belt packed with trowels and forks, stealing through the village under cover of darkness and making for the allotments.

'What kind of world do we live in?' I said.

Ott shouted, 'Look, Mummy! There's one!' I crouched to re-examine the remains of the last beanstalk. It had not been stolen, but eaten. By what I don't know; there were no telltale signs of silvery slug trails, no paw prints, no bird droppings. Nothing, indeed, with which to conduct a forensic investigation at all.

I consoled myself; at least there was backup in the form of the directly sown beans. All was not lost.

The bean seedlings may have disappeared but the weeds were once again already shooting skyward. The dandelions taunted, waved and nodded their heavy heads and Ott squealed with delight when she blew and waved them about, doing the wind's work for it, seeds scattering over the veg beds as lightly as her laughter pealed on the breeze. Maybe we'll get lucky, I thought, watching her skip and frolic. Maybe the dandelion seedlings will be eaten by a dandelion-loving slug.

That dream was shattered when a few days later, while Harry and Ott were at nursery, I pottered to the plot with Kit.

The earth was parched dry and crumbled to dust beneath my feet. I doubted very much that any of the tender seedlings planted last week would have had much chance of surviving. Even the raspberry, which I'd been promised would withstand a battering of battlefield proportions when it came to neglect, was shedding baked brown leaves and wilting.

It was soon obvious that water was the least of my problems.

Silky, slimy trails slithered between the pea leaves. They were full of holes as if shot to pieces and hung skeletal and useless from their shoots. Outrage turned to dismay when I saw that the few tendrils which were undertaking the gargantuan task of clambering up the hazel twigs to safety were far too immature to hold on to the smooth hazel bark and lay as if mortally wounded on the battlefield of my allotment.

'No,' I said to Kit with the sort of heartfelt drama one sees in courtroom television dramas. 'No, no, no. This is not how this ends.'

Kit blinked.

We scuttled back home to collect two containers of slug pellets which I scattered liberally around the whole pea area.

A slug consumes twice its body weight every twenty-four hours, usually at night when you are fast asleep and dreaming of prize-winning vegetables and how wholesome your children are going to be upon eating said veg. They – the slugs – are not particularly discerning in what they eat. From seedlings to lettuces, cabbages to lupines, if it's in front of a slug it's a goner.

Slugs and to a lesser extent snails are such a blight for gardeners that there is an entire industry surrounding controlling or deterring them. From copper tape to trays of beer, eggshells to pellets, the theories and methods abound.

Pellets are the rat poison equivalent to slugs but wildlife con-servationists argue that the secondary poisoning in birds or in the ground is enough to end their use. A slug pub is another deterrent. Bury a jar in the soil and fill it half full of beer. The slug, it turns out, is partial to a pint or two and easily lured to a beery death by drowning should said pints be strategically placed. I tried this once. It didn't work and the waste of decent ale after a particularly trying week was enough to send J into a pit of despair. I tried copper tape too; wrapping an entire planter in a roll of surprisingly expensive copper tape. The theory is that the tape, once crawled over, gives the slug a small electric shock. All well and good if the slugs aren't already in situ or if a child doesn't tear off the tape and use it as a belt. Eggshells, crushed, are supposed to be a good barrier as is ash or gravel but they are pretty useless when wet.

And then there are the nematodes, microscopic protozoa that can be bought as a powder and added to water. The way they work on slugs is rather gruesome and redolent of a zombie apocalypse film plot. They take over the body of a slug through its mouth or anus and release a bacteria particularly toxic to slugs, which multiplies, killing the slug host from the inside within two days. The slug corpse tissue is then eaten upon when the nematodes look for a new host. Nematodes are thought to be the most environmentally friendly and idiot-proof slug deterrent.

But I didn't know any of this as I sprinkled pellets far and wide. Besides which, the environment was not being particularly kind to my vegetables.

This was War.

I grow cosmos every year because, firstly, they are easy flowers to propagate and look pretty. But secondly and more importantly, they remind me of a garden in Kabul. Bagh-e Babur was a favourite haunt for Kabulis at weekends. It was a public garden which, having been used as a frontline in the civil war and subsequently left to rot, was nothing more than scrubland by the mid-2000s. Years of rejuvenation and horticultural expertise revived the garden to its former Moghul glory with water channels and plane trees, orchards and rows of roses and terraces foaming with delicate pink and white cosmos.

I was visiting the garden one day to learn about its reconstruction. Having had a particularly difficult few days prior to that working on a news feature about child abuse and self-immolation, and keenly feeling the pressure cooker of my job and the flailing security of Kabul, I was restless and disjointed. While I waited for my meeting to begin, I walked along the terraces amid the waist-high beds of cosmos. The flowers bowed and shimmered in the strong dusty winds which blew off the mountains behind me. The pungent and mostly obnoxious smells of the city were quickly replaced by grass and pollen and I felt momentarily at peace and, for a few minutes, unfussed by the world and everything it was cramming into my head. The cosmos seemed to me to brush the war away.

So I grow cosmos from seed to remind me of Afghanistan and to remind me that the world still turns. It might not have been 'very allotment' to put flowers where vegetables were supposed to flourish but this was *my* space and those were my comforts.

May is a month of past and future. Past because it is at the end of the lean months of winter and future because it's on the edge; spring is underway, the flowers are in bud and abundance is around the corner. With the allotment I began to think of May as the month of mayhem. A month of daily planting and watering, potting on, moving, re-propagating and digging in. It was a month of hard labour. Growing your own, as I was learning, was a full-time job.

My mother once said that children are born uncivilised and that it is up to you to civilise them. The same, I think, can be said of plants. It is down to the gardener to train them to do what you want or need them to do. But I was floundering trying to balance three children and scores of seedlings, and training them each to do what I needed them to do to survive.

Everyone needed me; that was the problem. Kit needed me to carry, comfort and feed. Ott needed me to understand her entangled two-year-old frustrations and tantrums, Harry needed me to play and to teach. And the allotment needed me to weed, feed and de-pest. It was a burden; another bloody chore like unloading the dishwasher or washing machine. I could not do it all. Something had to give. I felt caged and then envied caged birds because at least they wouldn't feel this heavy responsibility. And then I felt guilty and crap and I hated the allotment and all those seedlings for making me feel guilty and crap.

'I did warn you,' J said not unkindly. 'Just do what you can when you can and if it doesn't work then it doesn't matter.'

I nodded but felt condemned. I would do anything for my children but sometimes I missed the simple liberties of pre-children life and, truth be told, I had begun to think of the allotment as a new 'simple liberty'. Granted, it may at times have seemed like a bit of a chore like unloading the dishwasher or washing machine but the thought of *not* doing the allotment felt . . . well, *that* felt like prison.

It began to dawn on me at around this time that there was something missing from the village allotment sites. Other people.

The idea of a community is so entrenched in an allotment that there is a whole panel describing the types of eccentrics one might

82

encounter on a site in the RHS allotment handbook. The woman who obsesses over pumpkins, the man in search of the biggest onion or the bloke trying to grow the straightest leek. In allotment lore plot holders are a bit weird, a bit eccentric, almost parodies of themselves. But nice ones. Social media platforms are full of allotment groups, the members of which regularly post photographs of their successes, offer advice or help.

In popular culture the allotment is a stage and a lot more besides. The allotments in the soap operas *EastEnders* and *Coronation Street* were, over the years, an extra set on which dramatic storylines of drinking, drugs, arson and even murder unfurled. In the 2007 film, *Grow Your Own*, an allotment site is the backdrop for racial tensions between old-timers and a group of refugees who are given plots to enable them to blend in.

Indeed where there is community, there is also the potential for unrest. The 2013 BBC documentary series *Allotment Wars* explored the conflict seething among plot holders across Britain. It was not available to watch in full at the time of writing but the clips circulating the internet show a surprising number of petty squabbles among plot holders. In one clip, a set of garden gnomes goes missing only to be found dangling from a neighbouring shed's guttering a few days later much to the gnome owner's open-mouthed apoplexy (and my own amusement).

Only half the plots on the village allotment site were in use and although there were signs of snatched moments of work (a few extra beanpoles here, a makeshift cloche there) I had yet to encounter this sense of community whiling away an evening on the site. Not that I particularly minded; at the end of long days with children the quiet peace of birdsong and cows mooing in the distance and the rustle of trees was something I had already come to cherish. Even the gentle church bell chime marking time passing didn't bother me. This was my houseless back garden.

The morning dawned bright and early with the sun streaming through the windows and the children screaming downstairs. Which was unusual as Harry never went down on his own and Ottilie, still mastering the stairs, *couldn't* go down on her own. 'Happy birthday, Mummy,' they shouted before turning to J and saying urgently, 'can we have our croissants now?'

We gorged ourselves on pastries and jams, fresh orange juice and coffee and I began opening my cards.

'Hope these help you grow vegetables,' my brother's read. The delivery was delayed so this cryptic clue piqued my interest. What could he have sent? I hoped that whatever it was he had sent me would work some magic. The beans had not germinated; the soil I realised later was much, much too heavy with clay, the peas were still being decimated. The weeds were winning the battle for land and even the trusty and sturdy maize was looking yellow-leafed.

I received one other allotment-related present during the course of the day. A voucher from our green-fingered village friends Nico and Crystal for an hour each of their time to help on the plot. 'We just figured that time is something you really don't have much of.' Crystal smiled.

Nico chipped in, 'We'll do the strimming, clear the ground, weed.

Whatever helps.' It was one of the most thoughtful presents I think I have ever received.

I saw them working on the plot a day or two later hard at work with the gift of their own time.

The allotment had undergone a makeover. The borders were strimmed, the couch grasses razed to the ground and they were making me a no-dig bed too, laying down card and upending compost over the top. Crystal had weeded the other beds, tended the already straggly-looking butternut squashes, staked the raspberry and planted nasturtiums, and there was even a bucket of homemade fertiliser made out of nettles.

Nico was planting two mysterious plants.

'Yacón,' he said cheerfully.

'Fantastic!' I said. I had absolutely no idea what one of those was. It sounded like a computer operating system.*

They had achieved in one hour what would have taken me a week and they'd made it lovely and seem manageable. I had a vision of what the plot could be with *time* and I liked that vision very much indeed. There might not have been a community on the site itself but there exists among gardeners a spirit of togetherness and a generosity of spirit. There was hope.

Inspired and refusing to give up on the beans, while Ott and Kit slept Harry and I set about sowing the remaining packets of runner beans

---

* I later discovered that the yacón is a watery tuber prized in native South America for its thirst-quenching properties.

in the greenhouse, to give them a meticulous, safe and healthy start to life with smothering levels of attention.

We filled twelve small terracotta pots with fine seed compost that we dampened before placing a bean on each one. Harry practised counting as we did so, moving an outstretched finger slowly between each one and doubling back on himself. 'One, two, three, four, eleven, nine, three! Is that right?'

'Perfect,' I said.

This time, we would protect the beans and rummaged around for suitable material, alighting on some raspberry netting and ties. 'Like armour,' Harry said. I hoped it would be.

Later on in the afternoon, when Kit and Ott were awake, we picked the remainder of the broad beans from the planter by the sandpit. I demonstrated how to shell them and they delighted not only at the satisfaction of cracking each pod but also the fluffy interior of each one.

'They're so cosy!' Harry remarked. 'I'd like to be a bean just like this one.'

'This one,' Ottilie echoed.

He tried counting again and after successfully listing a few numbers in more or less sequential order resumed his shelling efforts. A lemon-yellow light filled the sky. Blackbirds and songbirds trilled in the woods nearby, pigeons cooed. Kit gurgled. His head was as soft as a bean pod and smelled as baby sweet as spring. Jiggling him on my lap and letting him clutch and gum an empty shell while watching the other two prod and poke their chubby fingers into pods and empty the contents into a saucepan, I thought this must be the stuff of magic.

'It's lovely and quiet, Mummy,' Harry said at length. And so it was. Until he announced he needed a poo, tripped over and wailed.

*

Hardy, and easy to cultivate, the broad bean was one of the first crops to be domesticated. Excavations have found traces of the fava in ten-thousand-year-old settlements in Syria. Like the pea, the bean was one of the most important sources of protein and stored dried, should there be a crop failure.

But it was not exactly cherished as a food crop and often given to animals. The Egyptians viewed fava – or broad beans – with a great deal of caution and believed them to be unclean. The angle-loving scientist and philosopher Pythagoras banned his followers from eating them, fearing rebirth as a bean and not as an animal or human. Meanwhile Pliny the Elder, author of the thirty-seven-book *Naturalis Historia*, arguably the world's first encyclopaedia (albeit a work of uneven accuracy by today's standards), believed eating beans caused sleepless nights and nightmares and that they generally 'dulled the senses'. Sowing broad beans, on the other hand, was thought to be as good for soil conditioning as manure. He was on to something as the bean is today considered an integral part of crop rotation owing to the release of nitrogen stored in nodules on their roots back into the soil.[4]

The later Romans thought differently and included this humble bean in soups, salads and sacrifices. The feast day for the goddess Carna, protector of vital organs, fell on 1 June when the beans were being harvested. They also believed that on death, our souls transmigrate into beans, making them an important if a little morbid funeral dish.

The Romans brought many cultivated vegetables to Britain but, as it turns out, the humble broad bean was already here and had been cultivated and traded for thousands of years.[5]

Having been introduced to the Americas by Christopher Columbus and his maritime colleagues who relied on broad beans and peas as provisions, broad beans are now a staple of Peruvian cuisine. The discovery of the prettier, juicer climbing bean in South America led to the slow decline of the broad bean's popularity and up until the middle of the seventeenth century the broad bean was relegated to fodder.

The 'not fit for human consumption' reputation was a hard one to shake and even today broad beans are rarely sold fresh in supermarkets. This is not to say they are not a valuable crop, however. There are a number of bean fields around our village with enviably tall spires and juicy beans. A local farmer explained to me a few months later that while some are grown for fodder, if unaffected by bean-loving beetles or blight, one variety of bean is sold for export to the Middle East where *ful* or *foul*, a protein-rich fava-bean-based dish, is served during Ramadan for a pre-dawn breakfast. The fava has gone full circle.

The appearance and harvest in our gardens or on our allotments of the lowly broad bean hails the start of spring proper. And *we* loved eating them cooked with bacon, feta cheese, oodles of olive oil and pepper. I learned later that a variation of this was the sacrificial dish offered to Carna. Lucky Carna.

I felt increasingly heavy as a shadowless, flat light had fallen across the month and refused to budge. The roses had bloomed early without my noticing and were already dropping their petals and, to top it off, a murder of crows had made the allotment their new home and were pecking at the ground for seeds, seedlings and worms, quite oblivious to my shooing. It was hard to maintain allotment momentum.

Just a few days after our afternoon of bean shelling, pestilence and plague ran helter-skelter between plot and children. Harry developed a fever and clung to me, arms like pea tendrils flailing for support. Kit's eye became glued shut with gunk and Ottilie could not stop coughing. When Harry was covered with a red sandpaper-like rash I took to Dr Google . . .

'Scarlet fever? Didn't Victorians die from scarlet fever?' J said unhelpfully.

I checked the symptoms. 'Raised rash; check. Blotchy red skin; check. High fever; check. Fatigue; check. Appetite loss; check. Tongue . . . Harry, open your mouth.'

He opened his mouth and half-heartedly showed a bright red and white blotchy tongue.

'Tongue; check. The only thing he doesn't have is vomiting.'

On cue, he vomited.

'Here. Three times a day,' a doctor said a few hours later and scribbled on the box of antibiotics. 'Good luck. You'll need it.' Whether she was referring to the taste of the medicine or the household pandemic we were about to face, or even the allotment I had mentioned in passing, I wasn't sure. Perhaps a bit of all three.

June

Lampshades, helmets and cloches – A muddled history of
courgettes – Companion planting – New arrivals – Digging
for DORA – A newborn baby allotment – Meeting a
Ukrainian gardener – History of the runner bean – Peas,
snacks and potatoes

'Delivery for you,' a driver shouted over the gate as Pullo snarled through the metal bars trying to take chunks out of his knees.

The box he handed over was vast but light and I wondered what on earth it could hold. 'Hope these help you to grow vegetables', the label said. My brother's present had finally arrived. I had imagined a library of vegetable growing books or a special propagating machine – if such a thing exists – or perhaps an army of . . . I ripped open the paper tape, lifted the flaps and frowned.

I scratched my head.

'Oooh,' J enthused, emerging from his office. 'What have you got?'

'I'm not quite sure.' Five bamboo lampshades encased in reams of protective paper stared up at me. I lifted one out and examined it.

'Why on earth . . .' I began. I knew enough from my sister that basket ware was on trend at that moment but lampshades? Five? I lifted one out and examined it. It was not very sturdy and I was at a loss as to how they would help me on the allotment.

'Well at least the box might prove useful,' I said to J, stuffing them back in their protective paper and turning my attention to Ottilie, who at that time was reddening unripely with something which looked a lot like a scarlet fever rash, and to Kit whose eyes were weeping with some sort of conjunctivitis. The childhood plague continued to spread through the children as fast as bindweed.

Housebound once again, we played with the enormous cardboard box.

'Oh, you've made a church?' J said a few hours later.

'No, Daddy. It's a castle,' Harry corrected him from inside the box-castle. 'And I am a knight.' He appeared wearing one of the bamboo lampshades over his head.

'I'm a knight, Daddy,' a Calpol fuelled Ottilie echoed.

We all beamed up at him. I was rather proud of the box-castle having sawn out crenellations and a drawbridge big enough for both Harry and Ottilie to crawl through, not to mention a few arrow slits hewn with a bread knife, and had set them the task of painting it while I made a flagpole out of a bamboo cane from the allotment.

'Why is it orange?' J asked. 'Why are you all orange, for that matter?'

'Ran out of grey.' I shrugged.

My brother is typing . . .

'Lampshades? What lampshades?'

My present, I typed. They arrived the other day. Love them. They'll look so smart when we hang them, I lied.

My brother is typing . . .

My phone rang.

He said, 'You think I'd send you lampshades?'

'Well, I don't know,' I said. 'I wasn't very clear about birthday wishes.' This was true. When asked what I wanted I had said, 'Anything garden-y.'

'You idiot,' my brother said. 'They're cloches.'

'Huh?'

'Cloches. You pop them over your seedlings to protect them. Winds, frosts, animals; that sort of thing. Thought these were a little better looking than the plastic ones you usually get.' He was laughing. 'You really thought I'd send you five oversized lampshades?'

That evening, with the children medicated, settled and calm, I bundled the cloches into the back of my car with a tray of courgette and chard seedlings and made for the allotment. Having sustained a period of yellowing, the maize, I noticed, was back to full throttle green and growing fast. The soil was warm too when I dug my hands in (of course I forgot the trowel, of course I bloody did) and set the lampshades, I mean cloches, over the seedlings.

With the sun sloping slowly towards dusk I had a good feeling. I looked at the now thriving maize. A very good feeling indeed. If nothing else here worked, the freshly planted seedlings now protected by cloches would surely flourish. I was an old hand at growing spinach and chard. So much so that two summers ago we had virtually lived off chard stalks cooked in liberal quantities of butter and garlic.

When Harry saw the cloches in situ a few days later he was not amused. We had taken a picnic down to the plot.

'But I thought these were helmets and visors?'

'Well they are in a way,' I said. 'Here. I passed him a sandwich and poured him a cup of water. 'They're the helmets and visors for the plants, aren't they?' It was a tenuous rationale but after chewing for a few moments he nodded.

We examined the peas when he had finished. Still flailing about on the ground but I was astonished to see that many of them had flowered and were producing tiny pods. 'Look!' I exclaimed, tying them to their supports with raffia.

Harry crouched and looked and was singularly unimpressed.

We set to work on the courgette seedlings. Placing them on the ground I showed him how far apart they needed to be.

'Why can't we plant them close together?' he asked. 'Like the peas. Like friends?'

'Because,' I began, 'they will need space. Peas grow upwards. They should do at any rate. Courgettes grow outwards. You'll see.'

Part of the *Cucurbita pepo* species, the courgette, summer squash – or the zucchini as it is known in Italy and America ('*zucca*' being the Italian for gourds and squashes) – has been a British favourite in the vegetable garden since the 1960s.

That it is an easy, fast-growing plant makes it a much-loved hit with novice veg growers like myself for whom there is instant gratification in those racing green fruits. But its history is long. With domestication beginning around ten thousand years ago in the New World it is a somewhat complicated one, too, owing to the interchangeable descriptions of hard-skinned ancestors which were often grown as much for their use as a receptacle – or gourd – as their flesh.[1] Indeed the word courgette was given by the French as a diminutive word for '*courge*', meaning gourd.

Throughout history squash and gourd were catch-all words. Botanists tried their best to classify them with more differentiation but it took two hundred years for someone to notice that a gourd has a white flower while a squash has a yellow one. Brought to Europe by Columbus squashes were originally thought, like many New World introductions, to be fit only for animals but, by the sixteenth century, they were a popular addition to the menu.

The squashes then were very much on the 'more like a marrow' spectrum but in the nineteenth century breeders in Milan gave us the slim green things we eat all summer long. The marrow-ness remains, however, for turn your back on a courgette for a few minutes and a marrow you will find.

'You've got your hands full.'

'You've got your work cut out.'

'You must be so busy.'

These are the sorts of things perfect strangers said to me when they saw me with three children so young and close together in age. There is no denying it was hard work and busy and all-consuming but I preferred to look at it in a different way. Companionship.

The thought occurred to me when I first saw Harry helping Ott do up the flaps on a raincoat and then later helping her undress for the bath. He was fiddling with the buttons on her shirt and talking gently as he did so while she looked up at him with absolute trust and absolute faith in what he was doing. On other occasions when unable to instantly tend to a mewling Kit I'd find Harry or Ott distracting him or comforting him, hushing him with soft tones. This is not to say they didn't fight and wind each other up – often – but for the most part, they were learning how to help each other. They were each other's companions.

Companion planting is just what it says on the tin; it is the theory that some plants perform better when planted alongside others. It is all about creating happy plant communities. Some plant combinations aid pollination, others boost growth or repel pests and a few are said to prevent blight.

The three sisters is a common combination and originates from Native American tribes. Maize, squash and (French) beans are planted together, the former providing the frame for the latter, the large leaves of the squashes planted at the base provide shade for the ground, keeping the soil moist and weeds at bay. This method is thought to date back five or six thousand years but there are dozens of other combinations. Carrots and onions, for example. The strong allium smell of the onions is said to repel carrot fly. Carrots and leeks also work well for the same reason. Marigolds repel whitefly from tomatoes while nasturtiums are said to lure aphids away from brassicas like Brussels sprouts. Borage flowers are a magnet for hoverflies whose larvae feed on the blackfly on broad beans.

The benefits of companion planting are largely anecdotal and some gardeners scoff at the notion. Not least because with companion vegetable planting there is little space for uniformity and neatness. The benefits of the children being so close in age were plain for me to see; when they weren't at each other's necks, scratching or kicking each other or snatching away toys, they were each other's companions and (I hoped) always would be. And coming up in the rear was baby Kit, the third in the triumvirate of companions.

*

I had been so preoccupied with potting on Harry to school that I had not given much thought to Ottilie let alone little Kit. Like the peas in their greenhouse plugs, Kit was bursting out of his Moses basket. Try as I might – and I did – I just couldn't wedge him in any more and with a heavy heart I packed it away into the attic and set about making up the cot.

I mourned this graduation to the next stage because however hard the baby stage can be, it is sweet and tender and oh, it goes so fast. Never again would I be able to carry said basket and a sleeping baby like a bag of shopping into different rooms when needed. Nor for that matter would I ever again cradle my own newborn baby in the crook of my arm or under my neck, nor would I fold impossibly small clothes from the washing line. And the baby blanket under which all three of them had slept would also soon be too small and relegated to dolls' prams and teddy bear picnics.

My children were growing and I had barely drawn breath to notice. Just stop, I wanted to say to the Peter Rabbit clock ticking loudly on the bedroom wall. Just stop ticking and tocking and inching forward and let me pause. Let me enjoy these seedlings of ours before it is all too late and they are lurching into independence seeking light and thinking little of their roots.

Village WhatsApp group admin is typing . . .

'Dear all. I am pleased to announce that we have just taken in a Ukrainian family. K and her two children will be staying with us while her father, Sergei, will be staying up the road. Please welcome them to the village.'

Village WhatsApp group member is typing . . .
'That's great!'
Village WhatsApp group member is typing . . .
'Bravo'
Village WhatsApp group member is typing . . .

Village WhatsApp group admin is typing . . .
'Sergei is looking for work and needs something to occupy himself with so please do keep an ear out for any work going. I think he'll do anything.'
Village WhatsApp group member is typing . . .
'Welcome all!'
Village WhatsApp group member is typing . . .
'The cows are loose on the playing fields again.'
Village WhatsApp group member is typing . . .
'I've called the farmer. Thanx 4 letting me no.'
And that was it. War in Ukraine had given a sleepy little village in Dorset some new residents.

When world war exploded in 1914, the empire was feeding Britain. 70 per cent of its cereals, 80 per cent of its fruits and all of its sugar was imported from as far afield as America, Australia, South Africa and Brazil. There was no immediate food crisis but hunger gripped the country in 1916 after a terrible crop failure here and in North America and when farming was at an all-time low. It didn't help that most of the farmhands (and working horses) had been deployed from field to front. Further pressure on the food chain came in February

1917, when Kaiser Wilhelm threatened to 'starve the British people until they who have refused peace, will kneel and plead for it'. German '*unterseeboots*', or 'U-boats', prowled the seas armed with torpedoes and they did not hold back. This unrestricted battle beneath the waves sank over a million tons of merchant shipping by the spring of that year. Britain was within six weeks of running out of wheat and just four until there was no more sugar.

The Board of Agriculture had already been collaborating with the Vacant Land Cultivation Society (a charity established in 1907 which gave wasteland to the unemployed to work) to develop a new land reform allowing the government to seize all unoccupied land for farming and allotments without the consent (or knowledge) of its owner.

Some landowners saw this as a horrific turn of events and the biggest challenge since the break-up of the feudal state. 'Was it for all this that their forefathers had enclosed the family lands?' they asked rather unpatriotically.

Nonetheless within a few months 'allotmentitis' gripped the country and 'Digging for DORA' (Defence of the Realm Act) was the new home front war effort and the country rose to the challenge, spade in one hand, fork in the other. Hundreds of new plots were created every week in parks and playing fields – anything available at all.

People went to extraordinary lengths to turn the lowliest scrap of nothing into productive land. Most famously, a rubbish tip in Battersea used as a 'chute' for dustcarts previously declared unfit for any other use was cleared by volunteers to become a beautiful, tidy and productive set of allotments.

Not everyone rolled up their sleeves, however. The well-to-do residents of west London initially resisted attempts to turn their gated communal gardens into veg beds. The London County Council was slow to create new allotment sites too; citywide there were waiting lists in the hundreds with an average of six applicants per plot – until the *London Evening Standard* exposed their apathy and reluctance and west London's parks were transformed.

And how. A model allotment was installed near the Albert Memorial in Kensington Gardens and another in Regent's Park near the zoo. The London County Council, now on board, installed another six in parks across London. The nation's leaders joined the fight too. The Prime Minister, David Lloyd George, grew King Edward potatoes while the Archbishop of Canterbury wrote a letter to newspapers sanctioning Sunday work. A directive from King George V replaced geraniums with potatoes, cabbages and other vegetables in the flower beds opposite the Victoria Memorial. He had vegetable plots installed at Buckingham Palace and Windsor Castle and there is a lovely photograph of him digging for potatoes at Windsor with Queen Mary in the early days of food shortages.

The war effort was also supported by produce exhibitions and competitions; the money from the sale of prize-winning exhibits was used to buy cigarettes for the war-wounded and surplus vegetables donated to hospitals, while competitions themselves helped to bolster a sense of patriotism and enabled people to feel a part of the bigger whole.

Prizes for produce were all well and good for charitable purposes but the prospect of starvation continued to be a real and present threat. The humble spud was in such short supply that restaurants and hotels were allowed to serve them only on Tuesdays and Fridays. Throwing rice at weddings was illegal as was adopting or feeding stray dogs. By the winter of 1917 queuing for food was the new normal. Luxury chocolate and sweets became outlawed and compulsory rationing limited the buying of sugar, meat and dairy products. The population was encouraged to eat slowly and keep warm – so as to need less food.

The message was simple – and often used in advertisements by seed companies. 'Grow more food.' The country couldn't dig fast enough; demand far outstripped supply. There were waiting lists for allotments in one Lambeth district of over five hundred names.

The Vacant Land Cultivation Society was doing its best to create more sites. Its chairman Mr R Andrews wrote to the *Bucks Free Press* saying that if people were willing, he would be able to secure plots in Surrey waiving any rental fee so that would-be plot holders had only to cover a tram fare to and from their plot so as 'not to wait indefinitely for ground'. In Brixton's now fashionable Brockwell Park portions were cut up for allotments and at one point even the bowling green was looking like a possible plot site but proved to be a step too far for the players who 'were prepared to stoutly defend every turf of it'.

Railway companies with spare wasteland joined the fight for DORA at around this time. Workers and staff in quiet stations were already allowed to cultivate small areas of land but the rail companies increased the number of their plots to six thousand, made them accessible for anyone inclined and even bought gardening essentials in bulk which they sold at cost to plot holders.

Newspaper articles describe new plots becoming available in the London suburbs of Norwood with plot holders working together over weekends to prepare the ground for planting potatoes, while others advertised new plots shortly becoming available.

Allotmentitis wasn't just confined to Britain. Garrison towns of northern France like Le Havre were home to a number of allotments in order to keep soldiers entertained and amused. They even had their own produce shows for it was hoped that a little gentle competition would help develop the 'right spirit' among those posted there. Inmates at prisoner-of-war camps in Germany were allowed to grow their own produce too. At the Ruhleben internment camp, prisoners set up their own horticultural society using barbed wire as trellis although they focused largely on sweet peas, dahlias and chrysanthemums sent to them by the Royal Horticultural Society and the Red Cross.

In Britain, the results of Digging for DORA were astounding. In 1913 there were estimated to be half a million plots. By the end of the war it was estimated there were one and half million.

Allotment societies, associations and federations emerged, as did a National Union of Allotment Holders, which gave growers access to cheap tools and an outlet for selling their produce. The war may have been devastating worldwide but by the time the armistice was drawn up, 'the Allotment' had become a well and truly established feature of our landscape and national psyche.

Which was just as well because peace did not bring stability. On the contrary, the world had changed beyond recognition.

A *Punch* cartoon of 1920 depicting David Lloyd George says it all.

The Prime Minister sits at his desk, frowning mid-thought with a pen in his mouth. Only his shoulders and head are seen above a tidal wave of papers, the headings of which include 'Irish Crisis, Polish Crisis, Strikes, Mesopotamia Crisis, Bolshevism, Soaring Prices, Cost of Living, Direct Action'.

With rationing, soaring unemployment, demobilised troops searching for jobs and peace, and a crisis down the coal mines, lean times ahead loomed and the need for self-sufficiency boomed.

Summer was very much in the air and in the ground; there was heat now, and a lot of it (which I loved and J despaired of), a lengthening to the days, a clarity to the sky at night which remained warm and, blow me down with a piece of couch grass, but the allotment was beginning to take shape. The carrots were growing, albeit in a wonky line, and the maize was inching up daily.

It was, I thought much later, like the early days of having a new-born. In those really early days after arriving in this world, babies don't do much other than sleep, eat and occasionally yell or wriggle if they find themselves unable to do either. Thus rather inert, they can lull the new parent into thinking they've got 'a chilled one'. The allotment was like this then and I felt smug. Having been planted, there wasn't a great deal to do apart from water. Nailing it, I thought.

Which was just as well because at home, alas, and despite erecting a paddling pool in the garden for raucous playtime, pestilence remained rife. I don't suppose it ever really left but lay dormant waiting to strike any of the children at their weakest points. Harry continued to look grey and required more antibiotics. Kit developed a fever and inflamed tonsils which even the doctor found alarming. Ottie oscillated between fever and a demented energy.

The house quickly resembled a Victorian sanatorium with me rushing between ailing offspring at pace with medicines and cold damp towels. And love – because when all else fails, when the bottom falls out of your world and there is no end to the discomfort and sickness, sometimes comfort is the best tonic of all.

Would that this was true for disease or blight-riddled plants.

'They're all full,' J was saying. 'From here to Dartmouth.' We were meant to be going to a friend's wedding in Devon in two weeks but were struggling to find a kennel for Pullo.

An idea popped in my head. 'What about Sergei?'

J frowned. 'Who?'

'The Ukrainian guy.'

J looked blank and I explained how I had met Sergei that morning at a village playgroup and how his daughter and host family had said he was looking for odd jobs. He'd turn his hand to anything, so I'd been told. And if he was up for it, I thought, he could do the watering in our absence.

'Well?'

'I guess he could only say no.'

'And he hates other dogs. He bites them,' J said into his phone a few days later and waited for an app to translate into Ukrainian.

Sergei nodded and seemed unfazed. Taking J's phone he spoke

loudly. 'It is best if showering ourselves,' the female robot voice translated.

He spoke again. 'Please can we walk showing,' and he used his two forefingers to mimic walking.

It was a bright, scorching day. We loaded up the pram with children, gave Sergei the lead and the dog and set off for the shade of the woods.

He described, as best he could through the app, that he had been in Poland before coming here but originally was from Kharkiv. My ears pricked. At that time, Kharkiv was at the centre of the conflict. I wondered how it must be to watch one's home town being obliterated from the relative comfort of an unfamiliar land thousands of miles away. But Sergei didn't strike me as the sort of man to want pity.

When the app started malfunctioning J asked him if he spoke any other languages. Sergei nodded. German, Polish and Russian, but of the latter he shook his head and crossed his arms. 'Taboo,' he said. We didn't need an app for that.

Back at home, while J rummaged around for a thirst-quenching few beers, I spoke into the app.

'Do you like gardening?' I asked.

I had been contemplating offering him the other half of my plot. If he was bored, I thought, and homesick and in need of reprieve, perhaps he'd like the distraction.

He shrugged. My assumptions were misguided. He was, however, willing to water it while we were away.

Later, during a cooler, balmier evening amid tick-filled grasses so overgrown again they grazed my elbows, I showed him the allotment.

With little to no phone reception at that end of the village translation was difficult but he didn't really need me to tell an app to tell him what was what. He got it all on sight.

'Pontatoes!' he mispronounced excitedly, looking at the volunteer spud poking through the ground. He frowned at the wonky lines of carrots and crouched down to look more closely. His body language said it all: 'What the hell is this?'

He turned to the corn and expertly removed the lower, yellow leaves and then moved on to the baby chard under a cloche which he checked for slugs, picking one off and flicking it into the next plot.

We Brits being 'mad-keen gardeners' use gardening as a catch-all phrase for growing anything from petunias to pumpkins but in countries where levels of agriculture are high and growing one's own veg is as much part of everyday life as eating them, 'gardening' really only refers to ornamental and aesthetic gardening.

Standing at the end of the plot where I could pick up a bar of reception, I called Nathan, a Ukrainian-speaking friend, and asked him to translate. 'Would he like half the plot?'

After a bit of a back and forth my friend explained that he didn't want it. Not, Nathan added, because he didn't want to grow food but because Sergei didn't expect to be here for that long. He would be going home in September when the war was over. Besides, Nathan explained, he was too late. The start of the growing season was too far gone to be properly productive.

We watered together, awkwardly passing cans and tripping on a fallen wire fence and stamping on nettles. He looked at the no-dig bed with its single yacón and was perplexed. I rather fancied that no-dig was not a concept that had yet made it to Ukraine. I shrugged my shoulders. It was the longest day, the title of which I'd always found odd given that it was also the start of summer. It depressed me to think of shortening days to come but I took comfort in the heat as we worked.

Before we left Sergei knelt to pick at the weeds, pulling them up expertly and deftly, roots and all, with one strong tug.

There was something deliberate and considered about how he worked his way through the plot. He understood the plants, he respected them, knew where to help them along and where not to.

I thought about his sudden departure from Ukraine. What if that was me with my family? Uprooted like a weed and forced to make a new home somewhere else. What would I do?

Triangles of bamboo canes supporting runner beans are an ubiquitous part of English allotments and vegetable gardens. Indeed it was the publican's bean row which drew me to the allotments in the first place, reminding me of Yeats' *'nine bean rows'* of his *Lake Isle of Innesfree*. But there is still some debate as to how the runner bean was first introduced to the United Kingdom in the sixteenth or seventeenth centuries.[2]

Often confused with the French bean, the runner bean is native to the chilly altitudes of Mexico and Central America where its wild ancestors grew and were foraged some nine thousand years ago.

The runner bean was the last of the New World discoveries to be brought back to the Old World by Cortés and his conquistadors where it was valued more for its pretty scarlet and white flowers than its beans. The climbing blooms lent themselves well to garlands and decorative displays fashionable at that time.

But while the French bean (which by the way is not actually French but South American, where it was often grown alongside maize and squashes as part of the three sisters of companion planting) is coveted the world over from China to America, Italy to Russia, the runner bean is beloved only in Britain. And even then, the jury is still out. Picked when small and juicy they are delicious but miss a day's harvest and those sweet little fingers will become fat and fibrous with strings which will easily lodge themselves between teeth and scratch their way down gullets.

But if the failures to grow thus far were anything to go by, we were far from having a glut.

Our bean seedling (or rather, Harry's bean seedling) needed transplanting to the plot and planting out. Third time lucky on the bean front. All we needed to do was find space amid the rampant weeds.

I had added to my tools a hoe that my father had kindly donated. The only problem was I had not a clue how to use it. A long handle, one flat square of metal like a small spade at an angle attached to a U-shaped piece. It wasn't obvious at all. I adopted what I thought might be a suitable hoeing posture and scraped at the ground but to little effect. I hit it and then I tried digging with it. No. Not obvious at all. Harry had a go too, but in the end we resorted to hand-picking out the weeds in a suitable-for-a-bean spot.

We began constructing a teepee-style frame using the old canes and tying them together using a length of old wire found conveniently in the long grass. Together we bedded in the seedlings, pushing the earth firmly around their roots. Beginning on the netting, we wrapped it loosely around the canes and used stones and rocks to keep it flush to the ground. The allotment might be the Wild West but this was the runner bean saloon of safety.

'I'm hungry,' Harry said as we admired our handiwork.

There were young mangetout hanging like emeralds from the pea sticks. 'Here!' I said, handing him one and holding my breath. I waited for a slow smile to spread across his impish face. This was what it was all about, I thought. Sweet tender home-grown veg from plot to mouth in seconds.

Harry chewed. He frowned. He chewed a little more and then he spat it out like chewing tobacco, declaring it disgusting and asking if I had any biscuits. The woodlouse at his feet was infinitely more interesting. I picked myself a bean. It was sweet, crunchy, juicy and oh-so-full of flavour. The boy was clearly off his rocker and I was disappointed but there was no point forcing the issue so I gave him a spade and together we dug a few more holes for the remaining corn seedlings.

'A potato, Mumma!' he yelped.

I looked. And there it was, a pale, gold orb of a new conscript potato, just sitting there and waiting to be discovered. 'And another.' Harry jumped up and down on a seedling. 'Another!'

I knew nothing about growing potatoes. Absolutely nothing about first and second earlies, main crops, chitting and seeding. Nothing about the way they grew as a family underground, nothing about their flowers and nothing about earthing up or digging up either. All that came much later.

Like explorers searching for the treasure of El Dorado we dug with a frenzy, unearthing more and more conscript potatoes. They hung together like oversized pearls and all thoughts of the shunned mangetout vanished. Harry jumped up and down at every discovery. Never mind mangetout or peas; this was our gold.

We ate the conscripts for tea as a potato salad and I'd like to think that they were the best potatoes we had ever tasted.

We were getting there, I thought as I laid my weary head on the pillow that night. It was both harder and easier than imagined to keep the plot going but the bountiful results of the allotment challenge were already visible.

We had been through almost a dozen sicknesses, survived slugs and rabbits and were out the other side stronger and wiser. This was to be a summer of glowing health indeed.

And then I was sick.

July

The plot awakens – The beginning of an obsession – A
history of brassicas – Poppies – Botany photography – In
search of a teacher – Allotment cheating – Seeking advice
from a stranger – Water shortage and drought – Carrot
porn – A history of carrots – Rain and reprieve – Brassica
advice – Winning as a novice

If June was the month of the plot as a sleepy newborn, still getting used to life ex-utero, July was the month it woke up and like its human counterpart it grew very quickly.

'It's so wonderful that now we can start eating what we've been growing,' J said, looking at the allotment in the stretched afternoon sunlight while he watered. Having spent a few days careering through motherhood fighting whatever sicknesses my children had passed on to me, dosed up on Day Nurse, Night Nurse and copious amounts of paracetamol, I had been eager to get down to the allotment. Seeing that I was not quite up to battle strength, J had offered to help.

I was gently hoeing (at least, that's what I thought I was doing – I still hadn't mastered the technique and had fixed upon a drag-and-poke method) between the courgette and chard cloches and looked up at him. 'We?'

'I mean, what *you've* been growing,' he said hastily. 'It's amazing that things can be harvested so quickly when you only planted a week ago.'

'Month ago,' I corrected. 'But yes, that was the general idea,' I said. 'Instant gratification.' Whereas a herbaceous border of stubborn peonies or beloved by slugs lupines can take at least a growing season if not three to establish itself, in the vegetable garden, tangible results are immediate and pretty satisfying.

Kit, who until then had been sitting contentedly on a tuft of grass gnawing on pea snaps, flopped forward onto his face and let out a wail. Righting him we continued; J pacing to and from the water trough and me with the hoe.

One of the courgettes had flowered and was starting to produce small fruits. I knelt down to admire the slender yellow fingers and, feeling ants swarming over my bare legs, leapt up again with a scream and started shaking my limbs feverishly. J laughed rather unkindly and I scowled at him.

Kit wailed again. The sun was in his eyes and as it was getting on for his teatime we hoisted him back into the pram and started the journey home. The vet and barrister's plots were abundant and immaculate. Bean canes already covered with flowers, a neat row of rocket and another of lettuces, potato plants in flower. The rainbow chard was so prolific it grew almost as a bush. It was hard not to notice their successes. It was hard, too, not to notice that once again they were ahead of the season having already started to grow winter veg. Lines of cabbages, kale and sprouts, maturing nicely beneath the exquisite summer sun.

The last time I'd tried growing winter veg it was on the back of an episode of *Gardeners' World* in lockdown. The presenter, Monty Don, was doing one of his 'plant along with me' challenges with red cabbage which he anticipated eating on Christmas Day. It took me two years to yield one small, tough and inedible plant which ended up as green waste at the council tip.

I texted Crystal. If anyone knew what should be planted for the winter, she would. And indeed she did. Sort of. She admitted to a similar anxiety enveloping her four weeks ago causing her to overspend on seeds. Her message and support buoyed me. But then it rattled me. *Four* weeks. That's almost a month. And a month in the garden is a long time especially in the summer. I must sow some cabbages and broccoli. Yesterday.

A trip to the garden centre beckoned. After the children and I had stared like cats at the oversized and velvet-tailed fish in the pond section of the garden centre and after we had investigated the massive terracotta pots and hidden inside them and after we had discussed the virtues of lavender and NOT AT ALL PICKED ANY we made for the vegetable seedlings. Harry at a gallop (he had taken to galloping everywhere like a *Monty Python* King Arthur with Ottilie stumbling after him). We bought red cabbage, broccoli, leeks and some lettuce seedlings which looked dejected and unloved. At around £1 a seedling the economics did not add up. Rarely are red cabbages ever more than £1. What on earth was the point? Besides which, brassicas are some of the hardest things to grow. But I did not know that then and, while beans were my bête noire of the spring, the ups and (mostly) downs of these leafy, waxy seedlings were to become an obsession.

We tend to lump all brassicas together as one great big rather difficult group of vegetables to grow. Because they are. Or rather, they aren't but they are a magnet for whitefly, aphids and slugs and protecting them from all of these is enough to keep one awake at night and plague thoughts to distraction by day.

The Swedish botanist Carl Linnaeus, known as the 'father of tax-onomy' thanks to the system of naming living organisms he produced in the eighteenth century, categorised the brassica family into seven groups and believed them to be native to the British Isles where they grew wild and well in the chilly coastal regions. He attributed their appearance in the writings of Pliny the Elder to the pre-Roman-empire trade routes between the British Isles, Phoenicia and Greece.*

However, recent gene mapping has proven otherwise.[1] Their domestication happened not in Britain but in the sunny Mediterra-nean. Because that's the thing about brassicas: they don't really care where they are. Hardy, determined, indelicate, whether grown in warm or cold climates, they are the undiscerning survivors. So long as there are no predators, as I was to find out.

If Pliny is anything to go by, the simple cabbage is a superfood. Quoting the fourth-century-BCE physician Dieuches, the philoso-pher Pythagoras and the green-fingered Roman senator Cato the Elder, he describes the varied medicinal uses of cabbage which, eaten raw or cooked and combined with a few other herbs, include a cure for intoxication, headaches, deafness, blindness, impetigo, spleen and stomach ailments, sprains, fistulas, bad dreams, insomnia and, amusingly, hypochondria.[2]

While the Romans probably ate the sweeter varieties in the Middle Ages the denser, more hardy solid-hearted cabbage was something of a staple in northern Europe and widely cultivated in Britain. As

* There is much academic investigation into the etymology of 'brassica' from the Celtic *'bresic'* and the Latin *'braske'*.

the key ingredient in sauerkraut, the cabbage was also responsible for keeping scurvy at bay on the ships of Captain Cook in the late eighteenth century.

The warm temperatures of the Mediterranean gave us something else during the selection process and development of cabbage-leaved plants. The long, hot, sunny summers resulted in bolting. But unlike a lettuce or spinach bolt, these flowers turned out to be rather delicious. The Italians called this flowering cabbage top 'broccolo'.*

The rest, as they say, is vegetable history.

Something was beginning to change in July.

The pigeons were cooing, the blackbirds singing and the plot was bathed in a glorious light which dripped like honey from every leaf and yearning pea tendril. I picked my first courgette of the year; racing green and sleek like a new car. I lopped the top off the first artichoke flower – probably already too tough to eat but never mind, I nibbled on a few pea snaps and cleared away some stubborn weed roots.

I had largely been viewing the plot as a means to an end – a way of lightening the load of a weekly shop – but as time passed I started to look forward to my evenings on the plot. They were full of toil but no less peaceful or calm for that. No pressures of housework, no pressures of children. No barking dog. It felt like the reset button at

---

* The cauliflower is another flowering cabbage and one whose roots may well stem from the Levant on the east of the Roman empire. For more information see Adam Alexander, *The Seed Detective*, 'Of Caulis, Krambe and Braske' (Chelsea Green, 2022).

the end of each day. This was the balm, I thought, pulling at a weed. This was the tonic.

As happens so often when my thoughts are allowed to wander and settle like dust, I thought about war. Despite covering many on assignment, I can't pretend to really understand conflict or its effects; I can empathise and I can learn about it, I can listen to people talking about how their lives have been ruined, but as a photographer and journalist I've only ever been a tourist, a backpacker if you like, meandering through its many landscapes at will, cherry-picking the bits to suit me. But I could – and always did – leave war. You can't compare motherhood to war but, just sometimes, the inescapable chaos and the lack of agency, the frustration and fury does feel like war. And an inescapable one at that.

While I watered, I thought about the gardeners I had met who continued to garden in war.

Photographing and interviewing ordinary civilians living in the line of fire and enduring war which was not their making I found an underlying thread. From Gaza to the kibbutzim, from Kabul to Helmand, from Kiev to Donetsk, from occupied territories to liberated ones, the understanding among gardeners was that the garden melted the world away. Whether it was a garden fit for a king or a few modest pots on a windowsill, the message was the same. Nature imparts solace, reprieve, air and a neutrality of mind. A garden was a refusal to accept a world defined by conflict. It was the creation of a mini-perfect world to which the gardener could escape.

I wasn't a gardener when I wrote down what they said but the more time I spent on my allotment, the more I understood it to be true. Down there I could escape the intensity of real life and the million micro annoyances of the day, the week, the month and I felt incrementally closer to understanding that daily need to escape. That small plot of mine complete with its blackfly or blight or weeds or whatever, it was MY space and mine alone. A place where I could do what I wanted without having to answer to anyone or explain.

On evenings like that one with its cidery warmth, time was mine and mine alone. No sharing.

Time in our garden seemed to have sped up overnight and the poppies I had sown in the spring showed their rich – almost livery – purple, velvet petals, still crumpled from their cocoon. *Papaver somniferum* in all its glory. I never actually saw the poppy fields in Afghanistan but I saw their legacy almost every time I went to Helmand or Kandahar provinces; pretty self-seeders shivering and nodding at the edges of wheat fields which until then had been used for the heroin industry.

Every gardener I met in Helmand had been involved in the opium trade because almost every single Helmander *is* involved in the trade in some way, shape or form. If not directly as a farmer, then as harvester or smuggler or landowner.

A doctor I met in Lashkar Gah in 2014 had, on seeing the public hospitals overwhelmed by civilian casualties (of a war funded in part by the opium trade) in the late 2000s, started his own private hospital with a little garden for patients to enjoy. It was a simple patch of well-clipped grass with a herbaceous border and we sat on plastic chairs drinking tea as the sun set and the needle-tipped stars began to emerge. I was curious about the funding of the clinic and the answer was simple. Drugs. His family owned land close to Gereshk. They were forbidden from growing poppy under the Taliban but its cultivation in their absence was easy thanks to the insecurity and his ancestral land was given over for opium cultivation. The proceeds of which funded the hospital.

Strange then that every year hundreds and thousands of paper poppies are sold across the country and pinned to lapels in remembrance of the sacrifices made by our armed forces through all wars. Of course for the soldiers wounded on the battlefield, morphine – an opiate – would have been the initial pain relief and heroin often a relief for newly civilianised soldiers trying to escape the horrors of their war.

I planted those poppies in my garden to remember in my own way. And for some curious reason, neither Harry nor Ottilie ever once tried to pick them.

My brother is typing . . .

'Doesn't look like Afghanistan to me.'

I frowned. I had been sending him photographs of the screen of my professional camera which I'd been using to photograph the produce of the allotment. I figured that as a bona fide gardener and designer he would appreciate my efforts, even if no one else did. But I didn't get the Afghan connection.

I replied:

'Huh?'

My brother is typing . . .

'Last time you got your BIG camera out it was for slightly different circumstances . . . in a slightly different place.'

He was right. I had not used my camera properly since Kabul and aside from the odd snap here or there of the children when they were newborn. Since becoming a mother my camera and eye-wateringly expensive lenses, memory cards, cables, flashes and batteries had lain somewhat dejected in a still-dusty canvas camera bag covered in transit passes in my garden office as a sort of Ozymandias of my career and of my previous existence. I had literally dusted the camera off one afternoon on a whim when I'd haphazardly dumped a fistful of peas and a small artichoke on a shelf in a shaft of evening sun.

They were beautiful. There were veins and angles, spikes and wayward leaves and colours I hadn't before noticed – especially not in bought and plastic-wrapped vegetables. It was all new to me and fascinating in a way that war and all its grimness had ceased to be.

Why not, I thought, lifting the camera to my eye having artfully arranged some volunteer potatoes. What harm could it do?

My brother is typing . . .

'Good to be back in the saddle again?'

It was.

I found myself enjoying the intensity of this new photography for photography's sake. In each frame there was something new to see and I lost myself to the pockmark on the potato skin, the vein running through a pea pod, the thistle emerging from the artichoke and the wonkily imperfect peas and shoots and chard already half eaten by god knows what. This wasn't just food but shapes, colours, veins, spikes, perfections and imperfections.

Since the fifteenth century there have been books focusing on the study of botanical specimens. These were illustrated with woodblock depictions of the plants but as the minute detail was hard to capture other botanists made *herbaria*, which fundamentally were pressed and dried plant specimens, stored on paper in a protective case. But it was in the early eighteenth century that botanical illustration flourished. There was so much exploration and discovery of a vast new world of plant life that there was demand for illustrators.

There is none of the symbolism to which depictions of flowers or vegetables in large oil paintings usually allude and none of the sentimentality in botany painting either. Pared back basics, they are beautiful illustrations of plants. Portraits, plain and simple, and I have always liked them.

Emulating the simplicity of the illustrations, albeit through a lens, was my own botany, my own allotment almanac.

An hour or so later J came into the house to find me trying to control a wayward pea. He shook his head and feigned interest when I showed him what I'd captured. 'Lovely. But are we allowed to eat any of it yet?'

With all the vegetables lying around Ott had peas with her porridge one morning.

I had left a bowl of them on the table post photo-shoot and promptly forgot all about them. It wasn't the most orthodox combination but as she ate the whole lot without complaint, who was I to stop her?

Harry and I cooked the artichoke for lunch. The purple thistle leaves and spikes which had drawn my eye turned out to be incredibly tough. It took about five hours on a rigorous boil to soften but I took great pleasure in sitting in the garden and showing him how to peel off the leaves, dunk them in melted butter and chew off the flesh until alighting on the thistle and ultimately the heart.

'It looks like dog hair,' he said when I pulled the thistle off in clumps. The thought then crossed my mind to feed it to the dog in retaliation for stealing a loaf of bread I had bought that morning. J, who at that moment was fiddling around in his workshop nearby, must have seen the look which crossed my face because he shouted, 'No, Lals. Don't even think about it.'

We have Zeus to thank for the artichoke. On his way to visit his brother Poseidon in the watery depths of the seas, the King of the Gods happened upon Cynara, a young beauty who was bathing and minding her own business on the beach. Feeling rather amorous, he seduced her, deified her and took her back to Mount Olympus. So far, so Zeus (this pattern of behaviour was pretty standard as he also had a penchant for swans and cows). Cynara, however, was not altogether happy about this turn of events and, feeling rather lonely and isolated and missing her mother, took to sneaking back home. Enraged and feeling betrayed, Zeus flung her from Mount Olympus and turned her into an artichoke.

The modern scientific name for artichoke is *Cynara cardunculus*, so this story *must* be true. Ahem. Myths aside, what scholars and botanists do know is that the modern artichoke is a variety of wild cardoon, a tougher, meaner, more voraciously prickly thistle origi-nally grown, according to Homer, Hesiod and later Pliny, in Greece,

Spain and north Africa. The choke enraged poor old Pliny so much he called it one of earth's most singular monstrosities.

He had a point, did Pliny. How anyone thought that eating a thistle was a good idea is slightly puzzling not least because a cursory glance at the artichoke and its culinary delights are not exactly obvious. Did a hapless group of Roman youths, unable to find cabbages to fend off the effects of intoxication, dare each other to eat a thistle? Was it a forfeit or a trick or even a punishment? Did anyone choke?

As vegetables go, the artichoke makes you work hard. A softening in boiling or steaming water followed by a painstaking removal of leaves and of course the thistly choke before finding the meaty heart. The Romans, who would have been eating an egg-sized version, would marinade them for at least a night in honey and vinegar before cooking and seasoning with cumin. Pretty impressive culinary dedication to a thistle.

A dedication which did not survive the fall of the Roman empire. The artichoke's popularity dwindled in agriculture and cuisine and there is only a cursory mention of the cardoon by the Sevillian agriculturalist Ibn al-Awwam.

During the Renaissance in Italy, however, art was not the only thing to have enjoyed a rebirth. Cooking was considered to be as essential to culture as art, and people – especially the nobility – took cuisine seriously. While the classical form and subjects inspired the likes of Donatello, Giambologna and Michelangelo to produce the works they did, classical recipes and foods inspired the cooks of the time. Unlike today's celebrity chefs they never quite reached a notoriety to match the artists but no matter; artichokes were once again popular. So much so that it is thought that a fourteen-year-old

Catherine de' Medici brought artichokes to France from Florence in the sixteenth century when she arrived to marry the future Henry II (presumably with a bag of spinach seeds). And from there it is believed the Huguenots fleeing religious persecution brought them to Britain although some attribute this to Dutch traders.[3]

And I for one was grateful as they remain in my 'top five' favourite vegetables and are sadly too expensive to buy in this country to feature much on the domestic menu. Next year I would 'go large' on the edible thistle.

J left for Afghanistan early one morning. The sun was streaming through the curtain at an improbably ungodly hour as he shuffled around getting dressed. I muffled something about a cup of tea he had promised to bring me and he muffled something about being late and that he had arranged for Sergei to walk Pullo every morning so at least I didn't have to think about that.

He scooped up Harry and hugged him. He scooped up Ottilie and hugged her. He scooped up Kit who was hungry and who wailed.

We hate goodbyes so it was short in the end. A hug and a kiss, a hair ruffle. A wave at the taxi driver and then that was it. He was gone.

Empty and morose we needed a distraction. The allotment.

'Where did all of this come from?' Harry asked when we arrived. As he had not been there for a week or so he was amazed at the growth which had taken place. The size of the courgette leaves alone were cause for open-mouthed awe. 'Whoppers,' he called them and something like glee spread over his tear-damp face.

In the distance a tractor beetled up and down a field and a fine dust laced the summer air. The beans, having curled up the bamboo frames, were very much in flower and the maize had begun to swell with ears of corn. The beetroots looked just about ready to pick and as for the chard, the bamboo cloches were overcrowded and bursting with dark green leathery leaves.

But as we stood there admiring the bounty I felt a growing sense of unease. Whether it was because J had just left for a remote corner of Afghanistan, or because the blackberries already seemed to be ripening rather prematurely in the hedgerows and the apples on our tiny trees in the garden were already golf-ball-sized, as if the end of summer was already upon us, or whether it was because I was dreading Harry starting school, or whether it was because, oh I didn't know. Perhaps it was everything.

'Who put it all here?' Harry asked, nibbling on a pea shoot and jolting me back to the task in hand.

'We did,' I said. 'We made this, Harry. You and me, and Ott and Kit and Daddy. We made it.'

But did we, I thought. There seemed to be very little skill involved on my part, just a lot of luck, a lot of sun and a fair amount of water. I felt like I was winging it and that the moment something collapsed or died or developed some sort of fungus or rot – which was likely because, well, nature – I would be in deep water.

The books could tell you only so much – if you had time to read them. What I needed, I thought, was a teacher. What I needed was someone who knew what they were doing to tell me what to do and how and when and why.

*

'I heard you cheated,' someone in the village was saying with a mischievous twinkle.

We were in the bar tent of the village fete where I was buying drinks for Ottilie and Harry. I had just been making idle small talk about how much I was enjoying the allotment and that I was finally seeing the fruits of my labour.

'But didn't you have some help?' he said, his grin widening.

'What do you mean?' I frowned and popped Ottilie on the bar while I rummaged around for my purse.

'I heard you paid someone to dig it over for you.'

I looked up sharply. 'What?'

'You paid the Ukrainian to dig it over for you, didn't you? Someone said they saw him on your allotment. So. You cheated.'

I inhaled sharply and ran through a Rolodex of things to say.

'Don't be ridiculous,' I said as Ottilie started hitting me on the head. 'What on earth would be the point of that? I dug it over myself. Fair and square with a mattock and fork.'

He sipped his beer. There was an awkward silence. Ottilie hit me again.

'Ow. Seriously, I did it myself. Got the callouses to prove it. Now if you mean Sergei, I asked – and paid for – him to water when we went away for a few days last month. Ow.' Ottilie hit me right in the eye.

He laughed good-naturedly, clearly unconvinced. But it bothered me so much because the very opposite was true. It would have been sensible to get someone to dig the plot over for me rather than doing it myself but it would have been too easy. If I wanted an easy life, I would have not signed up for a plot in the first place.

'And everything's going gangbusters! Peas, courgettes, beans.' I was aware this sounded pretty amateur. 'Ahem, some beetroots and artichokes. Carrots, obviously.' I wanted to at least sound like I knew what I was doing. 'Ott. Stop it. Seriously.' I rubbed the bridge of my nose. 'I think we'll even save money on the weekly shop!'

'Well then,' he said. 'Not many manage to do *that*.'

This made me more resolute in the quest for semi-self-sufficiency. 'If you had an allotment,' I began, 'what would you plant for the winter?'

He looked at me a little pityingly. 'Potatoes, obviously.' I was about to deep dive into the ins and outs of spud-growing but when Ottilie upturned her bottle of elderflower over my feet, fell over and cried, the villager quite rightly excused himself. We rejoined Harry, Kit and my father by the whack-a-mole.

But on the other side of the village green I saw Sergei with his daughter and grandchildren and recalled the way he pulled at the spent leaves on my corn and an idea began to germinate.

'Heavy yourself. Package so far. Pulp ki well,' I read from the translation app and frowned. I looked at Sergei (who had just dropped off the dog after his morning walk) who also frowned, shook his head and spoke into the microphone. We tried a few times ... he was looking for poo bags.

I shouted slowly into the phone, 'I can't find any. J hid them, I think. I don't know. He does that sometimes. Moves things around without telling me. But I'll buy some more.'

Sergei waited for the translation, frowned again and then waved the wretched machine away. Harry started scrabbling at my shorts trying to show us both a holly leaf. Sergei ruffled his hair and said, '*Malenky J.* Small J,' to which Harry beamed a smile as wide as the moon.

'Before you go,' I began to say when Sergei made to leave. 'Before you go, I wanted to ask you about vegetables.' The thought had crossed my mind at the fair that if Sergei was anything like the Ukrainian gardeners I had met all those years ago, gardening – or rather, growing vegetables – would have been as much a part of his life as breathing. He had demonstrated as much with expert dead leaf removal and weeding last month. 'Harry, let me talk to Sergei. Sergei, do you know anything about growing vegetables?'

He looked at me, head on one side as if I'd asked him to count up to three.

'Well, I need some help. I don't know anything at all,' I said into my phone.

He looked at it, and then me and then nodded. 'Tomorrow,' he said in English and turned on his heel before I could ask the app to ask him to be more exact.

The next day he found me down at the allotment watering. The children having been told to stay in the shade were gnawing on stale biscuits but they looked hot and quite on the edge of melting.

'What do you want to know about vegetables?' the app translated for Sergei.

I spoke awkwardly into the microphone, 'I don't know what I'm doing and I want to grow some for the winter.' I was shouting slowly and sounded like a robot.

He nodded.

'I know that Ukrainians are very good at growing vegetables so I was wondering if you could help me work out what to, um, grow. Here. We are not good in England.'

He nodded and said something. The app translated. 'I could shed you a mountain.'

'Ummm?' I said. He tried again.

'I could shed your eyes.'

The third try was a little bit more illuminating but still confusing: 'I could shed you a vegetable garden.'

He pointed at the watering cans and then the sun and then his watch and said, 'No. Evening,' in English.

The heat had hitherto been baking every*one* and every*thing* without reprieve. It was the first of three heatwaves to burn through the country that summer. In Britain we have never been great at handling anything other than a flat monotone of predictable, steady weather. Whole commuter journeys in London have been brought to a standstill due to autumn leaf fall on the Underground lines while a few centimetres of snow have grounded planes and disrupted travel plans for thousands, much to their disgruntled chagrin.

Thanks to a particularly dry start to the year (according to the Met Office rainfall was the lowest since 1976) the heat of that summer went down in the annals of infrastructural disruption and rightly so this time. Whole roads melted, there were electricity blackouts and a 200 per cent increase in wildfires. Seven hundred and forty-five of them burned across Britain during that summer and, in London, a grass fire in Wennington destroyed nineteen homes when it became uncontrollable.

Being a damp, rainy sort of island, when heatwaves do occur in Britain it takes us by surprise and we oscillate between celebrating a Mediterranean-type lifestyle and bemoaning the discomfort and disruption to our lives. But heatwaves are not uncommon; every few years there are periods of above average heat. As far back as 1808 extreme heat over a prolonged period has been recorded; most infamously, the summer of 1976, during which the mercury soared high from June to September. Extreme heat events naturally occur due to changes in global weather patterns but the frequency, duration and intensity of these events are steadily increasing. Thirty of the hottest days by UK averages have occurred *this* century and ten of the warmest years since 1884 have occurred since 2002. That first summer on the allotment was the first time temperatures of 40 degrees were recorded in Britain, which made it the hottest on record.[4]

A few degrees may not sound like a lot if you are lying on a beach or enjoying summer in the garden. But 2 degrees globally is all it will take to create droughts, famine, loss of habitable land, loss of ecosystems and throw hundreds of millions of people into poverty.

Being then in the throes of a heatwave and hearing the whispers of a hosepipe ban beginning to circulate, 'water' was the *mot du jour*.

There are so many ways to preserve and save water. Turning off the water while brushing teeth is an obvious one (and probably the root cause of many a bedtime argument between couples), taking a small bath instead of a shower, not flushing the loo after every wee, saving domestic waste water ('grey' water) and collecting what little rainwater there is in a water butt were just a few of the pieces of advice in circulation around this time.

In the garden adding mulch to soil aids water retention. Paradoxically, given the need for water for extra plants, planting marigolds and nasturtiums to blanket the area around lettuces and courgettes provides shade and keeps the sun from parching the earth. And watering in the coolest part of the day mitigates the immediate evaporation of water.

Which was all very well but with J away and my evenings housebound, when else *could* I water?

I shrugged and pointed at my three blond seedlings.

'I,' Sergei said. 'Something-something-something *polyv*.' I remembered the word. Water.

He was offering to water for me but, still smarting from being thought of as a cheat, I shook my head. I had to do the watering myself.

So. We arranged more or less to meet at some point, somewhere, at some unspecified time to talk all things vegetables. Maybe. At some point in the next few days or weeks. Perhaps.

The summer heat intensified and, as the weeks wore on, some gardening experts were talking about more drought-resistant allotment crops. Okra, chard, root vegetables and sweetcorn, to name but a few, do well in hot climes. Beans and lettuces – which are mostly water – not so much. I wondered how our vegetable landscape and our cuisine would change in a hundred years and fearing a reliance on okra (which is the work of the devil, right there on your plate), with Harry and Ott at nursery, I scuttled down to the plot one torrid afternoon with Kit to sling some extra cans of water over everything.

As it turned out, I don't think anything suffered that much and the heat for my sun-loving vegetables appeared to be working like steroids yielding daily results of courgettes, summer squashes and chard.

The conscript potatoes had all but given up in the heat, however. Their foliage dried to a crisp in the parched earth and because I had not understood the rudiments of earthing up, the last lot of stragglers lay on the dry ground, sallow greening eyes closing.

The maize was ripening and, thus far, there was no sign of badgers and the peas were now all podding. That traumatising introduction to life on the plot seemed not to have stunted their growth after all. Later I would shell and cook the peas. They would not exactly be plentiful enough to be described as a glut but a side order of peas was a good start and they would be delicious.

Actually they would not be delicious at all. Overripe, fibrous, overcooked and pulpy and not unlike an overboiled potato and it would be almost impossible to tell whether it was those early days at fault or intermittent watering which had made them so revolting.

As for the carrots, their tops were poking through the earth supporting thick foliage. Having never grown carrots before I felt immensely proud. They were there, I thought. I did it! I knelt at the side of the bed, put my hand at the base of the leaves and pulled. Out the carrot came and I held it aloft for dramatic effect.

And then I frowned. It was a very small carrot of an indiscernible pale yellow colour which, having divided itself in two, looked like the waist-down part of a body with two chubby legs trying to do the splits. Undismayed, I tried another even bigger one but this turned out to be smaller still and more like a knuckle. On a face. A third looked like two crossed legs with enormous genitalia and a fourth appeared to have three Barbie-thin legs and what appeared to be huge breasts. They reminded me of a music video by the pop singer Robin Thicke in which naked – or near naked – model-thin women dance rather awkwardly in a straight line while the suited and booted Thicke appears to take his pick. The video (and subsequent song) was considered to be so controversial and near-pornographic it was removed from the internet. My carrots had no such shame. There they lay, lewd and loud and unashamedly pornographic in their own gnarly orange way.

I sent a picture to AJ in Kenya for a giggle and she replied with surprising earnestness about stones in the ground or un-dug manure. 'Get forking, lady,' she replied and explained about root splits in clumpy earth.

It all comes down to soil preparation. The growing tip of the carrot is highly sensitive and will detect any obstacle in its way, changing path accordingly. And if the soil is heavy the result is short, stumpy carrot roots. Or in my case, carrots that looked like henchmen. What I didn't know when I'd bought the seedlings back in April was that it would have made much more sense to direct sow seeds into the (well-sifted) earth than to transplant post propagation. Carrots, I learned, were sensitive souls and didn't like being disturbed.

Until William of Orange, along with his wife Mary, took the British throne in a bloodless coup in 1688, carrots had been purple, white or brown. With a new Dutch king and queen on the throne, carrot breeders set out to create an orange carrot to honour the new royal family. Or so began the biggest vegetable propaganda campaign.

The truth is that the Dutch were cultivating orange carrots long before William took the throne. The myth has been a hard one to shake, however, and rather overshadows the carrot's origin story which begins in Afghanistan where the jagged Hindu Kush mountains meet the lofty Himalayas.

Some five thousand years ago the early domestic carrot was a primitive sort of vegetable with a split root and was probably used more as a dye than for its taste. Images of something looking like carrots were also found on drawings dating from four thousand years ago. The Romans took a shine to carrots but it was the seeds and leaves they preferred rather than the roots and it wasn't until the Middle Ages that the carrot was bred to be eaten.

Coloured red, white and yellow, the orange didn't come until Flemish breeders began experimenting with yield, flavour and colour in the sixteenth century. The darker the yellow, the more flavoursome and bolt-resistant they were. Five hundred years later and piles of orange carrots are the mainstay of supermarket vegetable aisles* and the Dutch still think of it as being 'their' vegetable.

*

---

* In recent years there has been something of a boom in 'heritage' varieties and a certain cachet attached to carrots of different colours, but it is more than likely that these are offspring of newer varieties as nearly all the carrots we grow and eat now are F1 hybrids, and were created to be carrot-fly-resistant.

Today they are a staple in our diets and in our kitchens, the bases for soups, stews, curries, cakes and salads, and a cheap staple at under £1 for a kilo. They are universally accepted as being animal food, too. Twenty-kilogram bags are sold at agricultural shops for under a fiver. But they little resemble the varieties brought to Europe by the Moorish invaders valued for their sweetness and turned into jams and puddings. I took the children back to the carrots a day or so later and they pulled at the leaves as if pulling a present from a stocking, laughing at the deformed roots. They were no less delicious when we tried them and the very small ones made perfect teething toys for Kit who gurgled with delight.

Heat wave or no, the weekly shop now was mainly domestic sundries and a few portions of meat and eggs. If you discount the exorbitant amount spent on seedlings and pea sticks, I was winning.

Water followed fire.

A storm came and went and left behind days of grey mists and sporadic rains and, as heavy drops continued to fall from frowning skies, I longed for the heat and light of previous weeks gone by. Shadowless days like those had the weight and cloying disappointment of the morning after a party and the mournful greyness made me miss J. He loved that sort of dank summer weather.

The children missed him terribly. At night we blew kisses at the rain-streaked windows and asked the dusk-trilling birds to take them to him. In the morning, whenever we saw stray chick feathers we thought that these must be the ones he had blown to us from a lost corner of Afghanistan.

The plot missed him too. Or rather it missed my evening watering sessions for in his absence I had no choice but to water hastily whenever I could. Which was neither thorough nor often.

Back in March, when standing on the empty plot with the gamekeeper's wife, I'd had a vision of a glorious summer spent watering, picking and playing and marvelling at the bounty nature had given us. We would be made golden by the sun and strong through mild toil. Our kinship would be reinforced by the shared experience of growing so much, so fast. We would be glowing with health, life and love – of nature and of each other. And wearing gingham.

Where I had envisaged Harry and Ottilie dutifully and carefully watering with me – doing what other children do on allotments if the photographs I had seen in books and online about getting children involved in an allotment were anything to go by – they sat together in a hot pile of limbs on a discarded plastic sack angrily munching the contents of a packet of oatcakes, squabbling about the water bottle and hitting each other on the arm with luminous green and lurid pink water pistols when they thought I was not looking.

I had no choice but to abort the daily 'family trips' and let the chores mount as fast as the weeds. I needed three arms down there. One each to control Harry and Ott (pre-mobile Kit was not yet a problem) and a third for the actual allotment work.

So when the heavy drops sploshed and splashed at my feet and the ground hissed with relief, feeling the moisture it so desperately needed, despite personally missing the heat and blazing sun, I could not be anything but grateful; one less chore to do.

*

Abandoning daily visits did not mean abandoning the whole enter-prise, however; I was still rearing a new generation of seedlings in small planters in the garden and so far they were thriving. Sergei would be impressed, I thought.

He frowned when I showed him my work a day or so later.

'Your carrots,' the app translated, 'are too bunching up. Start with again bunching light.'

It was my turn to frown.

He waved away technology and started to thin the carrots himself, easily ripping up tiny roots and discarding them over his shoulder. The penny dropped; they needed space to grow. It really was a back to basics lesson from him: don't overcrowd the seeds. Motioning with his fingers he demonstrated the correct planting distance between each carrot.

I said to the app, 'Okay, and the cabbages, leeks and broccoli? I don't know where to plant them or how to look after them. I know the white caterpillars will eat them if I'm not careful.'

He read the gobbledygook translation and nodded. 'But to keep them watered when you plant them,' the app said he said.

'And do I plant them here or in the allotment?'

He looked at the already-full-of-carrot-seedlings planter next to the sandpit and said, 'There's no city where you will plant.'

I got the gist; cities are crowded places. It was all about space and I'd made a ghetto for my seedlings. I showed him the two rotting planters next to my writing office on the other side of the garden, a neglected area of gravel, tricycles, broken tools, weeds and a place which rarely gets watered owing to its distance from the house and the too-short hosepipe.

Now completely overgrown with ivy and weeds, the planters seemed an unlikely nursery for leeks and brassicas but Sergei gave me a thumbs up. 'They can be planted in two stages. First here, then there to . . .' He puffed out his chest and arms miming how much they would grow. 'Maybe in ten or twelve days,' the app said. 'But Lily,' he said (he had mispronounced my name from the outset and it was too awkward to correct him), 'compostoas,' and he raked his hand over the dried ivy and dried-out topsoil of the planters. 'Compostas and water.'

I nodded. 'And the insects?' I asked. 'The white insects. Won't they eat them? Should I put a net over them?'

He shook his head. 'Just spray.' He mimed the action but didn't tell me what with. I would buy some netting. And some spray. I would buy all the sprays.

'One more thing,' I said. Sergei clearly knew his stuff and I was hungry for knowledge and wondered what to do with my lettuce seedlings. They were still in a propagation tray and looking very much like they ought not to be. 'Should I put them on the allotment or will they get eaten?'

'Half half,' he said, clearly hitting his stride. 'Half here for young leaves to snatch, half on the allotment to grow,' the app said.

There was some confusion as to whether he was to do the planting or me and, mindful of 'cheating', I said that no, it would be me doing the planting. I pointed at Harry. 'It's a nice thing to do together.'

'If you know what you're doing, crazy lady,' I imagined him thinking.

He was about to leave but then turned to the lettuces and then to the phone. 'Lily. Do you have the names of these lettuces? I want to plant some too,' the app said he said.

I rummaged around in the greenhouse and then on the kitchen windowsill and then in the 'useless drawer'. (Every kitchen has one of these; they start off life as 'the useful drawer' until being filled to the point of not closing properly with string, foreign currency, a curtain hook, some used wrapping paper waiting to be reused, several rolls of Sellotape, none of which have an 'end', three paper clips, a sandwich bag, batteries of various sizes, chargers for unknown, lost or broken electrical things, an old letter from the council telling you they're going to charge you more tax, some Playmobil hair, a SIM card, a toy truck, all the Allen keys amassed from self-assemble furniture and a flowery hammer. Oh, and in my case, old seed packets with most of their contents strewn at the bottom of the drawer.) They weren't there, however, but propped up next to the breakfast bowls and the radio on a shelf. I gave them to him gladly and thanked him again and again in Ukrainian.

After just ten minutes with Sergei I now understood a little bit more about bringing seedlings on and about spacing. It was as if a secret door had been not quite unlocked but certainly revealed.

'Dat's Sergy at the door'. Ottilie announced his reappearance a day or so later at breakfast when he came to walk the dog.

He pointed at the other side of the garden. 'Have you planted the seedlings yet?' I imagine was what he was trying to say.

'Not yet,' I said to Sergei. 'Not a huge amount of time.' We trotted over to the planters. I had at least emptied a bag of compost over the planters and watered them well.

He grinned and patted the compost as if feeling for a heartbeat. 'Yes,' he said in English. 'Yes. Good, Lily.'

Ottilie and I planted the broccoli and cabbage together after he had gone. I said I thought it looked like we were planting a forest for tiny weeny people or mice. She said she thought the thick dark compost looked like chocolate cake.

In the end I planted the leeks out alone. Sergei had been in too much of a hurry to explain the technique and only half showed me how to tease the roots apart. The message I understood was, 'Whatever you do, do it gently.'

I turned to my growing library. Books advocated using a dibber to create nine-inch holes into which you were to drop the leek and then water.

I searched for the dibber my father had lent me two summers ago. It was one of those things you always see lying around and think at the time, 'Oh, that's where that thing got to. What's it doing there?' Part of the daily clutter you cease to see until it is actually needed – like a safety pin or a chequebook – when it all but disappears.

High and low, near and far, upstairs, downstairs. Nowhere. Not even in the useless drawer. So I improvised and used a finger. It was not nine inches long. Nor was it particularly fat and wide like a dibber. The earth felt good in my hands and I fancied that some of that delicious damp nutritious compost was enriching me too. Or my finger at the very least.

By the time I'd finished watering, although I'd followed the instructions and pattern of planting, the little leeks looked like the unfortunate passengers of the *Titanic*, bobbing around hopelessly next to a sinking ship in a sea of watery compost without so much as a raft on which to cling.

Okay, so we might not be eating leeks till kingdom come but it was to these small planting out and potting on victories – of carrot and broccoli and leeks – that I clung. They made it all feel like I was winning in spite of J being away, in spite of the loneliness, in spite of the children mostly hating the allotment. So in spite of not being able to *go* to the allotment to do any allotment*ing*, I was winning on the allotment.

August

Not winning as a novice – History of the greenhouse –
TS Eliot, tomatoes and time – Allotments between the
wars – Weed reprieve from Afghanistan – Allotment envy –
A continuation of an obsession – An end approaches as time
marches on to autumn and boyhood

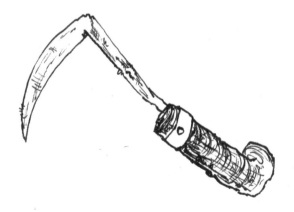

It would have felt a lot more like winning if it hadn't transpired that I was fighting a vegetable growing season on numerous fronts.

The most obvious was a lack of knowledge.

Sergei could only impart so much wisdom and I could only read so much. In the end it would all come down to experience. It would take season after season to really understand how things grew and why and how best to support a plant. So, not so different from being a parent.

The second struggle was the constraints and limitations of time which seemed to get more and more stretched despite daylight now lasting well into the evenings.

The third was a shared concern: nature and its unpredictable, well, nature. Too hot, too wet, too cold (as I would find out later in the year) and too random.

I had snatched a visit to the allotment on the way to the play park with Kit. With little time to do anything other than slosh some water over things I ran between veg beds checking on the state of things and taking stock. The beans we had protected with a net were in flower and the strong tendrils climbed at pace over the bamboo canes.

Those courgettes I had planted out with Harry and which had

been flowering were looking less and less like courgettes and more and more like enormous yellow pumpkins. Summer squashes, I later learned, but like nothing I'd seen before; variegated green and yellow and curiously enormous in size. So too was the plant's stem, a huge great big thing over an inch in diameter pushing menacingly against the bean netting as if to rattle the cage, threatening to break in and take over the canes and even the weeds.

I pulled back the stems and picked one of the globe squashes, wondering how on earth to cook the thing.

But a fourth front emerged as time wore on.

One fine August morning I was in the kitchen engaged in a chemical warfare against flies using a bottle of bleach spray (effective *and* clean) but went running out to the sandpit when I heard a fateful cry.

'NOTTILIE!' Harry shouted a portmanteau of 'No, Ottilie!' He was standing over her with a bucket of sand in one hand and a toy tractor in the other. Meanwhile Ott was holding, no, clutching a bunch of needle-sized carrot seedlings Sergei had recently thinned out.

'Like Sergy, Mummy Ott grinned. 'Tiny little baby carrots! Gentle, baby carrots. Where's Sergy? Carrots!'

This was the fourth front in the battle for veg. If nature was mercurial, children were positively impulsive the way they twisted and turned their attention and efforts. At any given moment the seedlings were vulnerable to a trampling, a sitting on, a decapitation, an overwatering and, now, an unearthing.

The lewd carrots we had picked the other day weren't faring much better either. Supermarket carrots can last for weeks in the bottom of the fridge but growing your own requires a rethink. They don't store well once picked and mine were looking increasingly wizened and rather depressing. What I needed, it turned out, was an earth clamp. This is essentially a hole dug into the ground, lined with a couple of inches of fine sand onto which picked carrots are laid, covered with clean straw and then buried beneath a layer of soil. This, supposedly, would keep carrots as fresh as the day they were picked.

It seemed like an awful lot of effort for the size of crop we had. There was nothing for it but to eat what we picked, brushing the fine earth off our trousers, and leave the remainder in situ.

We inherited the greenhouse when we first moved in and for a long time it was used as a shed for the odds and ends which needed shelter in the garden. Tools, large pots, lengths of string, various garden toys, a broken sieve, some shears which needed mending, a family of mice and, later, a dead rat that lay undiscovered for some months. Before having an allotment, if you were a seed on the way to propagation and you found yourself in my greenhouse, the chances of survival were minimal.

The whole thing had had an overhaul and deep(ish) clean (the dead rat had to go) earlier in the year and I came to rely on it as something like a shed or a 'she cave'.

So did the Roman emperor Tiberius. Actually he probably didn't even know what a 'specularium' was but he would have been lost without one. Apparently he loved cucumbers so much that it was his gardeners who invented a system of year-round cultivation. The cucumbers were planted in veg beds on wheels which were moved into the sun and on winter days were sheltered beneath transparent mica stone plates. Known as '*specularium*', these greenhouses became incrementally more sophisticated with plants and flowers being kept warm with fires lit around the outer walls to maintain internal heat.

The evolution of the greenhouse over time mirrored that of botanical exploration and in the thirteenth century large glass structures were built in Italy to house plants brought back from the tropics but it was really in the seventeenth century that they began appearing in earnest in Europe. Thanks to technological advances at the time there was better quality glass and metal available making construction easier. Which was just as well because the aristocracy of England, France and the Netherlands were developing a taste for exotic plants and fruits and a well-ventilated and heated greenhouse was fast becoming a must-have status symbol on wealthy estates. Etymologically, the French, with their penchant for housing and protecting orange trees, called theirs '*orangeries*' while in Britain the glass-house structures were places for 'conserving' rare plants; *the conservatory*.

With the Industrial Revolution came cheaper materials and when the window tax was abolished and glass was available at a tenth of the previous price, greenhouses were more accessible to the middle classes and soon were springing up all over the place. With the advent of plastics in the twentieth century, year-round propagation became available to everyone. Garden centres and online shops are today full of cheap and convenient ways to get one step ahead of the season.

My greenhouse was, let me assure you, not one of those grand Victorian affairs of wrought iron, clean glass and numerous staging shelves (I'd get one of those when we made our millions in selling allotment vegetables or bitcoin bullion, whichever came first) but rather a modest aluminium structure of about six square metres with greening glass. The roof apex was exactly three inches shorter than me and there were a few missing panes temporarily filled with cardboard and duct tape. Pretty it was not but it had been a good first home to the allotment seedlings before becoming home to the tomato growbag.

'It's a red one, Mumma.' Ottilie pointed and we looked. Indeed at her head height there was one red tomato. For weeks I'd been promising them that the green fruits would one day be red and ready to eat but the ripening had been slow. This was a joyous, momentous occasion.

We picked it. It was rotten. But there was a second one just next to it. My plan had been to slice it finely on a plate and let them taste it fresh and zinging but before I'd had a chance to feel smug about how wholesome the whole damn morning was looking, Ott had taken a chunk out of it and quickly devoured the whole thing, juice and seeds dribbling down her chin and onto the last clean T-shirt she had.

'Never mind, Harry,' I said, sensing his dismay. 'Try another one,' and I gave him the only other tomato visible, which measured approximately four millimetres in diameter.

Ottilie was already searching for another one, her head enveloped in the vines. 'I want a green one, Mumma. I want a green potato.' As the song goes (sort of), 'You say tomato, I say potato.'

We had watched these plants shoot since May and every time I picked out the leaves (an 'anti-bushing out' technique I had only that summer learned from Sergei) I gave them to the children to smell because the mineral, floral smell of a tomato plant is one of my favourites and a most potent memory trigger. With one inhalation I am transported to summer and to holidays in France where market tomatoes are as big as your fist and cost pennies. Nothing like the bland orange little things you buy plastic-wrapped in supermarkets here.

The French philosopher and writer Marcel Proust explores this 'involuntary memory' in *In Search of Lost Time*. I cannot pretend to have read the novel (I have heard it's on the longish side) but the legacy of one particular scene in literature, psychology, neurology and the subconscious is undeniable – even for those who haven't even read it. The narrator sips tea and nibbles crumbs from a madeleine cake and, inexplicably, his childhood memories come flooding back. This 'Proustian moment' has been taken as proof by philosophers, neurologists and scientists alike that smell, the most hidden of all our senses, works directly on the parts of the brain which deal with emotional memory and that olfactory memories tend to come from earlier life.

When out of habit one afternoon Harry picked a leaf and inhaled and Ottilie copied him, I wondered if this was a foundation of memory being laid. Their very own madeleines. In twenty years would this tomatoey smell similarly transport them back here to this summer and to this grubby little greenhouse of their infancy? Or was it just my own 'memory harvest' of my children's childhood which was ripening and reddening for me to pick while they were fresh and juicy with a flavour to be savoured?

*

With reds faded to amber and greens and blues blurring into each other with time, *Allotments and How to Work Them* is a lovely pamphlet to look at. There is a pen-and-ink sketch of a couple and a young boy that is not so dissimilar to the wholesome family-friendly images found on allotment websites now. The man leans on a spade. He is wearing a flat cap and a distinguished moustache. The woman holds a rake. She is wearing a blousy shirt with a large collar and neckerchief. The boy, presumably their son, is picking his way through a barrel of potatoes. Released in 1920, it is understandably a little worn but, as such, is something of an antidote to today's super-high-resolution images with overly saturated modern colours. There is an inset panel listing the contents: Choosing an Allotment; Preparing the Ground (Trenching); Manuring and Fertilising; What to Grow and How to Grow It; Potatoes for Profit, Pests and How to Fight Them; Monthly Calendar for Allotment Work (etc., etc.).

I delighted in the old typeset, the old currency, the ads for family medicine, the advice for brand-new chemical fertilisers and pre-made liquid manure. Inside, as promised, there is a plethora of advice about growing spuds and brassicas, on keeping bees happy and even about making your own hotbed.

There is a certain 'can do, will do' attitude about it and a lightness, too, as if encouraging the reader to step out of a dark winter. As well it might. After the intensity of life during those difficult war years, there followed in the UK a period of celebration and boom. A backlash against the trauma and deprivation of the First World War and the 1918 Spanish flu pandemic; nightclubs, jazz clubs and cocktail bars flourished in the cities, especially London.

Life was less inhibited and, for a brief period, there was a whiff of hedonism in the air.

It did not last; Britain was in debt and there was simply not enough money. Deflation and an economic downturn combined with hundreds of thousands of newly demobilised soldiers looking for work meant that unemployment rose to over two million. Poverty soared.

And so did the demand for allotments. *The Spectator* published an article backing the case for more plots, arguing that when staring down the barrel of hard times ahead, 'the products of allotments . . . may make all the difference for small families between comfort and want . . .'[1] Throughout 1919 there were over seven thousand applications to local councils for allotments. A week. Triggered in part by the newly acquired knowledge thanks to all the free advice offered during the war, the demand was so high that some sites divided the plots into smaller units to give everyone a slice of the action.

There was one slight problem. All that land seized for DORA in 1917 was being returned to their owners and councils were requisitioning public parks. The winding up of the Brockwell Park allotments was reported by a local newspaper and, reading the details of how the spoils were divided (there was a profit of £3 4s, four wheelbarrows and a superfluity of seeds to deal with), it is impossible not to feel that those involved relinquished the land a little reluctantly. Even the chairman of the allotments declared a little sadly that 'finding something to occupy his mind had saved his life as two years ago he was in a very bad state of health'.

There was another problem emerging, too, and one which laid the foundation for the ongoing battle for land still being fought today.

Thanks to the complete halt to building during the war and the rapidly expanding population there was a housing crisis. Prime Minister David Lloyd George promised to build half a million new homes in his 'homes for heroes' scheme. Some of the biggest housing estates of the country were built then including places like Becontree, just outside Dagenham, which for a short time became the largest public housing estate in the world.*

For the most part it was build, build, build. Allotment sites at this time were incredibly vulnerable but until 1922 there was little legal protection for a plot holder. Eviction with immediate effect remained likely. Another newspaper clipping from the *South London Press* in 1920 describes the discontent felt by allotment holders in Kennington who were being forced to give up their plots for the building of six-storey-high 'sky scrapers'. In fairness, this particular slice of land had been earmarked for building on before the war but having worked hard to produce, well, produce, the allotment holders were a little 'perturbed'. There was a little financial compensation but the years of toil, time and labour to make land productive were incommensurate with any remuneration.

This vulnerability lead to a downturn in demand for allotments. Without security of tenure, many plot holders were simply reluctant to commit to keeping an allotment. What would be the point if a

---

* The surge in building gave rise also to a new wave of urban planners. Ebenezer Howard, founder of the Garden City Movement, proposed the utopian idea of combining the benefits of both city and countryside. A perfect Garden City was planned on a concentric pattern with open spaces, public parks and six radial boulevards. Letchworth and Welwyn Garden City sprang up in Hertfordshire but they remained the only two.

local council could intervene and take it away for a new housing development?

The Ministry of Agriculture waded in in 1922 with a new Allotment Act which stipulated a six-month notice period if the allotment land was to be built on. Financial compensation was also increased. The Act prohibited the use of allotments for lucrative enterprises such as cultivating cut flowers for local markets. It stipulated that a plot should be 'wholly or mainly cultivated by the occupier for the production of vegetable and fruit crops for consumption by himself or his family'. This definition of allotment use is still in place a century later.

Another Act in 1925 stipulated that any ground purchased by local authorities for allotments became statutory and its use could not be changed without ministerial permission.

But the country was deeply entrenched in a post-war depression. The reintroduction of the gold standard by Winston Churchill in 1925 kept interest rates high and meant UK exports were expensive. Coal reserves had been depleted during the war and Britain was now importing more coal than it was mining, which meant that miners were being laid off or having their wages slashed while working hours were increased. The miners went on strike. Then everyone went on strike. Iron, steel, transport, docking and electrical and chemical industries stopped working.

Little good it did. During The General Strike there were zero concessions for the strikers; poverty, unemployment, starvation and homelessness abounded. Despair drove some back to work but many were sacked by pit owners, leading *The Times* to describe them as a million 'souls facing starvation'. By 1929 unemployment in Britain had reached three and a half million.[2]

Hope was at hand. The Quaker Society of Friends raised money, food and clothes for miners and their families before concentrating their efforts on providing allotments for the deprived in areas of Wales, Durham and Yorkshire. Allotments once again were seen as a means of self sufficiency and keeping up morale, and the Society of Friends subsidised plot holders with seed, fertiliser, lime and tools, selling them at half the cost price. Miners were initially dubious about switching picks for plots, fearing their unemployment benefit would be cut, but were eventually won over when the National Union of Allotment Holders ensured there would be no loss of benefits. By 1933 it is estimated the SOF helped a hundred thousand unemployed men to get allotments.

Benevolent societies throughout the Midlands began sprouting and setting up their own allotment schemes in the early 1930s. Elsewhere the nationwide depression had left its mark on the allotment.

They were increasingly seen as places of unsightly huts, mess and general neglect. *The Times* described plots unused and awash with rubbish – iron bedsteads, old baths, tin cans[3] – while a BBC broadcaster, SPB Mais, reported that nearly two thousand allotments in Sheffield were being well looked after but had been taken over by cutlers, moulders, razor makers, colliers, gun makers, knife makers, fish hawkers . . . the list went on. Industrious, maybe, but hardly a place of wholesome self-sufficiency in the face of starvation.

The Ministry of Agriculture waded in with booklets of tips on how to maintain a plot but the situation remained bleak. Numbers dwindled to just over eight hundred thousand plots.

Until, that is, 1 September 1939 when, shortly after dawn, Germany invaded Poland. Two days later Britain and France declared war on Germany who retaliated immediately by torpedoing a British liner in the Atlantic. The U-boat threat of the First World War was back with a bang and the British public was encouraged to dig deep to feed itself once again. 'Dig for Victory,' they said. Or die trying.

After months of back-breaking, blood-sweat-and-tears nurturing, August is the month to sit back and relax. The time for your allotment to look after you. Apparently.

The weeds on the plot were again out of control and making light work of subsuming the beans and butternut squashes. To be fair to the weeds, those butternuts had been doing a piss-poor job of establishing themselves for the forthcoming autumn. They lay akimbo, a weak afterthought with tiny leaves and stalks so stringy the whole plant looked more like a muddy set of festoon lights than the heroes of autumn casseroles and curries.

The battle between weed and gardener has been ongoing for centuries, if not millennia, and the methods deployed varied.

Hoeing, hand weeding and repeated cutting are some of the more prosaic methods of keeping them at bay. As is a blowtorch. This is actually a great deal of fun but best saved for weeds sprouting between paving stones rather than lettuce seedlings. Weed barriers are good up to a point; nothing is going to stop the seeds already germinating in a veg bed. The RHS also recommends weed suppressants like sheets of woven plastic or mulch. Being something of a sadist when it comes to weeds (a blowtorch *really is* good fun) I have had no qualms about reaching for the bottle of chemical weedkiller in the past. Finding none to hand I have, on more than one occasion, substituted with household bleach. But on an allotment where weeds often sprout uncomfortably close to a seedling this would be fatal. Literally. Indeed great caution was needed but with the weeds setting in faster than you could say 'Round-Up', speed was of the essence.

Weed reprieve came in the unlikely guise of J's return from Afghanistan. In addition to a new carpet decorated with drones (Afghan weavers have been incorporating contemporary images of war into their carpets since the Soviet invasion of 1979; early 'patterns' include tanks, grenades and arms, while the drone started appearing on rugs in 2015) he bought me a weeding scythe.

The handle was roughly wrought and the metal blade as sharp as a bespoke kitchen knife. I knew exactly where he had bought it and, holding it, could almost hear the rhythmic pounding of the blacksmith's hammer and the hiss of red-hot metal being plunged into water in the old city. I could hear the humdrum of market chatter; the rubber traders slicing tyres, the carpenters sawing, the call to prayer from the Shia mosque nearby, the fruit sellers peddling their produce as a holler, the smell of fresh flatbreads. For just a few seconds, I was back in Kabul and feeling very misty-eyed.

'You said anything for the garden,' J said.

I turned it over and felt the blade. Sharper than a razor. This would sort the pesky weeds out.

Weeds notwithstanding there was an abundance of courgettes (and rather tough and inedible summer squash). So far, so August. They were sprouting faster than Kit's teeth – which were appearing daily through his soft pink gums – and faster than we could eat. Our daily diet consisted of courgettes fried, steamed, grated, roasted, spiralised and sautéed in one way or another.

Imagine my surprise, therefore, when one day when I was unpacking my allotment haul of about seventeen courgettes J walked into the kitchen and asked where I'd found so many and why, for that matter.

'Well, duh,' I said. 'The allotment, dummy.'

'Oh.' He seemed to chew on this information for a few moments. 'If I'd known you were growing so many I wouldn't have bought any!'

He opened the fridge. In my absence he had been shopping and his list of sundries included three packets of courgettes and two heads of broccoli.

I reminded him of the allotment and cutting food bills. 'And broccoli?!' I said. 'That's a winter thing.'

'But you keep banging on about how yours keep dying or being eaten,' he said. 'And if it's so wintry then why do supermarkets sell it?'

He had a point. And if supermarkets sell broccoli year round, how was he – and all of us for that matter – to know about food miles and combatting climate change? What they don't tell you about imported fresh produce is how many nutrients are lost in transit. Most of our broccoli is grown in Spain and therefore travels a thousand miles or thereabouts to reach our shores, losing most of its goodness in so doing. Indeed the Food Standards Agency has for a long time advocated eating frozen broccoli (which is frozen on picking) over the imported and so-called 'fresh' stuff.

Gluts aside, there was to be no sitting back and relaxing throughout August. No idling the afternoon away in a deckchair nibbling on squash fritters and baby beans with a side of Spanish broccoli. The question of badgers and rabbits was never far from my mind and I found myself engaged in a number of plot patrols but so far the ears of maize were untouched and the lettuces seemed to be enjoying being left alone and un-trampled. But then there was the issue of the peas, which were browned and crisped. I had continued to water them when I could but about halfway through the month I admitted defeat. They were beyond help now; nothing would bring them back and when I cracked open a pod and found them to be tough, fibrous and bitter. The peas were over.

I did a few sums while devouring one of the corncobs with butter, salt and pepper back home (delicious, by the way). In the end the total yield of peas was about half a kilo. Which at a total cost of around £25 (pea sticks included) made them fifty times more expensive to grow than buying from a high-end supermarket. Economics lesson learned. Ish.

When it comes to the garden, there is nothing quite so depressing as other people's success. You can fudge it with income, you can fudge it with cooking, you can fudge it with your own intelligence. But you can't fudge it when it comes to plants. Success and failure are there, clear as day and plain for all to see.

J said, 'What's all this?' when I returned from the plot with an enormous basketful of French beans.

'Yes but how?' he asked when I'd pointed out the obvious. 'You said you'd had some problems with bean theft or slugs or some such.'

'The vet,' I explained.

I had been watering when the vet had arrived to his own immaculate plot. We had chatted by the by about the weather and exchanged a few courgette recipes. I'd said I was waiting for my beans to really get going while eyeing his abundant canes covered with flowers and beans.

'Honestly,' the vet had said. 'Please help yourself. You'd be doing me a favour. We're slightly sick of beans twice a day and if they don't get picked they just go stringy.'

Would that I had the chance to let them go stringy. Thus far, the total bean yield amounted to seven small beans.

The demoralising success of others didn't stop there.

A week or so later on the plot I heard a voice say, 'Well that's embarrassing. I haven't done any of this!' I poked my head up over the top of the maize where I had been checking for signs of a badger invasion. The barrister was standing in the middle of her own plot with her daughter, surrounded by success. There were lettuces and carrots and tunnels protecting Brussels sprouts and a cane or two of beans. There were gaudy gladioli and dahlias and sunflowers which, although browning and 'over', were so tall they seemed to touch the sky and exist very much as part of that plot's landscape.

'Why has he put so many flowers here?' the barrister's daughter said.

'He didn't,' the barrister said. 'I did. He just waters it whereas I never do. It's impressive,' she muttered to herself, 'what watering does.'

When she saw me I waved and gave her a thumbs up. 'Looking good!' I said. 'I don't know where you find the time. The cabbages are looking . . .'

She cut me off. 'It has nothing to do with me. It's Sergei.' She went on to explain that he had offered to water her plot on her behalf as a thank you for looking after his daughter and grandchildren who were living in her spare room. 'I didn't realise he'd actually do all this and take it upon himself to . . . look! Lettuces! He's planted more lettuces. Look! Wonder where he got the seeds. Good for him!' She smiled. I smiled.

'Yours is looking . . . lovely,' the barrister said consolingly.

We chatted in shouts at each other while I trotted to and from the water trough, perspiring heavily. I was happy Sergei had found a little bit of an outlet without having to take on a whole plot but I couldn't help feeling very envious when I bid them both goodbye and took one last longing look at success.

Envy didn't stop on the plots. My parents had planted rainbow chard in their flower beds and were dining out merrily. My sister, a self proclaimed non-gardener, had a glut of beans, cucumber and tomatoes while Nico and Crystal had so many strawberries in the greenhouse they didn't know what to do and their tomatoes were red and juicy.

Meanwhile Crystal, having already made a start on the next growing window, had a potting shed of young beetroots, chicory and winter lettuces. There was longevity there and certainty. There was a genuine 'we will be eating this in a few months' time'-ness about the whole thing. And not just from the freezer. And I envied it like mad.

If beans and successful growing thereof had been a mild pre-occupation of the spring, the brassicas were fast becoming a summer obsession.

Living now in the planters near my office and away from the sandpit, they were doing well. The leaves grew and multiplied and the stalks thickened and grew darker in colour. I was grateful for Sergei's instruction.

But things changed one weekend. We had gone to visit friends and I'd left everything unprotected with naïve confidence.

In two days they had become riddled with the tell-tale signs of caterpillars. Tiny things no bigger than a fingernail, they had finally found a continuous and uninterrupted food source. I started to pick them off by hand but had clearly missed a few as a just day later those I had missed had tripled in size and lay thick, supine, sleepy and brassica-drunk on the undersides of what was left of the leaves.

'Is there any hope?' I asked the garden centre staff later on. I described the mass munch and onward march of the caterpillars. 'I've tried netting, I've tried hand removal. Is there anything else I can do to save the seedlings? Would this work?' I held out a red spray bottle of bug poison.

The man looked at the ingredients which turned out to be toxic and instead recommended a much more expensive organic spray. 'You need this one,' he said. 'I don't bother growing brassicas,' he said a little unhelpfully. 'Never been able to keep them safe.'

'I was so determined to grow my own,' I began but stopped myself launching into an 'I've got an allotment, you see' speech.

'Well,' he said, 'with food prices the way they are going . . . if you've got the time and space to grow them then I would. It's going to be a hard winter if the headlines are anything to go by.'

That settled it. I added to the expensive spray another tray of cabbage and broccoli seedlings, bringing the grand total brassica expenditure uncomfortably high. I was definitely not beating the cost of living at this rate.

The time pest bit me later as I returned to the plot to make space for the newly bought seedlings. In the few days since my last visit nature's chaos had resumed. A rust was developing on the courgette leaves and the weeds were hitching a ride on the beanstalk. Frenzied and frustrated and so very, very dizzy with fatigue I pulled up the browned peas easily by the root and began scrabbling at the weeds. I tore the yellowing leaves from the artichoke and righted 'Harry's bean'. I lacerated my hands on the thistles and micro thorns and tore my arms on brambles.

'Where is the time to put in the real muscle and not just watering?' I thought.

I could just *not* do it, I thought, sucking a splinter from my thumb. I could chuck the allotment in and focus instead on the home front, stick to sweet peas and Swiss chard in the garden and return to the supermarket vegetable aisle and the ultra-processed stuff beyond. No one was forcing me to work an allotment and the responsibility of keeping seedlings alive was proving to be almost as stressful as looking after my children and not exactly a reprieve.

So why make life so much more difficult with brassicas?

Notoriously difficult to grow, there is a challenge in brassicas and one which I wanted to overcome. If I could grow them even from shop bought seedlings, I thought, then I could call myself a gardener. And if I could keep the allotment going then I could hold my head high above the parapet of motherland-trenches and not be subsumed by it all like the weeds on the butternuts or the caterpillars on the cabbages.

It turned out, I was not alone in my plight.

'You look like a medieval peasant woman,' J said a few days later.

With Kit on my back in a rucksack, I had scuttled down to the plot to water, harvest and plant the new seedlings. Not such an easy undertaking given the bending and lifting. J had appeared without my noticing and was tying the dog lead to a stake.

'No,' he added helpfully, 'actually you look like a Sherpa.'

'Well perhaps you could give this Sherpa a help?'

He took Kit, leaving me free to bend and scuttle around like a woodlouse. Planting Kit with a few flower pots to play with J grabbed the watering cans while I continued to pull up the remainder of the dead peas, cover the weeds with a tarpaulin and wander around harvesting courgettes and summer squashes.

'Shall we have ratatouille for supper?' I said. 'You know, with garlic and olives and everything.'

A look of panic flashed over his face and I'm sure he was about to say, 'How about a takeaway instead?' when we were both distracted by the arrival of Sergei on the barrister's plot. He was kicking her ginormous cabbages, shaking them and cursing. Caterpillars, he told an app to tell us.

Inwardly – and rather uncharitably – I smiled; so it's not just being a novice then.

I had a plan for the recently bought lot of seedlings. The plan was incarceration.

A few years ago, with a mistaken idea that a cottage garden was not at all an exercise in planning and instead something that just happened if you have a cottage, I'd bought and then been given a number of wrought-iron metal border hoops – the sort one might see in National Trust cottage gardens. For a while they looked good in *my* garden – professional almost, even if the borders of scraggly catmint and thuggish *Euphorbia oblongata* did not.

In the intervening years since then they had been no deterrent for determined toddler ambitions to reach the tantalising Other Side of the Flower Bed and, while the herbaceous plants did not survive, the hoops did. Now that they were redundant, I'd taken half a dozen or so down to the plot along with some fruit tree netting with which to make cages. Prisons or palaces, either way they were going to be caterpillar-proof. This was to be the last battle, and I would fight it to the end. If I lost, I said to myself, I would fall on my sword. Or I'd just buy the nutrient-devoid stuff from the supermarket.

I'd calculated two and a half metres of space would do it. I was wrong. I needed five. But by the time I'd finished pulling the netting over the hoops, watering the seedlings and tugging out a stray weedling here and there, I felt sure that this time, this time it would work. I sprayed the expensive spray liberally. It would be us and not the larvae or caterpillars dining out.

In the end, we never did. The final front wasn't with the caterpillars but a different and altogether more volatile element of nature. But I am getting ahead of myself.

August is high summer and for me it doesn't get much better than that. This is the pinnacle of what we have been working towards all year. But there was something mournful about that particular August. It was not simply that with so many people on holiday the village was even quieter than usual, but as the month wore on I found there to be something Sunday afternoon-ish about it. Technically still the weekend but with Monday hanging closely overhead. August sits on the cusp of change; soon the long, languid days would shorten and become cold, wet, wintry ones.

With Harry's first day at school fast approaching I had been buying his uniform over the summer. One morning we laid it out on his bed and tried it on. Everything was slightly too big and hung off his skinny frame. His legs poked out from his PE shorts like Twiglets and the sleeves of his sweatshirt dangled lower than his wrists. It was peculiar to see him still so small, young and unruly in something as ordered and neat as a school uniform, as if playing the part of an older boy; it felt like theatre.

Harry stuck out his chest and patted it, grinning widely. When he saw his own reflection in the mirror his grin widened even more so. I think I will always remember him like that – standing on the landing with beanpole legs poking out from oversized shorts, floppy blond mop of hair falling into his eyes.

'I need to show Daddy,' he said, putting on his new leather shoes and bounding downstairs and out across the gravel to J's office, stones splaying with every bounce.

He bounced about Big School and he bounced about his PE kit. He bounced about the sturdy-soled shoes and he bounced about his book bag. He bounced about his blue jumper and he bounced about his shorts and, despite becoming breathless with so much bouncing, he could not stop smiling.

J and I had passed the test of parenting and kept him alive and intact. We had nurtured him from seed to seedling to fledgling child, picking off the caterpillars, weeding around his roots, watering him and training him to climb the bamboo canes. It wasn't all laughter and sunshine, bubble bath and acquiescence. At times it had been difficult. Indeed, at times it still was; there were sulks and scratches, moments of lashing out and meetings at loggerheads. But he was taking the next steps – or bounces, in this case – in life and he was ready; independence was imminent.

It was bittersweet, however, and when he bounced over to the dog outside, J and I agreed that we mourned the arrival of this stage. With independence comes parental redundancy and, if the speed of time passing was anything to go by, we would have an empty nest before too long.

'Savour it,' people used to say when Harry was first born and we were wrangling with a new life and our own new identities. 'Savour every moment because each moment passes so quickly and then it is gone.'

I kept imagining our small cottage, then so desperately hard to keep tidy, suddenly very tidy and very, very empty. The splodgy mulberry juice handprint on the carpet, the scribbles on walls, the lost pieces of Lego, the Playmobil god-knows-what found in empty drawers, the torn books, the curtains that never quite hung properly, the scummy bath toys and squidged-out toothpaste – a permanent fixture of the basin – the chewed-up crayons, the potty and bathroom step, the toy tractors and trailers, the train sets and sandpit, the sippy cups with lids you can never quite open and Peter Rabbit breakfast bowls squabbled over; soon they would all be gone and their memory as faded as the height markers of each child drawn on the side of the kitchen door.

While Harry bounced back to J, I went to the children's bedroom so messy with scattered clothes and stray socks and looked at the paint peeling from the old window frames and at the neighbours' rooftops. In ten, twenty, fifty years' time, someone might sit in this very room and never know the madness of these years and oscillating emotions. We will be a thing of the past and these bricks and mortar which we now call home will hold no memory of our lives but instead be a temporary host to someone else's, like a greenhouse to seedlings.

Time used to be static. Before having children it was I who moved through it at will and with all the abandon of intractable dandelion seeds puffed from their stalks. As a freelance photojournalist I would travel back and forth through international time zones, wasting time, spending time and neither savouring the minutes ticking on from the clock as it moved forward, the days when they ended nor the years as they progressed.

In *Four Quartets*, the American poet TS Eliot examines the relationship between man, time and the divine. He was a devout Catholic and the religious overtones of his poem are obvious but the investigation of the past, present and future was far more beguiling to me. 'Burnt Norton', the first of four meditations, focuses on the passing of time. The opening lines, 'Time present and time past are both perhaps present in time future, and time future contained in time past', illustrate this complex interplay of time. If time is linear it moves forward never backwards, and we face the direction of travel: the future. And I supposed that this is what gardening does – it commits to the future.

In the garden the passing of time is marked by linear progression: the growing of things. Seedlings that push through the ground hunched over with the effort within days, the leaves that broaden and roots that poke through the bases of small pots within weeks. The climbers covering windows and grasses which thicken over months and the growth rings encircling trees year on year. A seed becomes a seedling, becomes a young plant, becomes something established with flowers and fruits. An acorn becomes a sapling becomes a tree. Time moves on and forward.

And so it moves with children; forward and never back, whirring and blowing with such a pace I could barely keep up. The newborn becomes a baby becomes a toddler becomes a child. The sounds become gurgles which in turn become a string of gobbledygook which before too long becomes words. The T-shirts that no longer fit, the shoes that pinch, the jumpers with sleeves suddenly too short, the trousers that skim ankles. These are the visible growth rings of children.

All I wanted to do was press pause or to convince myself that time is not linear at all but more a series of events happening alongside each other through time and space, their own little planets spinning for all eternity.*

A few days later we celebrated Harry's fourth birthday. It was a grey wet day but we chased away the blues with a small party, a cake shaped like a castle and a few party games. That evening, fighting a sugar-crash fatigue, I made my way down to the allotment. It had only just stopped raining and the moisture in the air had rendered everything crisp and clear and green of every hue, from the acids of ripening apples to the darker greens of fern and bracken. The sounds, too, clutched at a clarity only the moments after summer rains can achieve. Goats bleating, tractors humming and pigeons cooing. The crows squalled, the house martins swarmed, ducking and diving at the insects humming and cloying the air. In the hedgerows there were auburn-coloured berries instead of flowers and blackberries ripening in the brambles. They hailed the onward march of time and of autumn and of inescapable change.

But the heavy clouds were slowly parting above me and showing blue and there was a stillness. My back stopped aching and the malaise felt earlier seemed to lessen as I picked my way in now sodden espadrilles around the vegetables and wrestled with that idea of parental redundancy.

Mothers of young children often describe feeling trapped and losing their identity – and for good reason: the birth of a child equates

---

* For more information see 'Quantum Mechanics'.

to the death of one's previous existence and simultaneous birth of a new mother (and father). From the day you give birth there is no going back, no undoing. And as the baby grows into childhood you grow with it and adapt to its needs and whims, learning on the job as you go. The job description changes over time as your offspring-seedlings teach you how to be a parent, but on the allotment, letting my thoughts percolate I realised that I was wrong about redundancy. From the first gasp of a newborn baby, you never stop being its parent. And while Harry might be stepping into a new stage of life, Ottilie and Kit were very much in the flower of infancy.

I picked a few yellow courgettes and nibbled on Harry's runner beans, righting the canes again, pressing them firmly into the soft ground. With the tunnel of brassica seedlings in place the allotment was looking more . . . well, better. It was more knitted somehow. Neater, woven. More uniform. The allotment of someone who knew what they were doing.

I was learning. No expert yet by any stretch of the imagination but trial and error had led me to certain points: the tunnel to protect the brassicas, the net around the beanpoles in the same way my children had taught me about nappy rash and fevers, about Calpol and emollient creams. Watering had given us courgettes, corn and lettuces. Time was growing the beetroots and had given us carrots. I understood its whims and fancies and the progression of slugs and the aggressive cabbage whites. The allotment was teaching me how to look after it just as my children were teaching me how to be a mother and, well, a grown-up.

September

The beginning of things – Pulling up and cutting back . . .
or not – A history of lettuce – Dig for Victory – Advice
on what to grow now – A history of garlic – After-school
carrots – A second rising – Worms, wormholes and
dandelions

'Yay!' J said, springing out of bed with hitherto unseen morning vigour. He loathed the heat and the long light-filled days of high summer and would often be found in the coldest, darkest part of the house wrapped in a blanket as if willing the return of winter and rain. 'It's autumn! So long, summer! Thanks for coming.'

I groaned and threw a pillow at him. September had indeed arrived and brought with it the loom of winter. But I tried to remain upbeat. Autumn might mean the end of growing, of holidays and of heat, but it also marked a beginning: the picking and preserving of things, the return of things. Namely people as European destinations emptied of tourists and the country became full again with the cogwheels of a new academic year grinding into action.

'I'm ready,' Harry said early one morning a few days later. He was wearing all the right bits of uniform but in the wrong order. His shoes were on the wrong sockless feet, his sweatshirt was back to front and his grey shorts, well, they were nowhere to be seen. He was at least wearing his new dinosaur pants and clutched his favourite toy rabbit in one hand and his book bag in the other. It was his first day of school and 5.30 a.m.

His excitement was infectious, however early the hour, and we lumbered into action slowly pulling on our own clothes, wrestling Kit and Ottilie into theirs and making a breakfast fit for a king. Which it was; if the king was mad-keen on slightly burned porridge and raisins washed down with milk. Between spoonfuls Harry talked at ninety miles an hour about being four, his unicorn (uniform), Lego and his book bag.

J helped load everyone into my small banger after I had made a few portraits of this new schoolboy next to the front door. 'I didn't think I'd be so emotional,' J said to me as I too sniffed back some tears. 'I didn't think I'd care this much.'

I'd likened the start of school with potting on and planting out the peas on the allotment earlier in the year. I'd worried about their survival in an abstract way. When I arrived at Big School I quickly realised it was nothing like planting out peas. Nothing at all. Already over and lying dead in a crisped brown pile, the plight of the peas in those early days had nothing on the emotional roller coaster of a first day at school. The peas were not my first-born.

There exists a universal familiarity of all primary schools. The tables and chairs so small, the corkboards stapled with last year's artwork or empty and waiting for new ones. The brightly coloured paints and fat bristle brushes, the creased and well-thumbed library books waiting to be read, the named tray for each child's work and the named metal coat pegs, the type of which I have only ever seen in schools. And then there was the unchanged and universal smell of all schools which is part stale cooking, part new carpet and part sticky plastic chairs and crayons. But some things were different. There was an interactive whiteboard instead of a blackboard, markers instead of chalk and the register was taken from a tablet. But for the most part it was primary school utterly. This, I thought, taking it all in, is his new bed. Here he will grow and learn and root himself with knowledge.

That said, I don't think I was alone fighting tears as I left with the other parents. I never cried over my peas.

'How was it?' I said when I picked him up from the playground later. There was still warmth to the afternoon and he was flushed, dragging his book bag and sweatshirt behind him. A horse was whinnying in the field adjacent to the school and the trees shook with turning leaves.

Harry grinned wild-eyed; a look he used to get when he had not the faintest idea what was going on.

'Don't know.'

'What did you do?'

'Don't know.'

'Did you play with anyone nice?'

He shook his head.

'Did you play with anything?'

'No.'

'Was Mrs G nice?' Mrs G was his teacher.

'Can't remember.'

He seemed to be wilting like a newly planted-out seedling on the plot after a few days, unaccustomed to this new wild world. He was also ravenous and ate a J-sized portion of food plus seconds.

Eventually he stopped chewing, put down his fork and said, 'Mummy, I just want to sleep.'

179

And so he slept. It was four o'clock in the afternoon.

When professionals plant things out or on they usually add to the hole dug a bit of something extra to nourish the roots, as if to smooth the shock to the system. I never did that because, well, as a novice it didn't occur to me. On the first days of being planted out on the plot back in May, and having had their roots bruised and snapped and without an extra boost of nourishment, the peas had flailed around on the dry ground, desperately looking for something on which to cling and failing. Asleep in his bed, grey and sallow, Harry reminded me of the peas. He might have been wearing a uniform but underneath he was as muddled and uprooted, as lacklustre and as frail as a seedling planted out in the Wild West of my allotment.

'Don't worry,' his teacher said. 'This is the biggest change he will ever have consciously experienced. It takes time to adapt.'

This was to be a month of harvests and misty, dew-soaked mornings and silky chestnut shells. The last hurrah before winter. I'd organised a family party for J's birthday. The sun came out at just the right moment, adding to the cheer of the day, and it was Indian-summer warm. We ate outside and we ate well on slightly over-barbequed meat but perfectly grilled allotment corn and courgettes I'd picked that morning.

In the evening I returned to the plot to tidy up and to dig up the now redundant maize stalks. I pulled at one of the smaller ones with ease and lobbed it onto the pile of dew-damp spent pea stalks. The next one was not so easy; it had talons instead of roots and they gripped the thick soil, reluctant to let go, reluctant to give up.

Holding on to summer, I thought, as its papery leaves and bristly stalks lacerated my hands.

It seemed improbable that all of this had grown from a kernel the size of a tooth. I never imagined that one day fifteen of us would feel full from feasting on their harvest. It had been such a lark, such a plunge into the unknown. It didn't occur to me that uprooting the maize would be so difficult.

You win, I said to the stubborn plants as I left them there for posterity's sake.

With so much change afoot I took comfort in the constant of the allotment. It continued to yield impressive and seemingly limitless supplies of vegetables for us. Courgettes, beetroots, carrots and finally beans. The lettuces proved to be a surprise win for J.

Usually deeply suspicious of anything leaf-like, green and in our fridge it was with trepidation that he spooned some salad onto his plate one evening.

'This is lettuce?' He chewed ravenously.

I nodded.

'But it's . . . it's really nice.'

I felt very smug about this because in the ten years we had known each other J had never once had a good word to say about lettuce. Which is not really surprising given that most people's interaction with the green stuff is either a feeble cannonball of a watery iceberg or bags of pre-washed leaves, J included.

The problem is that delicate leaves like lettuce lose nutrients by the hour once picked and so, much like the broccoli driven over from

Spain, the pre-washed supermarket salads have little to no nutritional value. It is estimated that up to and over a week could have passed from lettuce-leaf picking to plate. To keep them looking fresh, these miserable little leaves are also packaged with a mixture of gases. And as for the pre-washing, a labour-saving attraction for shoppers and cooks, the water isn't exactly fresh and sparkling but more of an industrial vat of chlorine and water which isn't changed for hours. The chlorine is vital to kill bacteria which in the past has led to outbreaks of E. coli and norovirus – not exactly a palate-quencher. But then neither is E. coli.

The varieties available are pitiful too. Cos, romaine, iceberg and little gem are the mainstays but I'll hazard a guess that a blind tasting of supermarket-sold leaves would show little difference in taste between them. They do, however, more or less represent the four types of lettuce: loose leaf, crisphead, romaine and butterhead.

We have the ancient Egyptians to thank for lettuces. Around four and a half thousand years ago they transformed it from a plant whose seeds were used for medicinal oil into a food crop with juicy leaves whose milky sap was considered to be an aphrodisiac, so much so that the plant was used in sacrificial offerings to Min, the god of fertility and procreation. The Egyptians passed their knowledge on to the Greeks who in turn passed it on to the Romans who named it *lactuca*, meaning milk.

Pliny regarded lettuce to be 'soporific, and can check sexual appetite, cool a feverish body, purge the stomach and increase the volume of the blood . . . No other food,' he wrote, 'is more effective in stimulating or diminishing the appetite.'[1] A bit of an all-rounder then.

The Romans introduced lettuce to the rest of western Europe and to Britain where it thrived owing to the lower temperatures which prevented early flowering. Following the turbulent years after the Roman departure, little is known – or recorded – of the lettuce in this country although its popularity continued in Europe. We do know that by the thirteenth century English gardeners were once again growing leafy vegetables and by the fifteenth century lettuces were an established part of large kitchen gardens with cut-and-come-again varieties favoured for their sweet, tender baby leaves.

Which is what we were eating and J was pronouncing delicious.

'The matter is not one that can wait. So let's get going. Let "Dig for Victory" be the motto of everyone with a garden and of every able-bodied man and woman capable of digging an allotment in their spare time.' A catchy slogan indeed and one which became the heart of the war effort emblazoned on posters, leaflets and magazines, broadcast in films and repeated on the radio shortly after war broke out in 1939.

Despite the austerity of the Great Depression complacency had set in and Britain was back to relying on imported produce. Fearing a repeat of the near starvation of 1917 the agricultural sector was put on high alert two days before war was declared. Which was just as well because German U-boats were already amassing around merchant ships in groups of ten to twenty.

The War Agricultural Executive Committee (mercifully shortened to War Ags) distributed equipment to farmers across the country and as there was a dearth of tractors, organised mobile crews to work the land. Retired carthorses were sent back to work with old ploughs recently mended by blacksmiths while many farm labourers were held back from soldiering so as to carry out 'essential services'. Farmers even worked by moonlight to ensure the wheels of agriculture were turning at full capacity.

But it was not enough. The city dwellers needed to get digging and indeed they wanted to but allotment numbers had stagnated. Experts at the Ministry of Agriculture quickly worked out that half a million plots could support a million adults (or one and a half million children) for eight months. There were other statistics in circulation: one hundred acres of potatoes could feed four hundred people for a year, one hundred acres of oats would feed one hundred and seventy. Beef, however, put out to pasture on the same acreage would feed just nine people.

The War Ags was given powers to reclaim land including inefficient farms and areas which could be put to better use and ploughed with abandon.*

Rationing was inevitable and in 1940 standard weekly rations included 340 grams of sugar and margarine, 225 grams of cheese, 110 grams each of bacon and tea and around 450 grams of meat and one egg. A year later this was halved.

No spare patch of land went un-dug. Tennis courts, playing fields, verges, playgrounds and land surrounding the railways were put to better use. London's parks were once again turned over to oats and

---

* This left its mark permanently; thousands of acres in the Welsh mountains were churned over, the Norfolk fens were drained while, in Wiltshire, a vast swathe of heathland was ploughed up never to return to its former self.

root crops or individual plots. Palace and museum gardens found themselves ploughed up again while allotments sprang up around the Albert Memorial, Oxbridge quads, London Zoo and the dry moat at the Tower of London. People even grew sun-loving courgettes and marrows on the roofs of Anderson shelters.

There were one or two major flaws in the plan for food security. Not everyone knew *how* to grow vegetables. The Dig for DORA campaign was over twenty years old and the knowledge and understanding achieved then had not been passed on. Furthermore, not everyone wanted to start growing vegetables and getting their hands dirty. In the 1940s the cinema was a much more popular pastime than allotmenting – despite the war effort – and in stark contrast to today's bookshops crammed with hundreds of books giving advice on gardening and vegetable growing, gardening books were not mainstream. The Ministry of Agriculture addressed this with a series of leaflets giving instructions on every aspect of vegetable and fruit cultivation, soil health and propagation. Ten million or so pamphlets a year were distributed advising on everything from crop rotation to sowing and thinning spinach, to understanding the difference between centipedes ('fast moving friend' and illustrated flying a Union flag) and millipedes ('slow moving enemy' and depicted waving a swastika), to looking out for pea tendrils needing sticks, to making mulch from garden waste and storing vegetables over winter.

Cecil Middleton, a 'wireless gardener' who from the mid-1930s broadcast a BBC programme on Sunday afternoons called *In Your Garden* which gave advice about growing lilies and lavender, changed tack and switched his focus to leeks and lettuces. 'These are critical times,' he told his three and half million devoted listeners, 'but we shall get through them and the harder we Dig for Victory, the sooner the roses will be with us.'

Week-long Dig for Victory events with popular personalities went on tour. The War Ags reinstated the model allotment in public parks first seen in the Great War beginning with one in Regent's Park Zoo. An expert or two would be on standby to help and advise would-be growers, and to mitigate mistakes or crop failings new growers were told to actively seek advice in person or to join horticultural societies. Pretty soon, everyone was at it including Oswald Mosley, the interned British Fascist leader, who was said to have tended a patch of vegetables in Holloway prison.

The Ministry of Food began producing war-time recipes to help the public overcome the challenges of rationing. Public information films called 'Food Flashes' were regularly shown at cinemas while 'Food Facts' regularly appeared in printed media. The public were encouraged to grow and eat potatoes (unpeeled) instead of bread and Potato Pete, a cartoon character, appeared to reinforce the message. A glut of carrots soon led to the invention of Dr Carrot (designed by Walt Disney). The emphasis on their night-vision-giving properties suited the blackout culture well.

The demand for tilling earth gave rise to a motorised hand plough which could do, in two hours, what it would take a man with a spade two weeks. The rotavator, or roto-tiller as it was then known, was born. And as manure was already hard to come by due to an increasingly mechanised agricultural industry and potash (hitherto imported from Prussian or German mining towns) was unavailable, an artificial fertiliser – National Growmore – was readily available as early as 1942 and became the mainstay of the bleak post-war years. But I am getting ahead of myself.

Every propaganda campaign has its critics. Those wary of Dig for Victory were concerned with the allocation of sport pitches to veg patches. The Central Council of Recreational Physical Training argued that sport was integral to fostering stamina, determination and mental alertness in young people while others were worried about what would happen to all these allotments when the war was over. After the requisition of so many allotments after the last war surely all this digging would ultimately be a waste of time and resources and negate the hard work people put in to making compacted ground fertile. Interestingly, the controversy held sway and both the London County Council and Manchester Corporation forbade the destruction of sports fields for allotments.

With vegetables being such a highly valued commodity, thefts soared. There was no spare wire to cordon off sites. Pilfering other people's plots was punishable with fines and weeks of hard labour. A man in London was fined £20 (the equivalent of about £600 today) for stealing an onion and another 10 shillings for trespassing. Across the city a woman was fined £10 (£300) when caught with a basket of onions, tomatoes, carrots, parsley and a few apples and pears. In Worcestershire, the theft of a load of carrots was deemed to be so serious that the police took plaster casts of the footprints left at the crime scene.

By 1942 half the population was involved in digging an estimated one and a half million allotments which, combined with the front and back garden plots of suburbia (lawns became a rare sight in the 40s), were estimated to be responsible for producing nearly a million tons of vegetables and halving annual imports.

There are plenty of photographs from that time and looking at them, it is curious to see familiar landmarks like the angular neo-Gothic Albert Memorial or the open expanse of Clapham Common, Hampstead Heath and Hyde Park disguised as farmland and allotments. Instead of a flat, clipped-grass monotone typical of public spaces, there is churned mud as well as rows of vegetables, bamboo stakes, clipped paths and people busily preoccupied with a spade or a rake, a fork or a trowel, some seeds or ripe crops. Children were at it too. Up and down the country boys and girls were taught how to grow vegetables and the results used in the school canteen. There is a photograph, too, of two young princesses, Elizabeth and Margaret, studying the Ministry of Agriculture's cropping chart for their allotment at Windsor Castle.

Not for nothing was the country deemed never to have been so healthy.

The most poignant images, however, are those of the bomb crater plots. During the bombing campaign of the Blitz between 1940–41 and thereafter, thousands of bombs rained over the country. The photographs of its devastation are famous. Houses ruined, St Paul's Cathedral standing tall, whole neighbourhoods razed to dust, cities on the brink, tragedy and terror reigning over families torn apart. Smoke, ash, dust. You can almost hear the deafening crush of buildings collapsing. Some bomb craters, however, show something else. They show life.

In one image,[2] shot from a height of a second- or third-floor window, a man waters his tomatoes. His plot, an almost perfect circle comprising neat rows of beans, lettuces, tomatoes, onions and potatoes, is isolated in an expanse of concrete which was broken up by a falling missile in the grounds of Westminster Cathedral. All that was needed to bring it to life was a bit of fertiliser, some seeds and elbow grease. It's a middle finger to the opposition if ever there was one.

Another shows an allotment built in the grounds of a bombed-out house in Kensington. A Union flag flies among the beanpoles. Another shows a group of people sitting in the rubble of a bombed-out house in Chelsea having a picnic before starting work to create an allotment site.

In these images of life against the odds, there is a quiet resolve to do battle and to win that no other images of war could ever match. The people and gardens photographed reminded me of so many of the people I had met in Afghanistan, the Middle East and Ukraine who did not, could not, leave the war and who gardened for mental reprieve from war or to feed their families or simply as resistance to the opposition. In Gaza I met a shopkeeper, Naif Djubaily, whose back garden had been destroyed three times during various Israeli incursions. F-16 rockets landed so close to his house that his garden WAS the crater. But it didn't stop him dusting himself off and starting again.

In wars which cross continents and time, the metaphor is obvious. Out of the ashes, out of the chaos, out of the hell, great things can grow. There is life. We WILL survive.

Britain wasn't the only country digging for victory. In Germany, the small garden movement played into the idea of National Socialism.

It was thought that allotment gardeners had a duty to fulfil and to sustain the nation. Summer houses and chalets were torn down to make way for more produce until they were used as refuges from nightly bombings and, after the war, as homes for those who had lost their own. In France, war-time allotments reached a record high of six hundred thousand across free and occupied territories owing to acute nationwide food shortages.

In Britain, the result of Dig for Victory was that as a nation we had never been so fit, lean or healthy. Everyone had been eating wholefoods, vegetables, and lots of them. Sugar was still rationed well into the next decade and people were maintaining a level of physical activity previously unseen. The children of the 1940s were the tallest and strongest the nation had ever known and, in 1944, infant deaths were the lowest ever recorded.

One might assume that the connection with our food, the seasons and weather needed to grow it and our own personal health would have lasted long into the mid-twentieth-century.

But one would be wrong.

'This is the time of year when all I can think about is what to plant,' Crystal was saying. We were in our tiny sitting room one Friday evening and J, hell-bent on having a fire to celebrate the semi-darkness outside and in spite of it being still really quite warm, was striking match after match in the general direction of the tower of kindling. I had just bemoaned the end of the summer and impending re-reliance on buying vegetables instead of growing them.

'No no,' Crystal said as a flame eventually flickered and curled around a bank statement. 'I disagree. Now is the time to plant and prolong this growing season. We can make the year live on.'

Being Australian, September for her is the start of spring – albeit on the other side of the world – and as such she was beginning a new crop of onions, garlic, salad leaves and microgreens in their greenhouse.

'Salad in the winter?' I asked.

She nodded. 'If there's warmth and light, they'll keep on coming.'

'Garlic? Is it really that easy? Do you just get a few cloves and shove them in the ground? On the allotment?'

'Exactly,' she said. 'You can get it from the garden centre but your weekly shop garlic would also produce good results for a fraction of the price. You won't regret it.'

This all sounded perfectly within reach and something positive to work on in the face of a gloomy winter. The thought of the allotment languishing empty apart from a few brassicas, celeriac and leeks had filled me with an intense feeling of dissatisfaction. I had visions of an abundant spring of garlic. We could even plait it like they do in French markets, I thought.

'Bring it on!' I said as a spark jumped out and smouldered on the floor.

A member of the onion family, there are well in excess of over five hundred varieties of garlic but only two main types – hard neck and soft neck. As their name suggests, hard necks are characterised by a central woody stalk surrounded by a single row of larger cloves.

Soft neck garlics produce smaller, more tightly packed cloves and are the most widely grown garlics in the world because they are amenable to mass production, store well and do well in warm climates. Hard necks are considered to have the best culinary flavour.

There is some debate over the origin story of garlic as it is truly a global food. Garlic remains thought to date back six thousand years have been found at the Cave of Treasure close to the Dead Sea in Israel. Similar remains dating back five thousand years or so have also been found in the Tian Shan mountains of Kyrgyzstan as well as areas of central and eastern Europe and north Africa. It is indisputably one of the oldest and most commonly cultivated crops in the world and over the years has been used as food, medicine, an aphrodisiac, money and defence against evil and plague.

In Egypt the builders and slaves, recognising the fortifying qualities of garlic, consumed it widely during the construction of the Pyramids. The Greeks followed suit and gave garlic first to soldiers to enable them to fight better and then to Olympian athletes to perform better.

Writing a little later in the first century AD our friend Pliny described the benefits of garlic against 'ailments caused by changes of water and location'. Its smell was also effective against snakes, scorpions and 'every kind of wild beast'.[3] Quoting the Greek physician Menander, he explained that the smell on one's breath can be alleviated by immediately eating roasted beetroot.

Across the world and over the millennia, garlic has been recognised as an effective treatment of cardiovascular disorders – a reputation which still exists today. Historically, in China garlic was prescribed to aid respiration and digestion and possibly depression.[4] It was also used as a food preservative and for treating intestinal worms. Sanskrit documents dating back five thousand years also describe the healing qualities for cuts and bruises when applied topically.

The Middle Ages saw garlic very much as a medicinal herb for the upper classes and effective against constipation, the plague, cholera and tuberculosis in addition to other ailments. It was used latterly to ward off evil spirits, vampires and foul-smelling diseases and its healing qualities were still recognised and deployed as late as the First World War during which it was used on wounds as an antiseptic and to reduce dysentery in the trenches.

In twentieth-century Britain, however, garlic as food was not widely used and invoked a fair amount of anti-foreign sentiment. 'Garlic eater' was a slur commonly directed at the Italians and French. But thanks to pioneering cooks like Constance Spry and Elizabeth David, who introduced everyday Mediterranean recipes during the food and cooking revolution of the 40s, 50s and 60s, garlic increasingly became a staple in kitchens and gardens nationwide. And it is certainly something I could never be without, although given my own mother was taught to cook at Constance Spry's cookery school and she imparted some of her wisdom to me while growing up, perhaps this is not surprising.

With the rigidity of school hours, gone were those trips to the plot with Harry while the others slept when we'd tend the vegetables and look for worms. There was also little time for garlic planting. The heat of the summer belonged to a different time and place altogether and when the children and I finally did manage an after-school trip to the allotment it started to rain as soon as we'd left the house. It was a fine autumn mist rain rather than an angry monsoon so we braved the elements and held our faces up to the sky, letting them get wet, open mouthed and squinting.

We did not hear or see another soul all afternoon and when the rain stopped it seemed to me as if we were enveloped in mist. The world was ours and ours alone. We pulled up carrots which tasted earthy and not just because they hadn't been washed properly. They tasted of nutrients and flavour. They tasted honest.

All I could hear was the sound of tiny teeth crunching baby carrots when Harry said, 'Mmmm, I love carrots.'

'I love carrots,' echoed Ott.

A week or so later I was back on the plot tidying and cutting back. Time sped up and autumn had tightened her grip. There was none of the steroid growth of summer but much of its dryness despite the damp days. Life was drawing in as fast as daylight and the plot was quickly resembling its March self, as if bookending the growing season. The courgettes were mere fingers and not particularly glossy ones either and weeds were now poking through even the no-dig bed and the solitary yacón was looking sadder than ever. The beans were small but stringy and the butternuts still resembled a heap of broken light bulbs and clearly hated the plot so much that they were making a beeline for the allotment next door where someone was growing some rather magnificent pumpkins.

I looked up to the hills in the distance while I pulled and wrenched the rest of the maize from the earth's grip. The sun dripped gold in the ancient oak trees and was peachy in the tufts of clouds overhead.

Pheasant hens were clucking somewhere and pigeons were cooing as if it was dawn. The long grasses which had hidden Ottie just a few weeks ago were now damp and becoming mulchy. It wasn't cold but the rains had brought a freshness to the air which caused me to shiver. Someone, somewhere, was having a fire or a bonfire and the smell was as comforting as toast or cut grass or strawberries. And although I was pulling things up and clearing away in the looming shadow of a new season, I was making space for the next lot of crops and the next cycle of things to come and there was hope in doing so.

There was nowhere I would rather have been.

New life emerging in September was not just confined to overwintering garlic and leeks. Something else was happening in the planters by my summer-house office.

Being a lazy sort of gardener, when I'd seen the red cabbage and broccoli seedlings decimated by caterpillars in August and their planter resembling a Somme-scape diorama, I did not dig them up. I was too disappointed so I walked away and averted my eyes on the rare occasions I found myself at my desk.

One evening, however, I noticed a greening taking place. I grabbed a torch and investigated more closely. Minuscule shoots were pushing out from the eviscerated stalks. Undeniably, there was a new sprouting, both defiant and strong.

These were the survivors. This was life living again – a phoenix from the ashes of brassica failure.

The leeks in the other planter had bulked out just like Sergei said they would and were ready to be moved on. I carefully uprooted them into a bucket a day or so later and scuttled down to the plot with my basketful of tools including the dibber which in the end I'd found in the footwell of my car.

I hadn't seen Sergei for a few weeks and even the children kept asking where he was. I wondered if he and his daughter were back in Ukraine – I had heard that they wanted to leave. But the lettuces he had planted on the barrister's plot were being harvested. He was still here somewhere pining for his home.

The swollen skies threatened rain and I had no time to lose. First I had to clear the ground. The summer squashes were dying back and the few remaining flowers looked pretty non-committal about becoming a fruit. Besides which, we had become rather sick of summer squashes. The stalks were spiky and prickled but came out of the ground easily. After a few days of rain the soil was thick and heavy but the weeds were as easy to remove. I raked and then knelt to dib large holes for the leek roots. It started to rain hard but I didn't mind much, even when the drops chased down my back from my collar. At length I stood back to admire my work but was disappointed. Where the books had shown soldier-straight leeks in finely tithed earth, mine stood drunken and lax, flopping in the wet earth.

But I thought about the brassicas and I thought about the peas and then I thought about Harry in his new Big School and took courage. Soon row upon row upon column of tall, upright oniony leeks would flourish and the plot would look professional and tidy and definitely as if I knew what I was doing and not winging it, hoping that nature wouldn't notice.

*

'Look at the worm, Mummy!' Harry exclaimed one Sunday morning. We had decamped to the allotment with my basket of tools, two bulbs of garlic from the garden centre which were more expensive than I'd care to remember and some supermarket/petrol station garlic which had cost merely pennies. In addition there was a Thermos of tea, a box of breadsticks, three apples and a biscuit tin.

I had set Harry and Ott to work with a rake and a fork from their own garden toolkits while I turned the earth over. Kit meanwhile was happily putting one flower pot inside another over and over with earnest intensity marvelling at his own genius.

The sun was streaming through the turning leaves making them glow, the ground was wet with the autumn dew and the air smelled of woodsmoke. Where six months ago the soundtrack had been a chatter of blackbirds and thrushes, a chirping of great tits and a cooing of doves all sitting on nests or feeding their chicks, now there were pheasants clucking, matured ducks a-quacking and cockerels crowing croakily. The house martins and swallows were gathering on telegraph lines preparing to swarm through the skies returning to sunnier climes. It was spring in reverse. Except here we were still planting and trying to grow. Still holding on to hope that winter would not come. At least, that's what I was doing; Ott was never more than a foot or so from the basket of food while Harry was more interested in the insects at our feet.

'A wiggly worm, Mummy! Can I put it in my pocket?'

'Um, I don't think that's a good idea,' I said, putting down my fork and removing a shard of terracotta from Kit's mouth.

'Why?' Harry was cradling it in the palm of his hand. 'Sweet little worm. Shall I take you home?' he cooed.

'He might get hungry or be sad and miss his mummy and daddy and brothers and sisters if he's all on his own in your pocket,' I suggested. 'Maybe put him back in the ground so he can carry on doing what worms do best.'

'What's that?'

'Being worms. Here you go, Kit, try this instead.' I handed him a breadstick.

'Do you love worms, Mummy?' Harry asked in earnest. He had a habit of asking this about random and inconsequential things. Traffic cones, gates, steering wheels, dinosaurs, cobwebs, chair legs, Lego; I had been asked to delve deep and think about how I felt about all of these things recently.

I didn't have to think too hard about worms. 'I do,' I said. 'And do you know why?'

'Because they're so sweet?' he said.

'Mmmmph. Sort of. It's more that they're wiggly. Wiggly worms,' I began to explain, 'wiggle through the earth and make tiny little paths of air which is very good if you're a plant root as I'm sure it gets a little stuffy down there.'

Back then I did not fully understand that there was a hell of a lot more to worms than aeration. But as we worked the ground together I let my mind wander to wormholes.

J first introduced me to the idea of wormholes a few years ago. It was the night before Ottilie was born and, with a caesarean section booked in for the following day, I was putting Harry to bed for the last time as a family of three. Then just eighteen months old he was nestled fluffily in the crook of my neck, drifting off to sleep with no idea what was about to happen. 'I want to bottle this,' I whispered to J who'd appeared at the door. 'I want to bottle this moment forever,' and I stroked his duckling hair.

J smiled and said, 'I think it will be your wormhole.' And then he tried to explain. He found a piece of paper and bent it in half and said something about time not being linear and stabbed a pen, rather aggressively, through the middle.

'There,' he said. 'That's a wormhole. A link between the present and the past.'

J, for the record, studied archaeology, but it sounded plausible and so I indulged him. Indeed the *Encyclopedia Britannica* has much to say about wormholes. In Albert Einstein's theory of relativity they are hypothetical connections between two points in time or a tunnel between two black holes. There is an analogy of an ant walking across a flat piece of paper from point A to B. If the paper is curved so that the two points overlap the ant can short cut between the two points (J's pen holes), thus avoiding a long, tedious trek. If the paper represents time, the short cut is a wormhole.

Simply put, it is time travel.

I am no physicist but the idea of being able to travel through time to specific moments, specific memories indeed, is an attractive one. Of course this opens up the theory that we might currently be in a wormhole and that our future selves are looking back and marvelling, but with these years of my children's childhood passing at the speed of light I liked to indulge in the theory that any moment could be revisited at any given time.

In plant biology, a seed or bulb contains all the information for growing. Maybe this was what TS Eliot was driving at with those opening lines about time. A seed or a bulb is in itself its past, present and future. All it needs is water and a few nutrients. And if it's the earthworm that brings said nutrients with its wormholes and wiggling then surely this is a version – a very literal version – of the theory proven.

This highly micro-cosmical, allegorical and metaphorical explanation of worms is why I told Harry that I loved them. Or the idea of them, at least. Worms reminded me of past, present and future all rolled into one and that one day in the distant future, I would be able to look back at, say, this day, with absolute clarity and not feel old or infirm or alone in old age. I would be here, right here on the allotment with Harry and his worms, Ottilie and her snacks and Kit and his . . .

'No, Kit. Not the garlic, sweetie.'

I removed one of the bulbs he was eating like an apple and turned him around to focus on a beetroot I quickly plucked from the ground.

'I love worms,' Harry sighed to his palm. 'But don't pull off their tails,' he added sagely before setting the by now surely petrified worm free into the ground.

'Come on,' I said, sitting on the grass. 'I need everyone to plant some garlic.' They all sat and waited patiently while I split a bulb in two and gave them half each before showing them how to break off the individual cloves. We sat with quiet concentration, earnest breathing just audible over the papery white skin flaking around us.

'Smell it,' I encouraged and they inhaled deeply.

'Smells like mince, Mumma,' Ott said and went in for a second whiff.

Harry wrinkled his nose. 'Smells like wild garlic from the woods,' he said. 'Can we eat it now?'

Forgetting about the dibber I poked my finger deep into the earth and showed Harry which way up to put the clove. We planted one row and then another, in more or less a straight line. Ottie planted a row, dropping her cloves in each time saying, 'Goodbye garlic. See you later.'

We watered well and, having finished the breadsticks and biscuits, picked a few raspberries (three, not exactly a bumper crop) and then marvelled at the 'big whopper' brassicas which were by now thriving beneath their nets.

The sun was warm now and high and with our labour finished we packed up the basket and ran across the playing field with Kit in the pram to an apple tree to throw a ball around and to roll down a small hill with dried leaves sticking easily to our clothes and in our hair. Down we tumbled, giggling and warm and happy.

Tired, we lay on our backs for a few moments and Harry noticed a contrail high up in the sky overhead. He marvelled at it. 'Why is that cloud so straight?' he asked. 'And long! Is that a wormhole?'

Oh to not know. To not be burdened by the Big Wide World and to discover everything for the first time, I thought. I envied his innocence.

Then we piled on each other, all limbs and legs and laughing. We were euphoric.

I looked up at them with their flyaway hair, rosy cheeks, breathless and grinning corn kernels of tiny milk teeth, and I looked over at Kit who was on all fours, a pace or two behind but yearning and reaching to join in, laughing, ecstatic. I wanted to capture it, to bottle the joy of this point in time when we were all so happy together as one. Harry and Ott picked dandelion heads, counting as they puffed, Kit mimicking through pursed lips.

One o'clock, two o'clock, away the seeds blew, into the wind, up and down again on a whim. Three o'clock, four o'clock, they would land and take root, entrench themselves in that moment. This, I thought, looking at the sky with its single white contrail, and downy seeds floating, is it. Five o'clock, six o'clock, my very own wormhole; this was the seed, the bulb, the clove, and everything contained in it was my past and my future.

October

Tulips – A history of kale – Taking stock for a new
season – A history of leeks – Next season's broad
beans – Newcomers – Soil science – A mud kitchen – A
strimmer – The post-war allotment – Compost

High winds, storms and rains vandalised the allotment but, rein-spired by planting garlic and leeks and overwintering vegetables, I took Kit on a shopping spree to the garden centre.

I had my mind set on potatoes. I'd plant a whole platoon of them and I'd look after them, train them like a sergeant major rather than let them emerge like the criminally minded mercenary leaders of ragtag conscripts I had unearthed earlier in the year.

I rushed in, beaming with excitement, and asked a friendly member of staff, 'Where can I find the potatoes?!'

'Potatoes?' She frowned and cocked her head thoughtfully.

'Yes! I've got an allotment and I'm going to plant potatoes,' I said.

'Oooh.' She frowned again. 'You're a bit late. We won't be getting those in for a while now, love.'

'Oh.' I was dismayed. 'Late?'

'You'd never grow anything in time for Christmas if that's what you're trying to do.'

'Christmas? No. I just thought, well . . .' I had sort of assumed that winter vegetables were grown over the winter months. Buried deep in the ground until the spring. Hence the season's 'new potatoes'. I had assumed spectacularly wrong. Grown over the summer, stored *for* the winter.

'We'll get them again in the spring, love.' Seeing my disappointment she radioed through to a colleague. 'Got a lady here who wants to know about winter veg . . .'

Moments later another member of staff appeared with a spreadsheet.

'Right then. Winter.' She clicked her biro and moved it down the list. 'Broccoli, cabbage, cauliflower, chard, garlic, kale, leeks, sprouts . . .' she listed. 'Those are your best options, really.'

'It's okay. I've got some brassicas,' I said knowingly.

'Great! What have you got?'

'Um.' My mind went blank. Cabbages or broccoli? 'I can't remember. Some just came back to life.'

'Riiight,' she said slowly.

'Well.' I began to explain in a rather long-winded way about the months of trial and error and how Sergei had helped me to bring them on. 'He knows a lot,' I said.

'Uh-huh,' she said, looking pretty unconvinced, and a little confused, before staring back at her spreadsheet again. She made as if to leave. Before she did I asked about the perils of aphids in the autumn.

'I think you'd be all right now it's cooler,' she said, clicking her pen and reaching for her walkie-talkie that was fizzing. There was clearly another more serious gardener to be dealt with. I picked up a strip of kale seedlings being sold off for a quid and continued walking around with Kit searching for inspiration.

Finding myself in the sizeable bulb section and confronted with a pick and mix of tulips and daffodils by the bucket, an idea came to me. 'Sod it,' I thought. 'If I'm too late for overwintering vegetables I may as well bring joy to the house.'

Not exactly a money-saving exercise but I wasn't a bad tulip grower. Watching them spear through the ground in February only to unfurl as splashes of colour, precursors to the summer, never failed to cheer me on dreary March days. Yet again I left the garden centre with more than I had intended to buy.

I said to Kit, 'At least we'll have a rainbow of colour in every corner of the house.' The strip of seedlings wobbled and he tried to grab them. 'And some kale.'

The Italians favour cavolo nero, the English have the curly-leafed stuff, the Russians have their own red and green frilly-leaf variety which I've been told is exceptional when slightly pickled with vinegar. The Americans, meanwhile, have collards which are not dissimilar to the generic 'spring greens' we tend to apply to all brassica-ish leaves available to eat in the spring. Not surprising really because, as it is able to withstand winter, kale fills the nutritional gap on an allotment keenly felt in the early spring.

Kale is possibly the mother of all brassicas. Quite literally. Likely to have been domesticated twelve thousand ago in the Fertile Crescent for its oily seeds we have been eating its leaves for four and a half thousand years in various forms which include cabbages and cauliflowers and everything in between. And while we tend to favour the flowers or heads of both of those, kale grows as a leafy frond rather than a dense head. 'Acephala', its cultivar, denotes exactly this. Headless.

Easy to grow, nutritious and so hardy it can withstand hard frosts, growing kale was encouraged by the Dig for Victory campaign of the Second World War but its popularity soon waned and for a long time kale was relegated to the back seat of cuisine, used by agriculturalists to desalinate soil and by caterers for frilly green decorative display purposes. It was the bitter, forgotten green of the kitchen, as fashionable as turnips and with similar negative associations.

But in the 1990s nutritional research revealed its benefits to a new generation of foodies and by the mid-2000s, thanks to high-profile celebrities extolling its virtues, everyone was eating kale either in salads or blended into drinks or made into salty crisps. In 2014 the pop star Beyoncé appeared in her own music video '7/11' wearing a sweatshirt (and little else besides a bikini and, inexplicably, sweatbands on her knees) emblazoned with 'KALE' in the style of a Yale University branded sweatshirt. The leafy brassica was thus cemented into pop culture and millennial eating habits in one fell swoop. 'Eat kale, tell everyone you're eating it and you too can have an Ivy League IQ', or so the merchandisers hoped. Oh the irony. With lookalike sweatshirts retailing at anywhere between £20 and £60, it was clear that kale could do no wrong.

It was hoped its popularity would rub off on its cousin, the sprout, and in a bid to revolutionise those much-loathed balls of evil, breeders have come up with a sprout/kale cross: the kalette. A small, frilly-leafed mouthful of cabbage flower it is perhaps the first new variety of vegetable to be created this century.[1] But do not be fooled. These balls of purple promise are a sprout in wolf's clothing.

Sprouts aside, those polythene bags of rather tough and woody stems with a few spliced leaves we can currently buy in the super-markets belie kale's many varieties. It all depends on the length of the stem (short, medium or long), the type of leaf (curly, bumpy, spikey, plain, spear or ornamental) and the colour (light green, medium green, dark green, purple green and purply brown). I waver between favouring cavolo nero (literally 'black cabbage') and the more generic light green curly-leafed medium-stemmed stuff which (when left alone by cabbage whites) grows leaves larger than my hand but remains juicy and flavoursome. It's a nice problem to have.

Unperturbed by the drop in temperature I made for the allotment. It was finally time to do away with the butternut squashes. Grenade-sized, they would certainly not be feeding us through the winter and there was no hope of a growth spurt. At a push they might make a decent side dish, roasted.

Turning the soil over I planted in their place the newly-risen-from-the-ashes seedlings and the now wilting kale. The garden centre lady had said that the aphids wouldn't be a problem at this time of year so I patted the earth around the roots and left them unnetted.

It was a wet day and the soil was thick, cold and heavy. While I didn't mind the solitude of the weather, I was muddy and wet and just a little bit cold when I'd finished. I poured myself a cup of coffee from a Thermos and watched the steam rise into the fine mizzle of rain.

It is hard to stand back sometimes and see a garden or allotment with fresh eyes. Familiarity breeds acceptance and, over the summer, there was too much going on to notice the space available. Now was the time to start planning and thinking about next year and generally taking stock while the allotment held its breath as autumn pulled a blanket over it.

Resolved to plan a little better than March's pencilled scrawl of a bed each for veg, flowers and raspberries, I'd searched online for 'allotment plan' and ended up in a rabbit-hole vortex of advice and after an hour was none the wiser.

All I knew thus far was that I could be certain of some wonderful broccoli and cabbage in a few months and that I would 'go large' on broad beans having had such success this year.

I paced the length of the other half of the allotment. It was immensely overgrown and a bramble thicket loomed on one side. I wondered if it would be total lunacy to dig it over for next year.

I thought about a no-dig half plot. I'd need a lot of card and a lot of compost. I'd need to get a strimmer too; those waist-high grasses would be impenetrable without one. It already sounded like a lot of work. I shelved the idea but continued pacing, noticing for the first time a volunteer leek – at least, that's what I thought it was – in the middle of the grasses. Its white flowers were going to seed. No-dig might be an experiment too far but leeks from seed I could get behind, especially now that I was an expert leek grower. It would be months before I got around to shaking the seeds from the heads.

Nothing says allotment like a prize-winning leek. There are photographs of produce shows and competitions from the 20s and 30s showing piles of dead straight, enormous leeks. The vertical sculpture of the ground, they are a thing to be proud of indeed.
Hailing from the same family as onions and garlic, the leek is syn-

onymous with Wales but its ancestors are much more exotic. The leek is an old vegetable indeed and would have been grown widely across Egypt and Mesopotamia some four or five thousand years ago as a domesticated plant. Depicted in Egyptian hieroglyphs, leeks also appear in the Old Testament and it is said that the Emperor Nero loved eating them so much he was mockingly nicknamed 'the leek eater,' or porrophagus in Latin, by his subjects.

Its wild relation is even older and estimated to have been foraged long before the Egyptians got creative with images and communication. Indeed, the wild leek probably arrived in the British Isles in prehistoric times while the cultivated variety was likely brought to Britain by twelfth-century Augustine monks. It was embraced as a reliable hardy oniony plant, which could be harvested through the winter. Its health-giving properties through the ages have included being used as an aid for labour, a deterrent against being struck by lightning, a moth and insect repellent and as an aphrodisiac. Presumably not all at the same time.

Most of the leeks we now buy in supermarkets are bland offspring of the older varieties. In the 1990s male sterility in leeks was exploited by breeders and led to a hybrid variety with guaranteed uniformity which supermarkets loved.

I didn't know what variety had been left on the plot, or if it had any of the prize-winning properties of its forefathers, but I had little doubt that when propagated, they would be infinitely superior to the sad-looking thing which had been languishing in the vegetable drawer of the fridge for longer than I cared to remember at the time of writing.

*

It slowly dawned on me that what I probably needed was not a plan but a system of crop rotation. This would mitigate the need to choose and decide what and where to plant.

Crop rotation is a fine art but it's also a science. Plant the same thing in the same place twice in a row as a monoculture and you run the risk of soil-borne pests and diseases. If only one crop is grown in the same ground year in, year out, the soil loses fertility and nutrients. It's the plant world equivalent of an unbalanced diet.

Crop rotation doesn't have much of an impact on airborne diseases like carrot fly or cabbage whites but, if followed, it thwarts soil-borne pests. The RHS allotment 'bible' advocates a four-course rotation with each bed growing in order: potatoes and tomatoes in one year, root veg and onions in the second, peas and beans in the third and brassicas in the fourth. Squashes, corn and runner beans can slot in where convenient. Adhering to this will supposedly keep your soil healthy and meet its nutritional needs.

Some cultures take the land's needs even more seriously. In Israel there is a form of crop rotation so strict it includes a period of soil sabbatical. Every seventh year, pious gardeners observe 'Shmita', a year-long holiday for land advised in religious scripts. A seven-year cycle might be a bit excessive for a small plot like mine but I had finally come to appreciate that rotation was the Rubik's cube of life and is as much about the soil as it is about the produce. None of this 'shove it in and see what happens' I'd prescribed up to now. I vowed I would dig out some books at home and plan my own rotation, I vowed.

By the time I got home it was indigo dark. J had taken the children to visit family and the house was uncomfortably quiet. I drifted between bedrooms picking up toys and replacing books on book-shelves, straightening pictures which had fallen askew on the walls and folding spare blankets on the sides of their cots and bed. It felt very empty.

I distracted myself from the uneasy silence with a plan for the plot, cross-referencing books about crop rotation while I ran a bath. I pulled out some paper.

By the time I was finished the bath was cold.

I used to skim-read the advice about soil conditioning in books or newspapers. All I knew was that adding manure to your soil was important. I didn't know why or care that much either. 'Yes, yes, boooooring. Let's get to the good bit about colour and frilly flowers.' This year, however, I had seen the results of good soil. Or rather, I had been reminded of it. I'd fed our corn to J's family on his birthday. My mother-in-law's had failed. 'You've got good soil there,' she had said.

I'd given a lettuce to my own mother. 'You grew this?' she asked in disbelief. When I beamed proudly she said, 'You've got good soil.'

I had shown a film of my whole plot to my brother who texted back. 'Good earth you've got there. Look after it.'

Three little words.

Look.

After.

It.

My father appeared one Sunday with a car full of poo. Twelve bags of it. The clocks had yet to go back and the afternoon was slipping into the evening, as quickly as the temperature was dropping, but there was poo to be transported to the plot.

When we arrived at the allotment I noticed a new pile of tools and a sturdy wheelbarrow. The grasses which had hidden Ott in the summer had been razed to the ground. Ground which was marked out with posts and string. There were some newcomers to the allotments. Who on earth could they be?

My father and I unloaded efficiently and when he left I looked over my plot and wondered where on earth to start. There was suddenly so much to do. The manure needed spreading, the broad beans needed planting and supports needed to be made. Then there were the weeds and, oh look, the couch grass had tripled in size and was again encroaching into the beds and I still had the tulips to plant.

'Look,' my brother said over the phone the following morning. 'I wouldn't agonise over it too much. They're just seeds.'

I had been asking him about planting broad beans directly in recently manure-enriched soil. 'And then on *Gardeners' World* they advised against planting straight in the ground because of bad weather if it's an exposed plot. It's like the Wild West down there sometimes,' I said breathlessly.

'Just put them in the ground and see what happens,' he said. So I dutifully packed a Thermos into my basketful of tools and gloves and seeds and tulip bulbs I'd found in the greenhouse and set out into the sunny Sunday morning.

After miserable rains it was autumn absolutely again. The sun glinted sharply off the acid yellow of an ash tree still clinging on to its leaves and where green had clambered over village houses all summer there was now red. It smelled of woodsmoke and cut grass, humus and premature leaf rot all at once.

When I arrived at the allotments I set to work immediately spreading manure, cutting back and tidying. Inspired by Crystal's promise of winter greens (but against the advice on the seed packet), I began direct sowing chard and spinach into the ground. In hindsight, this was a complete and utter waste of time and money. With no warmth and not enough energy-giving light there was no chance for them to germinate, but the act of planting was spirit-lifting.

As I rolled each jagged ball of life between my thumb and forefinger before placing it in the earth I supposed that this was the joy of an allotment. This was the way to learn and if a year on an allotment was to do nothing else, it was to teach me how to grow.

'They're only seeds,' my brother had said. He was right. But secretly I hoped that they would become much more, naïve novice that I then was.

I had a brown paper bag full of *aqua dulce* broad beans but, prior to planting, sawed lengths of bamboo in half and staked the ground before winding a network of twine between each one to create my own supports for them to clamber through. The end result was a messy maize of string not unlike the laser maze of the *Mission Impossible* films. I planted the beans, sometimes pressing with my thumb, sometimes using the dibber and, invigorated with a sense of achievement, planted tulip bulbs in the grass edges.

The theory of autumn sowing and overwintering is that the plants are more mature and the sap less juicy by the time the aphids start hatching out and seeking sweet sustenance in the spring. When a colony of blackfly establishes itself on a plant, it is pretty darn difficult to remove. For the last two years in planters at home, I'd had nothing but success with my modest sowings of broad beans. If this lot survived, I thought, we'll be eating beans all the way through the summer.

I was just reaching for my Thermos and a congratulatory cup of tea when a young couple with their daughter arrived.

'Hello,' they said cheerily. It had been weeks since I'd seen anyone else down here and I'd become so used to being the queen of the plot, working in silence and letting my mind untangle itself, that I was taken aback. The newcomers of course.

'We're the newbies,' they said, waving a pitchfork. They were from Lithuania, they told me, and lived in the town a few miles away.

The man introduced himself as Dalius and described how he had previously worked a small 8x6-metre plot in town but wanted to scale up and had been looking for a larger plot. On hearing about the spare ones in the village he contacted the gamekeeper's wife and was given his allotment almost immediately.

'In Lithuania,' he explained, 'you are brought up with your hands in the soil; even if you were a city dweller, you would still drive or bicycle out somewhere to tend a vegetable plot. We're peasant people in Lithuania,' Dalius said.

'We were all peasant people once,' I replied. He grinned.

Allotments in Lithuania echoed our own allotment movement of three centuries ago. They were created for the urban population who had been lured to jobs in factories in towns and cities in order to maintain a degree of rurality and their knowledge of the land. They were also a means of supplementing household foods, with fresh produce being something of a rarity in the former Soviet Union. Like the chalet gardens of Germany and the dachas I had seen in Ukraine and Russia, Lithuanian plot holders were allowed to construct size-able buildings.

'We had a stove for cooking and for warmth and could happily sleep there,' Dalius told me months later over a cup of steaming coffee. Supermarkets in the Soviet Union weren't exactly brimming with fresh produce but they were entirely food-sufficient and only bought what they couldn't grow by selling surplus produce. But Dalius didn't enjoy helping his parents with their plot. Neither did he particularly enjoy helping his grandparents who also worked the land and lived well from it. The really lucky allotmenters, he explained, had plots near lakes. 'We'd go as teenagers, have a swim, socialise, sleep. For me it was less about weed control and more about fun outside.'

Moving to the UK almost twenty years ago with his wife in search of adventure neither of them had thought much about self-sufficiency at all. But when his wife developed health issues and was using a form of therapy to recover that relied heavily on totally organic foods and juices, something shifted.

'We saw benefits very quickly and I too felt more energetic. When you start to look at how produce is grown you see how many herbi-cides and pesticides are used in our food and the whole agrochemical industry is totally self-serving with seeds developed to be dependent on specific chemicals. People are more aware of this now but farmers are caught in the middle.'

As a family they continued to eat organic food but not only was it proving fiendishly expensive, as the laws for organic food can vary, you don't often know just how organic your organic food is. Indeed, for a product to be labelled as organic in the United Kingdom it has to contain 95 per cent of organic agricultural ingredients. The remaining 5 per cent could be asbestos, as far as the law is concerned. Okay, maybe not quite asbestos but there is 5 per cent of grey area.

Dalius and his family were reliant on a weekly delivery of organic vegetable boxes which do not come cheap.

'It was our biggest household outgoing,' Dalius explained. And with the cost of living increasing recently, something needed to change. 'I could get a second job to support my family, I could try and get overtime. Or I could grow what we needed and cut that cost entirely, know that 100 per cent was toxin-free and have fun at the same time. It's a win–win. We didn't spend a penny on vegetables over the summer and we're still living off our potatoes.'

There was an added environmental benefit to their allotment. 'I heard 40 per cent of produce grown commercially goes to waste. It's damaged in transit or it is too misshapen to be sold or it's just left in the ground. You don't have that with an allotment and there's no packaging to get rid of whatsoever. Any food waste goes back into the compost. There's something magical about waste regenerating into something good and I am trying to teach my daughter about the cycle of food.'

It would be impossible to be totally self-sufficient now, Dalius supposed. 'But it's something to aim towards especially given the food shortages and price hikes. I'm a bit jealous of my grandparents' lifestyle to be honest. It's great therapy away from your desk and computer, keeps you grounded and it makes me feel proud. When I was younger I used to think why bother growing your own when you could buy peas in a tin. But now I know.

'We are starting from scratch,' he explained to me on that October afternoon. 'It was really overgrown but Phil strimmed it for us. He's pretty serious about allotments.'

'Who's Phil?' I asked.

'That allotment's guy.' Dalius pointed to the newly strimmed grasses which hitherto had been taller than my children. 'Phil's got one of those professional strimmers.' he held his arms out widely as if holding an enormous machine. It sounded like just the sort of machine I needed.

Dalius and his wife returned to their work, chatting away in Lithuanian to each other while I carried on digging in the manure, turning it over loosely with a fork before getting my hands into the mix.

The church chimed two o'clock and my stomach rumbled. I looked at the unkempt half of the plot with waist-high grasses and brambles encroaching slyly from one corner. I needed to find this man with the strimmer.

That afternoon something strange happened. Despite being physically tired from the manual labour, I had a bizarre surge of energy all afternoon bouncing around achieving micro chores. I felt euphoric, as if I had taken some sort of drug and was riding a ten-foot-high wave with the world mapped out ahead of me. This almost chemical sense of elation carried on into the early evening. I asked Crystal about it.

She texted back immediately. 'It's got something to do with the bacteria, I think.'

Soil. Earth. Mud. In its basic form it is clod and sod and so far from being an accepted natural household addition like a flower or fruit or even pretty feathers that it annoys us when it is smeared on clothes, cemented under fingernails or trodden into a carpet. Even more so when it clogs and breaks a Hoover filter. It's the stuff that in recent years we have encouraged children to play with (but not too much) and are too eager to wash off their hands. There is a whole movement of people dedicated to exercising to the extreme in mud and fetishising the muckiness only to wash it all off as soon as possible because, if seen on a person, mud and dirt is a sign of being unkempt. Quite the opposite on a vehicle – notably the big SUV-style 4x4s. So much so that in the mid-2000s in the United Kingdom people would be prepared to spend £20 for mud in a spray can for their 4x4s to give the impression they'd actually been off-roading and were therefore more adventurous or posher than they actually were. And it might be grubby and muddy and dirty but it is the protector of objects buried, the stuff archaeologists look at in great detail for clever things like carbon dating. Aside from that soil is dirt and grub and filth and squalor and woe betide anyone finding mud on supermarket produce.

Dig deep with soil and you go back in time. In its deconstructed form it is an ancient thing. Years of erosion and a combination of clay, mineral particles, *Mycobacterium vaccae* (that's cow shit to you and me), geosmin, leaves, eroded insect dust, petrichor; it is a living, breathing being. *Mycobacterium vaccae* is believed to help reduce depression (among other things) by mirroring the effects on neurons that chemical drugs like Prozac can provide so it's a clever thing too. The elation felt on that sunny afternoon was all down to the soil I had been handling and manhandling.

But the outlook for soil is shaky. The United Nations reckons that by 2080, 60 per cent of the world's topsoil could be eroded. There are other alarming statistics about the number of harvests we have left and an impending total eradication of soil fertility.

The change in farming methods following the Second World War, intensive agriculture, monoculture farming, urban sprawl, the overuse of fertilisers, shorter fallow periods, climate change or just the continued and systematic laying of tarmac over the earth has dramatically altered the global reserves of topsoil. Add to that a growing population and all of the infrastructural needs this entails and the picture for soil is a little bleak.

This should not be underestimated. Overly intensive agriculture has been linked to the collapse of the Mayan civilisation and the kingdom of Mesopotamia – both of which were the places of origin for almost all of the vegetables we grow today. In both cases a good climate supported the growing population with productive farming systems. But when farming moved to more marginal land, stressing available soil and water resources, the systems became vulnerable.

The Mayans ended up with too many people living in too small an area competing for scarce resources while in Mesopotamia the soil salinised, causing havoc. In the latter case it took around one hundred years for land that was fit for cultivation to fall to just 6 per cent of what it had been five hundred years previously.[2]

No surprise then that good soil, organic matter, rotted-down manure or shit, whatever you call it, is not only vital in gardening in general but is the backbone of edible gardening.

If you plunge a spade into earth and it comes up wriggling with worms, you've got good soil. But good soil is not just earthworms. It is centipedes, ladybird larvae and slugs, it's spiders and springtails and ants – all in the first 10 centimetres or so of good soil. In addition to the fifty or so earthworms per square foot – if you've got good soil – are the billions of microscopic organisms: the bacteria, fungi, protozoa and worm-like nematodes. Forget a spadeful of soil, a teaspoonful should contain a billion bacteria, several yards of the filaments which make up the mycelium for fungus, thousands of those single-celled protozoa and a few dozen or so nematodes.

This all feeds into a soil food chain and it would be easy to presume that plants are at the top of this soil web; the kings of the jungle feeding off the lowly microbes and amoeba through their roots.

Easy but wrong.

They do but plants – vegetable or otherwise – also give back. They produce and secrete chemicals (specifically exudate) through their roots. It's the plant equivalent of sweating. This exudate in turn attracts bacteria and fungi which in turn attract bigger, hungrier microbes – those single-celled protozoa and the wormly nema-todes. What *they* in turn excrete is then reabsorbed by the plants as nutrients. It's a huge microscopic factory down there with well-oiled wheels and cogs. Not just mud. And it all comes down to poo.

Chemical fertilisers, pesticides, insecticides, while useful and con-venient, are an easy remedy. But much like sugar they are a quick fix, a pick-me-up, a plaster on the problem. Too much and the plants bypass the microbic-assisted method of getting nutrition. The microbes leave, the worms, perhaps anxious and irritated by the lack of food, follow. What they really need is manure – rich and well-rotted manure.

When I understood all of this it was as if a key had opened that magic door initially revealed by Sergei's instructions. It was creaking open and onto the natural world, to the garden.

Spurred on by the positive effect mud had on me I put my mind to creating a space for the children there. If having hands in the soil is as good as it was for me then it must be for them too. A mud kitchen; I would make them a mud kitchen.

My father, the perennial hoarder of all things not quite broken enough to be completely useless, was only too happy to help.

'I made some cold frames out of old roof slats.' He pointed to the rafters of the carport where hung three rickety, splintery-looking tables. The autumn glory of the morning had been washed away by sideways rain coming in damp drifts through the afternoon. There was still light left in the day but it felt unnaturally dark and more like late December than mid-October.

'I was just experimenting,' he said as we looked up, rain dripping from our hair and shoulders onto the concrete floor. One 'table' was enveloped in plastic but the others looked promising. All it needed was a piece of plywood on top and there would be a toddler-height table.

'And in here . . .', he opened the old piggery which had been given over to shelves of wine. (None of it fine, you understand; mostly the five-quid Sainsbury's Sauvignon which is always on offer and bought with the mindset of 'in case we run out'– my father being of the still-rationed post-war generation.) A heap of wine boxes lay in a corner next to a collapsed shelf. 'You can have that,' my father said of the shelf. He had found it, he told me, in the garage of their last house they lived in in London. 'Someone made it for shoe storage, I imagine.'

It was covered with mould and cobwebs and although there was an IKEA sticker on one of the sides it was mostly comprised of a few nasty splinters and plenty of rusty-looking nails and a hinge just the right size to hurt if fingers were in the wrong place at the wrong time. It was perfect for my children.

Restoration began a few days later, much to J's despair. While he battled it out on the phone to clients and colleagues, solving the international development issues of hunger, housing and heritage, I fiddled around with a saw, some nails, a hammer and a few odds and ends from the recycling bin.

The bottom of a few black plastic flower pots served as 'hobs' and jam jar lids as knobs. I hammered and cut, splashed some weather sealant on the roof-slat table and, half an hour later, the mud kitchen was finished and I stood back to admire my work. A bit wonky but no less jolly.

All I needed was the space on The Other Side of The Plot to set it up. And for that I needed Phil.

'A strimmer!' Ott said as we approached the allotments a day or so later. It was another fine October day, surprising given the deluge of the last twenty-four hours, and we had been talking about leaf colours and the sounds of the season.

'I think you must be right,' I said with exaggeration. I had contacted Phil and he was not only happy to lend me his machine but said he would do the strimming for me. However, the noise we were hearing sounded much heavier than a strimmer.

Indeed it was. Two men were pushing what appeared to be an oversized Hoover up and down the recently strimmed swathe of grass, churning the mud and grass, roots and all, with big, heavy blades like a plough. A rotavator. So that's what one looked like. It was noisy and gnarly but made light work of such back-breaking toil.

I planted Kit on the ground and settled Ott with her dolly and a few breadsticks on a bucket next to him and went off to meet Phil.

'I'm rotavating because, well, it's faster this way,' he said and explained he had hired the machine for a day to get as much done as possible. 'We'll deal with the consequence later.'

The consequence being that any small roots of bindweed or similarly invasive weeds – once churned into freshly aerated earth, teeming with all those microbes looking for a party – would have a field day.

'What do you need strimmed?' he asked, squinting in the sunlight.

I showed him the wild mass of grass, brambles, weeds and bamboo frames. 'Easy.' He grinned. 'I'll do your paths too if you like.'

Phil told me that he used to grow vegetables and herbs in pots on his small patio when he lived in neighbouring Yeovil. He showed me photographs on his phone months later and I could see the appeal of an allotment for him. Not a square inch of his patio to be seen and despite moving to the village a few years ago his garden was even smaller.

'I thought about taking over an allotment in lockdown but I had no time.' Indeed working in clinical waste during a pandemic, this was not surprising.

'I used to look at these allotments when I went for walks and wonder how many would have been snapped up after lockdown. But over the year they looked more and more overgrown and like no one was really using them so I thought why not?' It was a logical progression in his vegetable-growing journey.

A first-time allotment holder, his motivations were also rooted in the provenance of produce shipped in from around the world. 'We ought to be eating seasonal produce,' he said. 'If you grow your own, you know where it's from. And any surplus you can give to friends and neighbours. And there is nothing nicer than freshly grown vegetables.'

The allotment site for Phil was a place of community too. 'You meet all sorts of people passing with their dogs and wanting to talk. There's nothing quite like a good chat!'

The other man rotavating turned out to be Bob who had, with his wife Pat, taken over the adjacent plot to Phil, his neighbour but one on the other side of the village. Having just moved and with no real outdoor space, the allotment was to fill the void left by their previous garden.

'I looked after the lawn, Pat took care of the fruit and vegetables.' Recently retired, for them the allotment benefits were not just tasty vegetables but fresh air, exercise and something to do. 'And there's always something to do in the garden,' Pat said.

Later on, when Kit and Ott were napping, I returned to set about tearing down the three large wooden posts that had supported the bamboo bean canes. Rotten, they moved easily and I stood back to look at my plot with its ramshackle mud kitchen and soon-to-be strimmed other half. I was making it my own now. I was here to stay.

When peace was declared in 1945 it brought an end to six long years of shortages, destruction and instability. But tough times lay ahead; the austerity and hardships were to hang around for an awfully long time. Dig for Victory disintegrated but there was still a huge enthusiasm for growing vegetables. Cecil Middleton, the nation's favourite war-time gardener, produced another series of guides in 1945 under the title 'Dig on for Victory', but the terrible winter of 1947 followed by floods resulted in mass crop failure and many allotment holders simply lost heart.

People were really tired and worn down. Six years of patriotic self-sufficient duty while bombs fell and loved ones died had reaped little reward given the ongoing rationing and shortages. Enthusiasm for digging and sowing and weeding and watering ad nauseum had tailed off.

The Ministry of Agriculture – keen to promote food production in these times of austerity – was at loggerheads with local authorities who needed their parks back for walking and recreation. There were valiant efforts by the National Allotment Society who compared the amount of land used for recreation against allotment gardening. A fifty-acre golf course, they argued, could be used by just sixty people at any given time, whereas a mere two-acre allotment site could give eighty-one people leisure and pleasure.

But the war-time spirit which had galvanised so many had worn thin and, in the two years after the war, almost half a million war-time allotments were requisitioned or built on.

Post-war reconstruction and the redevelopment of city centres continued to gnaw away at allotment sites for new housing, schools and hospitals. Local councils and town planners saw allotments as a hindrance to such development schemes and many sites were simply sold off to developers.

With the future of allotments sitting so precariously a new Act was brought in to protect plot holders in 1950. It stipulated a twelve-month notice to leave instead of a six-month one and it had to expire during the winter months not the productive summer ones. But it did little to keep people interested and the constant threat of eviction turned people off.

The image of allotment gardening was also suffering from associations with poverty, charity and the austerity of war-time needs. People wanted to distance themselves from the rusty reminders of some pretty dreadful years. In the 1950s there were advances in living standards. People had more money, food was cheaper and more abundant. Convenience food in the form of sliced bread and frozen peas came in by way of America and was very popular. There were cars on the roads, supermarkets slowly made their way into the high streets. By the mid-1950s allotment numbers had slumped from around one and a half million in 1945 to just under 730,000.

The allotment's image problem was hard to shake off. Those sites not requisitioned or built on were often sandwiched between railways or gasworks with sooty squashes and courgettes and smut-smudged lettuces and squashes. Tenants adopted all sorts of things for use on their plots including sheets of iron, window frames and bathtubs. This recycling of rubbish – or upcycling in today's parlance – became synonymous with allotment sites which began to resemble shanty towns. The addition of plastic to the horticultural world in the 1960s – flower pots, seed trays, watering cans and hand tools – added to the look of neglect over time.

Some plot holders used their allotments for alternative purposes too; keeping pigeons for racing or keeping livestock. Neither of these were particularly harmonious additions to sites and vegetable growers often found themselves at loggerheads with pigeon fanciers over crop decimation or with livestock owners over the vermin, flies and maggots which followed the animals or their waste. Most often, the gardeners lost the battle and their land fell vacant.

While the war-time allotments were worked by young, old, men and women alike, by the 1960s around just 3 per cent of plot holders were women.[3] The average plot holder then was most likely to be male and over the age of forty-five and, although they would have made a valuable contribution to the household budget this was not the primary motivation. During the 60s, the allotment underwent a sort of about-turn in the nation's psyche. Keeping a plot was a low-cost, keep-fit hobby. For pensioners, it was also a way of overcoming the boredom of retirement and provided an escape from the pressures of modern living. The grinding necessity of self-sufficiency which had given the original allotment movement its impetus was a thing of the past. Keeping an allotment had become a hobby.

Contrast then the use of allotments in East Germany and the Soviet Union at this time, which were initially viewed with deep suspicion until it was realised that allotments and their gardeners could make up the shortfall in fresh fruit and vegetables. In 1963 private allotments covered 4 per cent of all the arable land of Russia's collective farms which produced half of all the vegetables of the USSR.*

Drastic action was needed if the allotment was going to survive the twentieth century in Britain. In 1965 Harold Wilson commissioned Harry Thorpe, Professor of Geography at the University of Birmingham, to review the provision of allotments. Thorpe and his committee were responsible for establishing a new vision for post-war allotment provision, a radical shake-up with allotments to be seen as a rewarding, leisurely recreational activity.

Thorpe compiled a questionnaire which was distributed to nine hundred urban councils and eight and a half thousand parish councils. There was a separate questionnaire sent to plot holders and, after four years of inquiry up and down the country, it was clear to Thorpe and his committee that despite a brief resurgence of vegetable growing in 1967 when the pound was devalued, the poor state of

---

* There was also a huge demand among urban Soviets for weekend retreats or 'dachas', which were similar to the chalet gardens of Germany and Sweden.

allotments owed much to the movement's origins. 'Dig for Britain' had been launched but did not last long; that rather un-idyllic image of railway sidings was unshakeable. 'The stink of charity had attached itself to allotments as beneficent grants to landless labourers during at least three centuries of enclosure.'[4]

The committee, on seeing that the role of an allotment had changed and that people were growing vegetables as a hobby rather than as self-sufficiency, suggested that there be a name change to reflect this break away from the old image of charity. 'Leisure Garden' was floated as an alternative. The Thorpe Report suggested that allotment sites be more like the chalet gardens of Germany, Denmark and Holland with flower beds and shrubberies in addition to a lawn. Thorpe believed each site should have a play area, demonstration plots and a community centre in addition to a main site building with a lecture hall, office and loos. The goal was to create a strong and inclusive gardening community attractive to men, women, families, children and pensioners alike; a sort of allotment utopia.

Bristol District Council forged ahead with a pilot site complete with chalets, curtained windows, seating areas, loos and car parking facilities. The idea was to combine recreation, rest and cultivation. Similar schemes sprang up across the country including the Bordesley Green Ideal Allotment Holders' Association in Birmingham which was held as hugely successful, with many tenants prepared to travel miles in order to grow vegetables.

Thorpe's findings and recommendations held little sway in the end. While he characterised the average plot holder as 'an individualist who considers his allotment to be as private as his home garden', plot holders blamed councils for failing to provide essential basic facilities: fences, water and locked gates. Plot holders were also reluctant to give up their individual sheds too. Sites now were nothing more than scruffy shanty-town gardens made of corrugated tin and broken junk and viewed as unkempt and a blot on the landscape; a reminder of the hard times after the war. By 1970 there were just half a million allotments left in the country.

'A mud kitchen?' Harry looked at me in disbelief. This was the stuff of professional playgrounds and nursery school enclosures. 'For me?'

'For all of us,' I said as we four trotted down to the allotment after school one day to investigate the new addition to our patch. He ran ahead with Ottilie and when they saw it in situ, their smiles beamed brightly. By the time I arrived with Kit moments later, they were already filthy but deeply engrossed in the earnest work of making chocolate mud cake, mud soup and mud bread. I gave them dried leek flowers and weed seed heads to play with and Harry began digging a hole because, well why not?

The peace did not last. A fight broke out in the kitchen and Kit fell into the hole. It was darkening and cold and I suggested that it probably was time to go.

Harry pouted. 'I love the allotment now. Can we come tomorrow?' Surely this was the happy bacteria working its magic. Or was it just that it was free rein to dig and delve with abandon and in so doing . . .? 'Is that a space rocket?' Harry chirped, interrupting my thought. He had noticed for the first time a large plastic container on the corner of the Lithuanians' plot.

When I had first met them that Sunday afternoon they had been unpacking and assembling something which looked not unlike a Dalek from the *Dr Who* television show. They had been chatting to each other in Lithuanian. Occasionally a word would land here or there. '*Kompostos*' was the one that blew over most often. A seed of a word which landed softly, quietly, unobtrusively at first. And then it germinated: compost.

They had been making a compost bin.

If good soil is the gold leaf of healthy gardening, good compost is Midas himself. The numbers of organisms per teaspoon of compost are almost too large to fully understand; up to a billion bacteria, nine hundred square feet of those fungus tentacles, up to fifty thousand of those single-celled protozoa and, in some cases of uber compost, three hundred nematodes. Which is all pretty delicious if you are a plant.

I had thought about making compost when I initially took over the plot but the very first mention of the word induced a lot of pursed lips and paused 'Ooooh's from those to whom I spoke; chiefly, my mother-in-law, my mother and my brother. 'It's a lot harder than you'd think,' said one. 'Rats,' warned another. 'Faff,' said another. 'Unless you know what you're doing.'

As I emphatically did not I quickly forgot all about it.

But how hard could it really be? When I saw the other compost bins it looked like a mixture of vegetable food waste and some grasses and leaves. What would be the worst that could happen? A few rats gnawing through an old teabag? Hardly the bubonic plague.

*

The science behind composting is as dense as the bacteria found within it. Like baking, if the ingredients are in the right proportion and cooked at the right temperature, you'll have a cake. Too many eggs, however, and you will have an omelette. Too much butter it becomes more of a spread. Too much sugar and it's a syrup, while too much flour renders it inedible.

For compost the ingredients are roughly two thirds/one third measures of carbon and nitrogen. Carbon is the brown stuff: the twigs, wood chippings, woody stems, cardboard. Nitrogen is the green stuff: fresh leaves, grass clippings, flowers and (well-rotted in a bucket of water) the weeds. Into the mix you can add feathers, human hair, shredded paper, newspaper, branches and roots thicker than your thumb, coffee grounds, teabags and dog hair.

The three elements required to 'cook' it are water, air and heat. You cannot have protozoa without water. But not too much else they will drown. Air is to enable organisms to breathe. Compost aficionados advise getting the pitchfork into the cauldron of debris and giving it a twirl. Heat is life's metabolic activity. Once the microbes get going, it's pretty sweaty. This warmth creates an environment which increases microorganism population.

Get the right proportions and you have yourself a gold bar. With icing. Get it wrong and you can damage your plants with a stinking pile of sludge. And some rats.

Since the early Romans, farmers have understood the effect of composts and soil on plant growth. They used marl to enrich the soil, differentiated between different types of manure and made numerous composts and green manures. Their knowledge and expertise was taken to every corner of the Roman empire and their husbandries were read and adapted by Moorish gardeners of the tenth, eleventh and twelfth centuries. Back then different animal manure was readily available given the custom of fattening birds and animals in aviaries, dovecots, stalls and stables. The Greeks, Romans and Arabs could and did choose from the dung of birds, cattle, sheep, goats, pigs, horses, donkeys, mules and even humans. Pliny recommended human poo and urine as the best fertiliser – particularly when collected after a banquet.[5] How he came to this particular and unsavoury conclusion denotes a dedication to the study of poo and its effects which went above and beyond the 'mildly curious'. But that's Pliny for you. I have an absurd image of him hiding furtively behind the latrines nursing the effects of the night before (presumably nibbling on a cabbage leaf), hem of his toga lifted in one hand, resolutely waiting until no one was looking to take samples for trial in a miniature amphora held in the other.

I digress. Botanical experiments flourished in the mid-fifteenth century (some of them more science-based than others) but it wasn't until the nineteenth century that the essential constituents of plant food were identified. German chemist Justus von Liebig discovered the full cycle of nutrition first in plants and then in animals and by 1840 had identified the nutrients essential to plant growth and that plants could convert these nutrients into starch, sugar, fat and proteins. He also discovered that when they were ingested by animals as food and excreted as dung, these substances were converted back to their original simple components.

Liebig's horticultural experiments went on to stimulate the foundation of the artificial fertiliser industries of the late nineteenth and early twentieth centuries which at the time were becoming vital. The introduction of mechanised farming methods like tractors meant that fewer farms and homes had a ready supply of horse poo and that muck heaps were fast diminishing and being replaced by chemicals. Reliance on chemical fertilisers such as Growmore grew in the Second World War during the Dig for Victory campaigns. In the twenty-first century there has been a pushback against artificial and chemical additions to the garden but the advancement of the agrochemical industry has left its mark. It is hardly surprising, therefore, that even today shelves in garden centres can resemble a chemist's.

But I knew none of this as I set up a collapsible bin my father had found in his treasure trove of junk and started loading it up with grasses, eggshells, orange peel, the spent maize spears and roots, rotting courgette stems and couch grass tufts.

This compost bin was my own 'mud kitchen'. I would be putting back what I took out, trying to lessen the frightening statistics about the impending barren topsoil and reaping the benefits in so doing. At least, that was the aim.

Mud. Earth. Dirt. I thought. Call it what you will. It is the sum of all its parts. It is land which we strive to own and tame but never will for it is the first layer of earth, and the last we will ever know.

November

Going home – Potagers and French allotments –
The Good Life – Advice from a timber merchant –
Finding time with my seedlings on the plot –
Questions answered – The wilderness of motherhood –
Fog – Sweet pea – A parting gift

They were going home, Sergei explained. In broken English he was saying that he, his daughter and grandchildren would be returning to Ukraine at the end of the month. K, his daughter, had mentioned as much to me a few weeks ago but as there was no end to the war in sight I'd rather assumed they had changed their plans. He had the resigned look of a man having to choose between two less than perfect scenarios. Stay in the UK and be safe, earn good money but be culturally isolated, or go home to friends and family but live perilously. Furthermore, what would they find when they went home?

Both their physical and psychological landscapes would have changed. As the Greek philosopher Heraclitus proposed, no one can step into the same river twice – it is not the same river and you are not the same person. Home is never the way you left it after a period of absence. I wondered how they would cope. A lot of Afghans returning home after the fall of the Taliban in the early 2000s set about working on their gardens and when they could they planted a tree. On a practical level the tree would provide shade in summer, fruits for food and fuel in the winter. On a metaphorical level when a tree's roots bury themselves in the soil they hold on to the land. I couldn't give Sergei and his family a tree to take home but I could give them something else.

I was waiting for Frank next to the potager. It was half-term and we were staying with friends in France who were rejuvenating a crumbling house in one of the most rural and forgotten areas of the country thick with brambles, briars and boar. It was a beautiful house with honey-coloured brickwork, generous apertures and a dreamy turret or two. Inside it was capacious; there were whole rooms which were comfortably the same size as our entire cottage back in Dorset. Having been abandoned for some years, however, it was in a state of disrepair. There were windows without panes, shutters without slats falling from their hinges and electrical sockets perilously dangling at exactly Kit's crawling height. But while our friends were concentrating on the internal infrastructure and tedious things like septic tanks, structural beams and roof tiles, it was the kitchen garden which interested me the most and Frank, the land agent and the potager's new custodian, was going to show me around.

A potager originated as a plot of land on which were grown the essentials for a thick vegetable soup known as 'le potage'. As a bonus, any surplus could be bartered or sold at market. Later adopted by the monasteries of medieval France potagers became more formally organised on a four-bed cross design mirroring the religious symbolism entrenched in monastic life. In addition to vegetables for making soup, the gardening monks grew flowers, herbs and medicinal perennials.

With true French flair, the decorative kitchen garden was hijacked by the nobility during the French Renaissance. Humble vegetables were laid out to geometric patterns amid grand architecture and marble fountains. The Potager du Roi de Versailles, Paris, produced all the fruits and vegetables needed for the court of Louis XIV and covered twenty-five acres. The potager at the chateau of Villandry in the Loire valley is a little more modest at just three acres but no less jaw-dropping. Box hedges line geometrically designed beds each planted with flowers and vegetables in contrasting colours and textures. Through half-closed eyes it looks more like a tapestry than a kitchen garden.

In its heyday, houses such as our friends', while not as grand as Villandry, would have been a self-sustained entity running on hunting and farming with the potager, or kitchen garden, as its beating heart supplying the kitchen with ingredients for meals for those 'upstairs' and 'down'. They would also have employed numerous gardeners – each of whom would have had specific roles, from taking care of the greenhouses, to tending to the seedlings, nurturing the fruits and vines, to storing the produce.

In some great houses in England, there existed a weekly ritual of sending a supply of vegetables, fruit and flowers from the garden (along with dairy produce, poultry and preserves) from an incumbent family's country seat to their town house by horse and cart.*

---

* Beatrix Potter's *Johnny Town-Mouse* tells the story of Timmy Willie, a country mouse, who went to town in a hamper sent to a large town house every Saturday. There, he had a miserable time and returned home again a week later (in the very same hamper) to the safety and sanctity of his home in a kitchen garden.

In the potager of our friends' house, the remnants of such a garden existed. Contained within its walls was a low open shed containing a rusting rotavator, a few wheelbarrows, crates and tools. The broken bones of a cold frame stood, weed-filled, next to a line of espaliered fruit trees running down the centre of the site and a complex irrigation system tentacled out from an open well. Each veg bed was about the same size as my entire plot. They were also edged with timber which seemed to halt the steady march of weeds spreading onto them. It gave me an idea for my plot.

Frank, out of breath from having a morning's planned mushroom picking overturned by the bloody rampages of a fox inside the chicken coop (four chickens, one duck, one fat fox) the night before, showed me how he was preparing the soil for winter. Chicken poo, he explained, was a great soil conditioner, topped with straw to keep the weeds at bay. He would soon be getting some manure but there was no rush yet.

Indeed, with temperatures at an unseasonable 25 degrees Celsius, autumn still seemed to be unsure about when to make her grand entrance in the Loire region. It was so warm that the produce still flourishing in the kitchen garden included yellow courgettes, tomatoes, red and green peppers, aubergines and carrots the size of a child's arm. And artichokes. Glorious globe artichokes which put my piffling solitary grenade to shame. Half a dozen or so artichoke plants in one whole bed of their own. Now that was the way to grow artichokes. I took note.

His cabbages had already started to ball and looked succulent and slug-free and he was already blanching the celery deep in the soil.

Frank knew what he was doing and I envied his knowledge. I also envied the climate.

Back in England several things had changed: the day truncated into a black afternoon thanks to daylight saving. Secondly, it never ceased to rain. Hour upon hour the windowpanes blurred what little light there was with water. But it was not all gloom and doom. To my total surprise the brassicas were thriving. The cabbages were beginning to ball – not quite on Frank's scale but still. And best of all, the broccoli florets were just beginning to emerge like miniature saplings.

The broad beans had also germinated since my last visit, their first leaves pushing through the soil in search of light. This show of life just before the dark precipice of winter cheered me somewhat. Something else had germinated in my absence too. The allotment site.

The whole area looked like, well, a proper allotment site denuded of scrub and grass with neat paths between each plot – all of which were now in use. Blue water butts stood at the corners of some of the plots and there was a general feeling of 'work in progress' with black weed sheets laid over newly furrowed plots and upended wheelbarrows resting or sheltering new tools.

My own allotment plot had changed too. It had doubled in size. Phil, as good as his word, had been strimming. I was going to have my work cut out.

I turned to *Allotments and How to Work Them*, one of the pamphlets the Garden Museum had sent back in July. It contained a month-by-month calendar which I perused with the same sort of mild interest reserved for horoscopes, not really thinking that there would be anything of use imparted. My heart sank as I read: 'November is a month of preparation for the allotment holder . . . the really heavy labour – trenching, digging, manuring – should be completed before the first frosts set in.' Where on earth was I going to find the time for this 'really heavy labour'?

In the 1970s twenty years had passed since rationing had ended and, in that time, there had been an explosion of domestic labour-saving devices and convenience food. Even bread could be bought pre-sliced. People had disposable incomes and time for leisure activities like golf or tennis and there was no urgent need to grow your own vegetables because the supermarket freezers were full of frozen ones year round.

The number of allotment plots was down to just over 530,000. Still high by today's standard but alarmingly low. Sites were very much the frayed and jagged hinterlands tended by frayed and jagged blokes looking for reprieve from family life or from modern life.

But then in the spring of 1974, something happened. Tom Good, a plastic toy designer from Surbiton in south London, facing something of a midlife crisis on his fortieth birthday, decided to leave his rat race job in a utilitarian concrete tower block and turn his hand to 'the job of life', as he called it. With his wife and to the horror of his conventional-to-their-core neighbours, he transformed his suburban garden into an allotment with the aim of being entirely self-sufficient.

So began the iconic BBC television series *The Good Life* which starred Richard Briers as an enthusiastic white-collar-worker-turned-man-of-the-land Tom Good, Felicity Kendal as his supportive and patient wife Barbara, Paul Eddington as Jerry Leadbetter, Tom's colleague, neighbour and friend, and Penelope Keith as his rather humourless, shrill and social-climbing wife Margo.

The Good Life was a show of genius; the self-sufficient and wholesome Goods contrasting in perfect comic tension with the Leadbetters next door, who lived a wonderfully middle-class existence in suburbia complete with a patio, a wrought-iron pagoda and sunloungers.

I was not born when the show first aired but I vividly remember watching reruns as a nine- or ten-year-old in the early 90s and loving it. As the theme music faded and the animated white bird flew around an animated flower on the screen, I would sit in my nightie in a much too big armchair, tuck my feet under me and for half an hour be totally absorbed by the trials and tribulations of the Goods as they reared livestock, made electricity from methane, lived totally off-grid and of course grew their own food.

Indeed, watching it almost half a century after it first aired the magic remains. It is charming, good old-fashioned sitcom telly. No dramatic music, no high-stakes relationship drama (indeed the third member of Tom and Barbara's marriage was undoubtedly their garden), no special effects, no controversial issues.

It was an instant hit and went on to run for four seasons until 1977 (there were a few *Good Life* specials the following year) and was exported to Australia, Belgium, the Netherlands, Canada, South Africa, Zimbabwe and New Zealand as well as other Commonwealth countries. It was supposedly the Queen's favourite television show and in 2004 was voted the ninth-best British sitcom of all time.

The impact it had on the allotment movement was marked. The National Allotment Society welcomed over eight thousand new members in 1977 and around sixty thousand plots were created in the three years it aired, while waiting lists for plots surged to over a hundred and twenty thousand.

Shown at a time when public interest in green issues was increasing and against the backdrop of an oil crisis it would be unfair to attribute this boom in allotmenting solely to the show. But it was certainly part of a wider cultural trend of the 'back-to-the-land' movement of the 70s when Britain was growing 75 per cent of what it ate. Tom Good would have lived through the Dig for Victory campaign of the Second World War as a child so I couldn't help wondering if his return to the land in the face of middle age was some sort of attempt to regain some of that childhood innocence a little of us all crave and that this was why the show was so successful. We all hanker for a time when life was less complicated.

Either way, the legacy of *The Good Life* was more than just an increase in numbers of allotment plots; it demonstrated that self-sufficiency and allotment gardening could be dealt with by anyone from any background and not just working-class men escaping their families. In essence, it made the prospect of 'grow your own' infinitely more accessible.

Sadly, it was not enough. Councils were still under pressure to provide land for housing projects and, as *The Good Life* drew to a close, the demand for plots almost dried up. By the 1980s there were just three hundred thousand plots left which was a loss of more than twenty-three thousand a year since 1970. Allotments were relegated once again to the edge, the land no one else wanted, tended to by retired old men with time on their hands.

Thirty years or so later, *Amateur Gardening* magazine decided that with backing from the National Allotment Society and television stars Bill Treacher and Thelma Barlow (who played allotment-holding characters in the soap operas *EastEnders* and *Coronation Street*) it would launch its 'Allotments 2000' campaign. Its aim was to raise the profile of allotments, promote them and head up another inquiry into their use. They were going to press for more land for sites and ensure the protection of existing sites. Echoing the Thorpe Report of the late 60s, the Select Committee for the Environment, Transport and Regional Affairs proposed an overhaul of allotment law. All those rules about growing flowers and not selling produce for profit needed to go if allotments were to survive the twentieth century.

This time, the government sat up and took note. It sponsored a handbook, 'Growing in the Community', which saw allotments as part of a social contract and a way of delivering a 'diverse range of agendas including health, biodiversity and social inclusion'. The handbook aimed to revive public opinion of allotments and the 'Allotment Regeneration Initiative' was launched in 2003 by the Federation of City Farms and Community Gardens, attracting over a million pounds of investment. Headed by a group of experts, including Phil Gomersall, the current president of the National Allotment Society, it published a number of guides to help would-be plot holders and produced the largest body of advice on a wide range of topics covering the running of an allotment society and site. 'For ten years,' Gomersall told me over the phone, 'there was greater demand and big money to be invested in allotments. But throughout history you get waves of popularity in allotments. It usually depends on what's going on in society.'

Indeed, in the early 2000s, it wasn't so much an economic thing as a green thing. 'People were aware of the environment, and trying to be greener,' Gomersall said. At the beginning of the twenty-first century the environmental problems were numerous; the hole in the ozone, food chain problems such as mad cow disease and foot-and-mouth disease and fears over genetic engineering all played a part in the twenty-first-century 'grow your own' movement.

In addition, the obesity crisis and concerns over nutrition led to something of an overhaul of school meals and national understanding of food. Jeanette Orrey, a primary school catering manager in Yorkshire, kicked off a food revolution by cooking school meals in-house using organic, local food. When celebrity chef Jamie Oliver heard about it the issue of school food went national. A snowball effect led to the establishment of The Food for Life Partnership in 2006 whose aim was to transform food culture – while the RHS responded to growing public interest with its Campaign for School Gardening.

Food knowledge and interest in good health and locally grown produce was not confined to this country alone. Increasing uptake in allotments went as far afield as the United States with Michelle Obama, then First Lady, creating her own allotment site at the White House (and of course capitalising on the results in her book *American Grown: The story of the White House kitchen garden and gardens across America*[1]).

She wasn't the only woman in power to take to the spades. Home-grown produce had become so in demand and fashionable that in 2009 even the Queen installed a veg bed in the gardens of Buckingham Palace. It had taken a world war for a vegetable bed to appear in a royal garden last time.

Meanwhile, an urban gardening movement began to sweep through the younger generation and a handful of guerrilla gardeners started working on unused corners of towns. Another celebrity chef, Hugh Fearnley-Whittingstall, introduced the idea of Land Share, which allowed people to grow their own food without having to own their own land. Twenty-two thousand people signed up to Land Share within weeks of its launch and a further seventy-five thousand joined the scheme until its eventual closure in 2016 due to lack of momentum.

Growing your own had become a lifestyle choice in the twenty-first century rather than a necessity. A recreation and hobby, not a question of survival. Tom and Barbara Good chose the path of self-sufficiency because they were a bit bored and wanted to shake up their run-of-the-mill lives, not because they were on the breadline.

And let's face it, despite the best efforts of those campaigning for change, allotments still had a bit of a problem; the shanty-town wasteland next to railways was a hard image to shake.

But in late 2019, a wet-market vendor in China experienced breathing problems and a few months later the world stopped turning. Or rather, the world carried on turning but we were forced to stop and the value of allotments was pulled into sharp relief.

*

The young girl behind the counter looked at me blankly and then back at her screen.

'It's for the couch grass,' I said. 'I need to stop it.'

Inspired by Frank's potager of timber-edged beds I was in the local farm and timber wholesalers. Having a clientele comprised predominantly of farmers, equestrians and offspring thereof, I was not sure she would understand my need.

She did not. But a white-haired colleague munching on biscuits at a desk behind her did.

'Planters?' he said.

I shook my head. 'Allotment.'

'Couch grass is omnivorous,' he said with the sigh of someone who had learned the hard way. He stretched back, sucked his teeth and said something along the lines of, 'What you want is some six-inch-two-forty by four-point-eight or so at six by six although we do other lengths too.'

This meant nothing to me but the young girl turned to look at him before turning and jabbing away at her computer keyboard.

'You're going to have to dig a small trench,' the man reached for a Jammie Dodger, 'and then you'll be able to slot it in just shy of the surface. Roots are pretty relentless but at six inches deep you may just stand a chance. Eight to be sure.'

'Okay,' I said and so ordered two of the what-he-said lengths of timber and returned to the car where the children had been kept entertained by the toing and froing and incessant beeping of forklift trucks around the forecourt.

'Here you are, love.' A young man delivered the planks on his shoulder. They looked to be almost exactly the same length as my veg beds. Which made them almost exactly double and a half the length of the interior of the car and no amount of creative thinking could squeeze them in. I rummaged around in the boot for a solution and quickly found one. A saw. There was no time to question why there was a stray saw in the boot perilously close to the rear childseat. It was getting dark and had started to rain heavily so I balanced the lengths of wood precariously on the bumper and began to saw.

J examined the wood with some suspicion when we got home and shot me a 'what are you up to now – actually no, don't tell me' look and leaned them up against the house.

All I had to do now was wait for the weather to ease up. Which it did not. If the summer had been one of the hottest and driest on records, this was surely the wettest autumn on record. 'Good for the garden,' people always say when it rains. I thought of my plot and was dubious. Whole fields had turned into lakes, roads became rivers. Surely that much rain wasn't good for anything. 'Why are we in the sea, Mummy?' the children asked as we splashed through the countryside. 'Is this a car boat?'

Deluges notwithstanding, I worked hard and with machine efficiency throughout the month, squeezing in twenty minutes here or half an hour there between rain showers, school runs and nursery drop-offs. It felt like a race against time and the shortening days.

Because it was. But as soon as an opportunity presented itself, I would pull on my wellies and sprint through the village to the allotments where I'd hurry and haul the tarpaulins over the wet grass, weighing them down with heavy bags of manure, willing the rains away just for a few more minutes. When it was dry enough, I would take a basket of tools in one hand, Harry's hand in the other and we would skip down to the plots.

We planted the remaining tulip bulbs to hail the end of winter and we dug up the dandelions – no doubt the result of Ottie's dandelion-clock blowing and frolicking back in May.

You've got to hand it to the dandelion. Turn your back for a week and dozens spring up with roots as long as twelve inches. 'Big whoppers,' Harry announced.

If only we could live off dandelions.

As the month continued so did our combined efforts and inquiry into the world of the plot.

Harry and I dug small trenches for the timber and stamped them into place, falling on our bottoms when they wobbled. It wasn't quite on the scale of a potager of a grand French house but it was something.

Sometimes it was Ottilie working as my trusty under-gardener. We would check over the winter vegetables, shake slug pellets when we saw the telltale signs and then finish up in the dipping sun dunking biscuits into steaming hot tea as our shadows grew longer and the day shorter.

The children often busied themselves in the mud kitchen or making worm houses but, for the most part, they were happy just being outside. One always feels better outside than in. Perhaps a little colder and grubbier but undoubtedly better.

The allotment was almost a home away from home and as such a place to learn about the natural world. Ottie was entering the 'Why?' stage and I hoped that the allotment had some of the answers.

One afternoon she was sitting on an upturned flower pot eating stale Rich Tea finger biscuits while I sowed the remainder of the broad beans. The light was languid and befitting the late autumn day and, it having rained solidly for so long, the earth was soft and malleable and I made quick work of the sowing, pressing each bean into the ground with a forefinger. I showed her the six-inch-high bean shoots poking out of the ground in the bed behind us. Weaving lengths of string between the bamboo canes for supports I told her about the seasons and the cold winter which would come in a few weeks. I told her that it would probably be rather grey and there would be no leaves on the trees and that there would be frost but that, nonetheless, the seeds underground would be asleep until the spring, 'When you'll have a birthday and the world will become green and alive again,' and she held the ball of twine for me, investigating a worm here or there.

I don't suppose half of what I said went in but she watched and listened and cocked her head on one side now and then. When she slid down to crouch next to me to examine the ground, perhaps more was going in than I thought.

The warmth of that afternoon did not last long. In fact by the evening we were back down to implacable single-figure temperatures, gritty wet mud and slippery leaf fall befitting the month. We were increasingly hemmed in by the onset of winter at home. Without the heady freedom of summer, the playground of the world outside, the long evenings and warmth and we were stuck inside four walls with darkness falling like lead in the middle of the afternoon.

This is the restrictive side of motherhood no one warns you about when you go for those early scans and start shopping for impossibly small clothes. At times it is a barren island landscape where a parent's frustration and annoyance could run as rampant as weeds putting out roots over small things like spilled drinks or thrown food, missing socks, refusal to wear a jumper, the tower blocks of Duplo pushed over, the snatched toys, the plain petulance. The loneliness and boredom of afternoons cooped up could be stupefying. Watching the clock the house felt like a sticky, chaotic, messy place. And so noisy with the clamouring of three small children needing space to stretch and play and yearning to be free.

The minutes of afternoons like those ticked by with impossible slowness until at last it was bath time and the frantic race to wash, dry, clothe and envelop the final few minutes of their day with calm, soporific warmth. And then, as I heaved a sigh of relief and picked up the strewn clothes and toys on the landing, listening to each of them burble or snuffle their way into a deep slumber, I would often be hit by a crashing wave of remorse. Watching the bubble foam melt into the emptying bath, I would feel the tarnish creep of guilt that the day was not perfect and that I was not perfect and that I had willed the evening to come quickly just so that I could breathe. I would regret half blaming them for the physical and mental claustrophobia I felt and I would miss them so much that half an hour later I would stand at their door or by their bed and listen to the rhythm of *their* breathing.

This is the wilderness of motherhood and one which is endured for long stretches of time. As the season closed in, that warm and golden-lit afternoon planting beans with Ottilie seemed more like a dream or a segment of film which someone had edited into the wrong sequence than my reality.

And then came a fog. It crept through the night and settled around us for a few days. Millions of droplets of chilly condensation, thick, eerie, secretive and swirling in obfuscation, obscuring and abstracting light and distance, hiding cars, causing crashes, smothering the land. The village, sitting in a well of hills, was positively buried beneath fog. We had disappeared in it and lived in a forgotten, cut-off corner of the world, our own chilly desert island.

I certainly had no desire to go back to the allotments. Actually that's not true; it was ALL I wanted to do. There was something about the fog which drew me in. I wanted to be hidden by it, disappeared by it, lost in my own private, frozen world, absorbed and forgotten, mired in mud and far away from the four walls of the cottage and cross, bored, tired, cold children. I craved the grubbiness and labour of the land even more when another mysterious illness spread between Harry and Ottie and for days we were even more housebound and my mind bent inwards as I fought suffocation. I longed for the cold air and I craved light with the same intensity as people crave cigarettes, drugs or drink. Or chocolate digestives.

Unable to do the physical stuff I bent my mind back and turned my attention to allotment planning.

The more I read about crop rotation, the less my plan fitted together. I started afresh, using one of the Ministry of Food's war-time Dig for Victory plans. If it kept Britain afloat during the war years, it would keep us afloat during these lean years.

According to the Ministry of Food I should have my compost heap at one end of the plot along with my tools. Next to it I'd have a row of tomatoes, radishes and parsley followed by three rows of dwarf peas, two of dwarf beans and a whopping six rows of onions and two of shallots and broad beans. My head started to hurt as I read on. Next would come the root crops: parsnips, carrots, potatoes, potatoes and more potatoes. A small row of spinach, beetroots and seakale followed next and then finally the winter and spring green crops. No mention of garlic, artichokes, celeriac or tulips. There were no short cuts to planning next year's plot.

I had collected an entire paper bag of sweet pea pods at the end of the summer and having read a short excerpt in a magazine about the best way of propagating strong, early bloomers, decided to give it a try as a rehearsal for edible peas. It was simple. Fill a number of upended loo rolls with seed compost and sow two seeds per roll then water and leave on a warm, light windowsill.

I was doubtful. Not only would I have to put the tray so far out of reach of the children that I would likely forget about it, I had no idea if I had collected seeds at the right time or if they were even fertile.

I had instructed the whole family to save spent loo rolls and one afternoon collected from my parents a large plastic bag full of cardboard tubes. I set twenty or so on their bottoms, filled them with fine compost, watered, sowed and watered again. Then I put them on the windowsill and forgot about them.

But then, one rather cold and grey Sunday afternoon made marginally more jolly by a family tea party to celebrate Kit's first birthday, I noticed a greening taking place.

I gasped loudly.

'What happened? Are you all right?' My mother-in-law leaned forward with concern.

I leapt up and charged to the windowsill. Pushing through the black earth were the luminous green first shoots lurching into the new growing season, eager to leapfrog into spring. Quite what I was going to do with forty sweet pea seedlings was still up for debate. I'd had a vague notion of planting them as an arch in the summer but summer felt very, very far away, however, and the quiet austerity of winter was still to come.

But I didn't think about that then. I thought about the peas I would sow in January and the life I would create in the greenhouse and on the windowsills where elsewhere there was none.

A week or so later, having put the children to bed and listened for their contented snoring, I went downstairs, put on a warm coat, pocketed two envelopes of seeds I had collected and stepped out into the cold. It was an inky black night. There were no street lights in the village so I picked my way gingerly, relying on muscle memory of walks with the children to avoid the ditches and pothole puddles, allowing my eyes to become accustomed to the dark and the stars which were beginning to blaze overhead like scattered seeds.

Lights from other people's houses occasionally streamed onto the wet tarmac and as I walked I could hear and smell the vestiges of other people's days. A family watching the World Cup, meals – a curry here, a roast chicken there – being cooked, fires smoking up through old chimneys, piano practice. At the bottom of the village where the houses were less closely built together I heard the tiny stream trickling over pebbles and leaf rot and owls hooting amid the rustle of trees. I rounded a bend in the road where there was no light at all and slowed my pace until I saw the lights twinkling from the cul-de-sac of houses I was looking for. Although it was still too dark to make out the house numbers, number 14 was easy to find. A large blue and yellow wreath, the national colours of Ukraine, was as good a beacon as any. I stepped up to the front door and knocked.

Sergei was standing shirtless in his host's kitchen waiting for the washing machine to finish spinning.

He, his daughter and grandchildren were making the journey back to Ukraine via Moldova and I had come to say goodbye. Their arrival felt recent but five months had passed and while living in a sleepy village in England might be safe, they were almost entirely dependent on the wider community for lifts to and from work or playgroups or school or shopping. I had not seen much of Sergei since he started working on a building site in town but I attributed the success of my brassicas and leeks to him and his advice.

I spoke into his phone explaining as much and he waved away the thanks.

'So I just wanted to say goodbye and thank you and . . .' I waited for the robotic voice to translate my farewell. 'And,' I said, rapidly trying to find the simplest words so as not to confuse the app but to maintain a degree of emotion and authenticity, 'I hope you find . . . happiness there.'

Sergei listened and nodded. '*Tak*,' he said. 'Yes.'

That afternoon the news from Ukraine had been bleak. Much of the country was still without power, water and heat after a barrage of Russian missile strikes. Cities were in total blackout, hospitals struggled to stay open and with winter and sub-zero temperatures fast approaching the situation looked increasingly desperate. But Sergei and his daughter were adamant about returning home. I think if the roles were reversed, I too would have felt the tug and heard the siren call for home.

'*Tak*,' Sergei sighed and scratched his back. The washing machine rumbled on.

I fumbled in my pocket and pulled out the envelopes. 'I have some seeds for you,' I told his phone and shook them. I had translated their contents and written the Cyrillic letters as best I could.

запашний горошок

квітка космос

He squinted at my scrawl and handed me the phone to explain.

'Sweet pea,' I said.

'To eat?' he asked.

I shook my head. 'Same family but these are flowers and they smell lovely. I had a lot in the garden when you helped me water. *Polyv*,' I said, remembering the Ukrainian word.

The phone translated. He nodded.

I explained that they would grow tall and quickly come the spring.

'And these.' I shook the envelope. 'These are cosmos seeds. I grow them every year because they remind me of a garden I knew in Afghanistan. And, well . . .' I ran out of words and struggled to explain in simple terms about the Emperor Babur's garden in Kabul and the flowers which transport me there and that I missed that place.

I gave the seeds of this flower to Sergei, a refugee returning to a country blighted by war, in the hope that it would remind *him* of a country he called home for a short time and connect him to another country also blighted by chaos and war.

But I could not explain that through a literal translation app. I can barely explain it now.

But when Sergei leaned his head back and nodded slowly saying, '*Tak*,' I thought that maybe he understood what I was driving at after all.

'And the winter vegetables,' he said. 'Are they okay now?'

I nodded and beamed proudly. 'They're huge! They look very . . . professional. Very . . . Ukrainian!'

Sergei smiled a tad uncomfortably. The washing machine, which had until then been spinning and rumbling in the corner of the kitchen, was suddenly quiet and still. Without its whirring driving us to speak up and out, we too fell into silence.

'Well.' I suddenly felt very awkward. I think he probably did too. 'Goodbye from us all. I hope the journey is pleasant.' I held out my hand to shake his and he spoke into his phone.

'Give my kisses to the children and to the dog,' said the app robot.

We exchanged numbers. I don't know why; it's not as if we forged a lifelong friendship through badly translated bursts of conversation about my infantile attempts to grow a few vegetables. But I suppose it's what one does now, the exchange of telephone numbers.

'Thank you, Sergei,' I said without translation at the front door and hoping the darkness masked the sudden emotion creeping into my voice. 'Thank you for showing me how to garden. Thank you for everything.' We hugged, he kissed me on the cheek and that was it.

I stepped back into the darkness outside. As I retraced my own steps through the cold, dark village I passed the entrance to the allotments. Somewhere in there, I thought, are my vegetables. It was this war on the fringes of eastern Europe – among other things – which had led to a cost of living crisis. A strange circularity, therefore, that it was a refugee from the war who showed me how to persevere, who kept it all alive when we were beset by drought or when we were away, and who showed me, hands in the earth, how to plant carrots and leeks, broccoli and cabbages, lettuces and beets.

If in the First and Second World Wars the need for food was so great allotments and home vegetable growing were things of national importance, the same can be said for Ukraine in the early days of the conflict. When I went to Donetsk in 2014 supermarkets and grocery shops had all closed. With no imports coming from China or Russia and with transport routes in and out of the city severely hampered by the war, they sat with boards instead of windows and planks of wood covering their doors. The hungry population, many of whom still remembered life and shortages under the Soviet Union, returned to the old ways of self-sufficiency and turned their gardens into vegetable patches. But this was in the spring of 2014 when the war was nascent. Eight years later it had intensified beyond anyone's expectation and it was the wrong side of winter to contemplate such self-sufficiency.

I thought of the black nights Sergei and his family would soon be living through and I thought of the black nights of Kabul, a city which almost always had power failures. The omnivident stars above me as I walked seemed to bleed into each other, blurred and confused. I doubted very much that anyone was planting *anything* at all. What an idiot I was to give seeds as a souvenir. What a ludicrous parting gift.

December

Christmas list – Pandemic gardening – Frosts and cold
snap – Picking celeriac – A history of celeriac – Another
cold snap and a Christmas harvest – Allotment presents – A
history of saving seeds – Allotment resolutions

'What do you want for Christmas?' J was asking one morning.

In truth, there was nothing I really wanted.

Actually that was a lie. Of course I WANTED things. Material things like new saucepans and oven gloves which didn't have holes and woolly – not cotton – socks and hand cream. Some new jeans would have been nice and maybe something cashmere. And a bigger house. But when I really thought about it, I didn't *need* any of it. And when I really, really thought about it, I didn't WANT any of it at all.

But then I realised that there was one thing I really, really needed this year: seeds.

Oh, and more light in the day.

Inspired by the recent sweet pea successes I set my mind to the seeds.

Economically it didn't make sense to grow peas; I'd worked out that the cost per pea last summer was something like 14p which adds up to a lot of pennies if you're fond of peas. Which I am. But this was about understanding the provenance of food. If Harry, Ott and Kit took delight in picking and eating them straight from the plot then economy could take a step back.

The only problem was, I had no idea where I had put the pea seeds.

They were not in the greenhouse tin of odds and ends. Neither were they in the infamous 'useless drawer' in the kitchen. They weren't in the old desk in the drawing room and they weren't in a basket on the windowsill. Nor were they in my 'allotment' basket which J kept putting on a shelf in the downstairs loo and they were not in my car – the Bermuda Triangle of all useful things including medical records, scratched CDs, the dibber, a jar of cashew nuts, toys and sometimes seed packets.

Scratching my head I added 'method of storing seeds' to my Christmas list.

The last time I had thought about seeds with such intensity was when the world stopped turning.

I was six months pregnant with Ottilie when a shrimp seller from Wuhan, central China, presented herself to a local clinic with flu-like symptoms one December morning in 2019. While Wei Guixian spent the next few weeks feeling increasingly worse with an intense lethargy and a soaring fever and flitting between hospitals, clinics and a market selling wildlife produce largely found in the wetlands of the Yangtze river where she worked, my head was stuffed with all the chores to be completed in the remaining period of gestation. Wei, as it turned out, was not the only one experiencing this terrible turbo-flu and as 2019 became 2020, doctors related the emergence of the coronavirus with the market and Wei, along with many other market sellers, was quarantined.

I listened to the news of this strange disease spreading through China and parts of Europe with mild interest but barely thought about it. As I painted the spare room a cheery yellow to spite the gathering grey skies outside, I thought about the spring to come and what we would call our daughter. As I painted small murals of birds on the bedroom walls to keep the new baby company while she slept, I recalled the bird-flu outbreak I had tried to document for Agence France-Presse when I worked for them in Dhaka. It was devastating for owners of birds and of course the birds but it didn't really affect ME. Not really. This coronavirus or Covid-19 or whatever it was called, I thought, would be the same sort of thing. A tragedy for those affected, something to note and talk about for those unaffected. A future trivia question in a pub quiz at most.

Three months later the story was different. The world quite simply stopped. It had to. Cases of Covid-19 were spreading so fast that, globally, hospitals were overwhelmed and death counts soared. Schools, nurseries, pubs, restaurants, sports centres, music and theatre venues, cinemas and non-essential shops were all closed. The only places to remain open were food shops. We were confined to our homes and allowed out for just an hour a day. Having just given birth to Ott by way of caesarean section she and I were doubly locked down and confined to my bed until I was able to walk easily (anyone who says that a C-section is an 'easy option' for childbirth has clearly never had a C-section). Quickly bored with watching rubbish television and frustrated with my limited ability to move I started fixating on a flower bed out in the garden. From my reclined position and as spring began budding and greening outside my window I fantasised about how to plant it – just as soon as I was able. My recovery and my daughter's growth would be easily measured against the growth of that flower bed. I began online plant shopping for lavender, nepeta and achillea – each representing previous gardens I had known and loved – and ordered seed catalogues. Their pages quickly became torn and dog-eared so intensely had I read and analysed them with the sort of earnestness usually reserved for salacious celebrity or parliamentary gossip.

From these catalogues and after *much* deliberation, I placed small orders for vegetable seedlings and seeds too – nothing complicated, easy croppers like spinach, chard, courgettes, and tomatoes. Enough to feel productive. Enough to acknowledge that there would be a future.

While the virus waged war outside and as my newborn baby adjusted to life, I would turn the other cheek to chaos and garden. At least, that was my plan. On week four of recuperation I somewhat overdid it with a spade and had to return to total bed rest for a few days.

Zealous digging notwithstanding, I was not alone in seeking distraction. Hobbies and pastimes surged during the pandemic as people adjusted to a new normal of confinement and limited human contact. Those not home schooling via computer took to baking and extravagant cooking, to online partying or art lessons or quizzes – sometimes all at the same time – and often followed the morning after by an online exercise class with the perennially upbeat Joe Wicks. A lot of people alleviated the boredom with an 'every day is Friday' attitude to drinking or excessive online clothes shopping. But while most of these activities involved more screen time and a virtual connection and required, at the very least, a smartphone, gardening did not.

If the increase in social leisure activities in the 50s and 60s sucked people away from their allotments, the boredom created by the pandemic naturally drew people back to the land. The Office for National Statistics reported that 42 per cent of Brits took to gardening during lockdown. Aided, no doubt, by a deliciously warm and sunny spring and a seasonally hot summer nationwide, people began planting their gardens, potting their balconies or roof terraces and using windowsills as seedling suntraps.

The attraction was obvious. Supply chains had been disrupted (we will all remember those absurd photographs of people piling loo paper and pasta into shopping trollies) and food prices had started to rise. With no guarantee of produce in shops people began to understand the fragility of the food system on which we had become so dependent. It was as if we needed to Dig for Victory all over again. People began to realise that food did not have to come from an overcrowded, understocked supermarket. Furthermore, to be self-reliant and grow one's own food mitigated contact with other people when it came to shopping inside and it also did away with queuing for hours. But more than that, and perhaps most crucially, it was about mental relief. When the world closes in and becomes very small, to know that it does in fact keep turning and that life endures and continues to grow is surely the biggest motivator to keep on going.

Gardening became so popular that the BBC's show *Gardeners' World* saw ratings soar to 3.8 million by June 2020, the highest ever seen. Formerly the preserve of an older and more settled generation, suddenly a new genus of novice gardeners were tuning in to Monty Don's gentle patter about training courgettes to grow up string, cutting tendrils from a sweet pea and creating a wildflower meadow. Thanks to online streaming platforms it gained a popular following abroad too. The *New York Times* likened the programme to a Covid news antidote[1] at the height of the pandemic and the *Washington Post* called it 'Pandemic medicine'.[2] With garden centres closed for the foreseeable future, seed companies saw sales soar by up to twenty times in the early weeks of lockdown.

A by-product of all this gardening (in addition to the mental reprieve and semi-self-sufficiency) was that while many people continued to connect online, gardeners and growers were able to connect in real time – albeit at a distance. People shared tips, seeds and produce with neighbours. Seed swaps in cities became a 'thing' and communities worked together to work with nature. Vitally there was also more understanding and appreciation of where food came from.

Allotments and self-sufficiency became part of the general public's Covid response. The pandemic severely impacted poverty; with supermarkets unable to meet the demands of consumers, food banks struggled. However, a food and farming organisation, Sustain, brought together fifty allotment groups from Reading, London and Manchester who together donated tons of fresh fruit and vegetables to food banks.

Post pandemic, the number of people turning to their gardens continued to rise. According to the mental health charity, Mind, in the two years following the first lockdown, seven million of us took up gardening with 63 per cent of adults saying that time in the garden had alleviated stress and anxiety as well as boosting well-being.[3]

Lockdown did something more than create a new generation of

gardeners, however. It created a need for space. One in eight people (one in five in London) do not have access to a garden – or balcony. Confined with no end in sight, something shifted in the national psyche. The humble allotment, still considered to be the preserve of old men and rickety sheds, was given a new lease of life.

Phil Gomersall of the National Allotment Society told me over the phone that allotmenting and gardening was as contagious as the pandemic itself. 'There were no leisure activities so people were looking over the wall at allotments and thinking, "Wow. How can I do that too?"'

Gomersall himself couldn't tend his own plot due to Covid vulnerability for eight months, but the other plot holders looked after it, delivering him his own vegetables daily.

An allotment was the ideal safe haven during the pandemic lockdowns. Combining fresh air, sunshine, fresh food and community – real-life community – it was perhaps unsurprising that applications for plots soared – by up to 500 per cent in one city – and waiting lists averaged at eighteen months or up to four hundred names. Ninety per cent of local authorities saw an increase in applications for plots. Having lain on the periphery of cities, towns and our subconscious for decades, the pandemic laid the foundation of a new, twenty-first-century allotment movement.

'It's snowing, it's snowing,' Ottilie cried when she poked her nose out of the front door one morning.

The sun was blazing brightly from the bluest of skies in a way that makes you feel glad and happy and that everything will be all right. But it was certainly not snowing. An easy mistake to make if you've never seen snow and you are two and the world had become white and crisp with a hard frost. Icicle-enshrouded blades of grass stood as still and large as sculptural reliefs, leaf fall looked decorative and the debris of garden 'stuff' to take to the council tip and bags of manure I was yet to take to the allotment were almost pretty under a layer of frost. Even my perenially grubby car looked clean, so hard had it frozen.

'Shall we go and look at the allotment?' I suggested to Ott. Having talked a big game to my extended family about home-grown celeriac sauce with turkey on Christmas Day, I had to be sure that they were ready and ripe.

When she agreed I scurried and gathered warm clothes, the pram, hats, breadsticks and in record time we were crunching over the gravel and trotting through the white village marvelling at everything made crisp and fresh by the frost. At the plots Ott charged ahead, excited to work the latch, hands half sticking to the metal as she opened it.

'Snowing, Mummy,' she said again. 'Lotment's snowy.' We slipped and slided over the icy grass and picked our way to the frozen plot where it looked so still and solid it was as if Medusa had been on the site, staring and glaring at all she saw turning everything to white stone. That said, it looked like a plot still very much in use; a plot in action weathering the cold and hunkering down with winter veg roots digging deep.

I said, 'Look at the garlic we planted!' Its leaves had poked through and were standing as if with hands on hips.

And there were the celeriac. Large, flat leaves made larger by the frost encasing them and sitting as a crown on the King of the Roots. Since they were first planted out so much had happened. We'd fried all summer as war rumbled in Ukraine. We had a new King, we'd had two new Prime Ministers. (One of whom led the country for such a short time – and so badly – that her leadership was pitted against that of a supermarket lettuce's shelf life. One–nil to the supermarket lettuce.) It had been chaotic and at times uncertain but the celeriac grew on doggedly. The world had spun and spun but in the garden there is always order and there is always a constant.

I was proud. This is what it was all about. A middle finger to the chaos of the human world, to food miles and to pesticides, here was my organic world with which I was feeding my children (apart from the edible bribes of biscuits) – even in winter. I felt so smug I was starting to annoy myself and so returned to the task in hand and knelt down to the one closest to me. Its roots curled like a knuckle around a clump of earth but it was disappointingly small when I pulled it up. I leaned forward to pull up another. This one was bigger and would have passed the supermarket size test but it gripped more firmly to the ground. The mandrake tentacle roots were stubborn and thick and unwilling to give way. Until they did and I fell back onto Ottilie and mud shrapnel splayed everywhere.

Ottilie wailed which set Kit off. 'Abort, abort, abort,' I said aloud, throwing the celeriac orbs into the bottom of the pram where they were soon joined by Ott whom I had wrapped in my coat.

Pushing the pram back through the village I left the celeriac on the doorstep to thaw. Which was a bit ridiculous given that it was –1 degrees without the added wind chill.

Hours later it was still frozen. As a student twenty years ago I once worked in a London branch of Marks and Spencer's, promoting a brand of peaches and nectarines. I stood at the shop entrance behind a butcher's block wearing an apron with crates of the fruit which I had to cut up and give to the general public in tiny cups. It was well paid but surprisingly difficult work, not least because the fruits were kept overnight in the supermarket freezer. Every morning I would arrive at the back entrance of the shop where all the delivered goods were being sorted and stored and open a heavy hydraulic door to a freezer as big as a room. As a result of being frozen and unfrozen over a period of a week, the fruits were the opposite of juicy. They had the texture and taste of cotton wool and no one bought any. Indeed, one lady was so repulsed she spat the whole masticated piece of peach into my hand. Ever since then I'd had an aversion to frozen fruits and vegetables – peas being the exception. Looking at the frozen celeriac, I wondered if all was lost.

A while later, when Ott and Kit were napping, I read up on celeriac and sub-zero temperatures. It would all be all right, I consoled myself. They *are* particularly hardy and a few frosts wouldn't do much harm. I sighed with relief. And then I saw the words 'earth up in the autumn'.

I'd heard about earthing up. It's what you do with potatoes – or so I'd been told. It protects against blight and light, bugs and slugs. You can earth up leeks and celery, too, to both blanch and stabilise them in high winds.

At least you do if you know what you are doing and I did not. There was nothing for it but to test the goods.

The soup I made was rich and heavy and as I sipped, I felt its warmth and goodness flow back into my veins. Not earthing up had made no difference to the taste (phew) and I could not help but think that I was, right then, eating the last six months.

When drinking fine wines people often say that they feel like they are drinking history. I hold my hand up here; I'm partial to a glass or two of wine but I've never become misty-eyed – at least, not when thinking of a wine's vintage on first sip. But slurping my home-grown celeriac soup . . . well, I understood the nostalgia attached to wine and to drinking the past. Every spoonful of soup contained the heat of June and July, the languid evenings of weeding and watering. Every growth ring held the DNA of those glaucous moments of late summer after the rains had cleared and steamed the twilight. It felt to me that each mouthful too contained the mists, mellow fruitfulness, fogs, warm spells and cold snaps of the last few weeks.

J was away for a few days so I had the rest of the soup for supper and went to bed early, soup-warm and sated. I would pick one more for Christmas Day to go with the turkey and leave the remaining celeriac in the ground until January, I thought to myself sleepily, when we will be half-starving ourselves after the excesses of Christmas.

This simple and poor decision was to be my undoing, our undoing. In fact it was to be the undoing of the allotment, but I didn't know that then as I drifted off dreaming of celeriac seeds.

If there was a beauty contest for vegetables, I think it would be safe to say that celeriac, with its gnarled, knobbly skin, wayward root tentacles and sallow, grubby colouration, would not be a contender.

Celeriac is slightly different to the celery we use in soups, stocks and salads with smaller stalks and leaves but the same family nonetheless with similar flavours; the root being very obviously more earthy in taste than the stalks and leaves. Celery and celeriac are believed to originate from the Mediterranean where celery was deployed for medicinal use. Its seeds were used widely in Greece, Egypt and Italy to treat colds, flu, arthritis and digestive problems. And it was a pretty bog-standard thing to have lying around one's garden or fields if my old chum Homer is to be believed. It appears growing wild outside Calypso's cave in *The Odyssey* and grows wild on the plains of Troy (modern-day Turkey) for horses to eat while its leaves were used in garlands and victory wreaths. And there the story of my favourite rooty-beauty fades until the Middle Ages when the Italians began the process of domestication and breeding out the wild bitterness. It was not recorded as a culinary ingredient until 1623 in France but by the end of the seventeenth century it was commonly cultivated in Europe.

Its earthy taste is exploited to maximum effect with the classic French dish *celeri remoulade*, a sort of delicious mustardy sauce in which sits a slaw of celeriac matchsticks.

And it never lasts long when I make it because when it comes to celeriac, beauty really does come from within.

Despite a new growing mound of harvested loo roll inners, I still had not yet found the time nor the inclination to begin on starting off the peas. For one, I still couldn't find the envelope of seeds – and I'm pretty sure it *was* an envelope I had squirrelled away somewhere and not a pot or a jar. But more than that; it was just too darn cold.

The cold banged at the door and rattled the windows and, finding them closed, was still able to penetrate the crevices and micro cracks typical of old buildings. It dried my hands and rubbed them raw. Hairline cracks appeared in my thumbs and the cold hurt my ears. It hurt my nose. It even deranged the dog.

Every morning was so frozen over that the car had to be doused with jugs of hot water just to open its doors. After the November rains, the roads in and out of the village were deathtrap slides of frozen water, leaves and mounds of rock-hard horse poo. The children, at first mystified by this new white world and beautifully rosy-cheeked, were soon tired of the cold too. Their noses and eyes streamed, their hands were constantly blue and they were growing thinner and wan due to so much shivering.

'Isn't this glorious!' J said one particularly miserable morning as he wiped ice from the inside of the bedroom window. I was too cold to react.

Winter has a point. It kills bugs in the air and, in the ground, it gives plants and animals a period of dormancy. Wipes the slate clean, so to speak. But it meant that even if I knew where my peas were, I simply had no inclination to sow them.

Imagine my joy at the passing of the shortest day. It never failed to fill me with a sort of bubbling anticipation for spring. From then onwards there is more light in the day, there is more time. There is hope. I refused to acknowledge that the shortest day also hailed the start of something else. December is a seasonal bridge beginning with one foot in autumn and ending with its toes firmly dipped in winter and if the cold snap of late had been anything to go by, the coming winter might just be hell.

It dawned on me in the early hours of one particularly icy morning that if we were cold – inside with the heating on and clothed – then what on earth would the allotment crop be feeling? With temperatures barely going above zero for days at a time, I began to feel anxious. They needed a winter blanket but how and where does one find one of those without traipsing off to the garden centre to part with already diminishing funds? Please let them live, I said silently to crows shivering on a neighbour's chimney.

As cold as it was I bundled Harry and Kit into warm clothes and slid down to the frozen allotments to check on the state of affairs and to unearth a celeriac for Christmas. Harry insisted on dragging a plastic dog on wheels behind him and it skittered and slid in the ice but the world was beautiful as the sun bled through the morning. Together we explored the frozen water trough, shook ice from the grasses and looked for animal footprints. We righted the tarpaulins which had blown off on the still-to-be-dug-over half plot and weighed them down with puddles frozen to disks.

The marvelling at this winter wonderland came to an abrupt end when I got down to business. The beans had survived and were looking quite pleased with themselves.

The broccoli florets were looking a little . . . charred. They looked as if they might even be in pain. If only I had covered them. But it would be fine, I thought. It would be absolutely fine. These brassicas of mine had weathered aphids, they'd survived the heatwave. A bit of cold would be nothing to them; they were made of stronger stuff.

The remaining red cabbage and kale seedlings appeared to have been striking and had done precisely nothing since being planted out but no matter. Come spring which, after all, was JUST AROUND THE CORNER, all would be well. I mentally patted myself on the back. I was getting good at this allotmenting malarkey.

'Let's pick this one.' Harry was standing over the celeriac. 'It looks like a monster.'

'All righty then,' I said, jolting myself back to reality. He had brought a spade with him and as I plunged the pitchfork into the ground he plunged it into the mud. He had grown a lot in the three months since starting school and in ways I had not appreciated but it was only then, watching him heave his spade, that I noticed. Life was more natural for him now and he was learning things. And every day he would come home to tell me that clouds were made up of tiny droplets of water which made rain, or that five is one more than four but one less than six, and that some cups are made out of plastic and forks are made of metal. He was learning to read and would exclaim with delight when he identified letters on road signs. He had new friends and he was growing stronger too.

He grunted one last time and we wriggled the root free.

'Delicious,' I pronounced. 'At least it will be soon.'

He looked dubious. Kit looked bored.

The cold thawed as quickly as it froze and Christmas Day dawned disgustingly mild, wet and humid – more like an August afternoon than the first week of winter proper. But it was Christmas and the children were awake early with excitement.

'Happy Christmas!' we croaked with fatigue.

'Is it snowing now?' Harry asked before vomiting three times and falling back to sleep immediately.

While he lay in the thralls of a sweaty fever which had crept up on him from god-knows-where, J, Ottilie and Kit and I breakfasted on croissants and jam and retreated to the Christmas tree to exchange presents.

'You said you wanted more light in the day so I took you at your word,' J said as I unwrapped a head torch. 'Now you can be down on the plot until midnight if it takes your fancy.'

I grinned and flicked the light on and off on my head until Kit found this too distressing and yelled.

I must have mentioned something about wanting to cook on the allotment because my mother had given me a portable camping stove which folded neatly away in a plastic briefcase. Technically we weren't allowed fires but there were no rules about such contraptions. I wondered about cooking the children's tea on the plot with them as my sous-chefs. What could possibly go wrong?

J also gave me a trailer that the children insisted on being carted around in when Harry woke up. It was a beautiful thing with four wheels and a long handle and was exactly the right width for the pathways between the plots, which neither the pram nor the wheel-barrow could boast.

I was given a seed box by my mother-in-law a few days later and it was full of seed packets. Crimson-flowered broad beans, black Spanish radishes, yellow boulder beetroots, purple 'dragon' carrots, white Casper aubergines, purple dwarf beans, to name but a few.

The gift, unbeknownst to her, was twofold. Not only are seeds the gift that keep giving – if you collect and store the seeds of seeds at the end of the season – for me the sudden influx of seeds took away 50 per cent of the plot-planning decision battle. Not being much of a decision maker this was one of the greatest presents of all. Now I had the seeds, all I had to do was work out what should go where. Which having been given no less than two books about war-time vegetable growing, both of which were illustrated with numerous plans and ideas for crop rotation, would be easy. Or at least, easi*er*.

Days later I set about sorting seeds. It posed a bit of a category conundrum. If you are going to sort properly you may as well do it as you might clothes. Jumpers in that drawer, socks over there, skirts on the hangers, new black suede boots as far away from children as possible. But unlike clothes, vegetables fall into category upon category: seasons, when to sow, when they grow; when to harvest; alphabetically? Geographically? By colour? There were and are a million categories for seeds and the choice was making my head go fuzzy.

Frank had allowed me to pick a few fronds of basil from the potager back in November and I shook them into an envelope, inhaling the faint smell of a future summer as they tumbled out. I rolled leek seeds from their flowers (finding this fiddly, I later employed Ottie to help; small fingers worked wonders). Then it was a question of rifling through the additions to the seed library, for that is surely what it was by then, and working out the order in which to start propagating when the weather warmed up. Peas, broad beans and a funky-looking white aubergine were first in line.

My mind travelled momentarily to a seed bank – the first and only I have ever visited.

Fayez and Muna Taneeb ran a permaculture farm in the occupied West Bank. On land surrounded by the ten metre-high security wall and adjacent to a chemical factory whose plumes of black smoke belched out of chimneys just next door, their farm was a form of psychological resistance. And well it might be; having had to fight to use his ancestral land when the wall was constructed and losing 60 per cent of it, the couple were vocal and active opponents to Israel. Fayez had been arrested twenty-five times for 'unspecified reasons' when we met in 2016.

Fayez grew everything from tomatoes to cucumber to beans, strawberries, aubergines and peppers and employed not just an army of young men and women to keep things ticking over but bees to pollinate his crops. It was his seed bank of which he and Muna were so proud. A small shed with shelves on every wall and jars and bottles of seeds collecting on every shelf. Nothing fancier than that. 'This,' he told me, 'is the answer to Armageddon. When it happens we, at least, will have everything we need to start again!'

A century ago saving seeds was as much a part of gardening as soil conditioning. Thinking about that little shed in the middle of a hostile and heavily militarised area, and how simple Fayez and Muna's seed library was, made me realise how integral saving seeds is for food security.

Last year's New Year's resolutions were to not make any New Year's resolutions. But I didn't have an allotment then.

My list of self- and plot-improving aims was as follows and in no particular order:

- Be less scatterbrained especially on the allotment
- Read more about plants
- Remember what you plant and where
- Swear less, weed more
- Plan
- Frown less
- Look after tools
- Slow down
- Save seeds

Last year was a dress rehearsal, I thought. A mere dip of the toe, a soft scratch of the hoe. This would be the year of the allotment.

I plunged in.

January

Global warming in winter – Searching for spring –
Mortification – A history of crop failure – Janus and
lunar gardening – Sowing – The pandemic of gardening
abroad – A first snow and new germination – Cabbage
ravages – What was the point of the allotment?

January dawned with a drab and dreary indigo which lingered until well after breakfast. Perhaps it too was waiting for something better to come along than the first month of the year. And oh how it rained. The Christmas cheer of just a few days ago, the fairy lights adorning shop windows, the municipal decorations of local towns, our own decorations, they were all hanging akimbo like broken paper cracker crowns or smeared through water droplets running angry rivers over the car windows in endless drifts and droves of rain.

Which was rather incongruous with the temperature outside hovering in the mid-teens. It was both uncomfortably wet and uncomfortably warm. On the bright side, this mitigated the need for heating which, given the hollow sound bellowed by the oil tank the other day when Harry hit it with a stick, could only be a good thing. The downside was that temperatures this high in the first few weeks of winter only meant one thing. The planet was getting hotter.

'What is, Mumma?' Harry chirped from the back of the car. I was driving him to his first day back at school with Ottie and Kit and must have been talking aloud.

'Oh, nothing.'

'You said, "It's getting hotter." What is?' he persisted.

'The planet,' I relented.

I was not entirely sure he knew what planets were yet and watched him through the rear-view mirror trying to absorb this information.

'The moon?' he said at length.

'Nearly right. But no. The planet,' I tried to explain. 'Earth. It's all the countries in the world, all the seas and ocean, all the animals from the North Pole to the South, all the lions in Africa and tigers in India, all the horses in the fields and the cows and dogs and trees and cats and vegetables and flowers. The planet. It's where we live and it's getting hotter.'

Unseasonable weather and temperature fluctuations are not a new phenomenon. In 1668 the first frosts came in August and winter lasted for eight months. For twenty years England enjoyed Siberian-cold winters and the Thames was so frozen solid that it was strong enough to hold frost fairs and carnivals. The causes of this mini-Ice Age are still hotly debated but the data for a warming planet is irrefutable. Between 1659 when records began and 1750, the average temperature rose by 0.7 degrees Celsius. The Industrial Revolution can be and often is blamed for this change but there was no reversal and by 1900 the national average had risen another degree. By the year 2000 it had risen another.[1] It has been getting hotter.

The cold snaps we had experienced in late December were unusual. The first frosts usually came much later than they used to, if at all. Last winter we could count on one hand the number of times we had to de-ice the car.

Global warming is perhaps the most pressing and depressing problem of our time. Worldwide, wildfires and floods can and will decimate whole communities and create domestic refugees but it was the gradual creep of mercury up the scale which irked me the most.

That balmy early January morning was the meteorological sword of Damocles hanging over us.

'Tractor!' Harry said, pointing out of the window. 'Look, Ottie, tractor.'

'Oooh nice, big red Massey Ferguson, that one,' I said, swerving to avoid it.

I pulled into the school car park and waited for a free space. Harry waved to some of his new friends frolicking across the playground.

What world are we leaving for these seedlings of ours, I thought morosely.

With a long morning stretching ahead of us and no end to the rain in sight there was only one place to go: the garden centre. Still unable to locate the buff (I'm sure it was buff) envelope of last year's harvested and dried peas, I still needed peas for seeds and wanted to investigate potatoes. I'd been too late to the potato party back in October but according to the online and paper catalogues I was receiving daily, now was the time to get potato-ing. That quiet January morning seemed like the perfect time to find out what exactly a seed potato was.

Spuds and peas aside, mostly I wanted to escape the drab, wet morning of the first week of the year. During the pandemic's second and third – and winter – lockdowns during which garden centres were allowed to stay open, I would come to the garden centre every Friday with Harry and Ott. While 'non-essential' shops, cafes, playgroups and play areas remained closed it was easy to become glum and depressed but in the garden centre it was always spring. In the garden centre there was always life blooming or about to bloom.

It reminded me of Afghanistan where the winters are short but bitterly cold and treacherous for plants. Gardeners would overwinter blousy geraniums, tree lilies and fruit trees in great giant terracotta pots under polytunnels made out of little more than white tarpaulins, polythene sheets and bamboo.

Over the years working near Kabul's old city I came to know Kaka Khalil, a kind-faced man with a large family who had lived in the same building for generations (apart from a brief absence when the area became a frontline in the civil war). A local elder of sorts, he was liked and respected by the community and worked tirelessly to solve petty differences among neighbours and market stallholders. He was also a superb gardener and the courtyard of his house in the summer was a heavenly place of lawn, box hedges, roses, fox-gloves and pomegranate trees. When I last saw him there was snow on the ground outside turning to black ice as the wind whipped off the white Hindu Kush mountains. It was blisteringly cold. His greenhouse, a little way off from his house around a few alleyway corners, was not only crammed with overwintering pelargoniums but he had somehow rigged up a television to the city's electric grid masquerading as a slack wire between two telegraph poles. It was clearly temperamental – the plug lay rather alarmingly in a frozen puddle. When he saw me staring at the bare plug Kaka Khalil explained that the radio was more reliable for news. I frowned when he explained. Why would he be listening to the news in his shed, I wondered. Noticing a shelf on which stood a Thermos, several glass tea cups and a bowl of dried fruit, it dawned on me that this was something akin to an allotment shed – in spirit at least. This was where he escaped his wife and children and all the chattels of the world. A man cave. But it was better than a man cave, I thought. So much better. Standing there and surrounded by plants and greenery, life and colour while the outside screamed a dreary, flat grey, it was perennially spring.

'Leave Kit in the car?' Ott jolted me back to reality.

Manhandling him into a trolley (he had become a muscular and somewhat determined little baby) we darted through the rain, soaking our feet in puddles, and dashed inside. We caught our breath and ambled towards the now-skeletal Christmas display. For the duration of December and November half the garden centre had been given over to a wintry wonderland of talking reindeers, of gnomes and elves and wrappings and ribbons, of old-fashioned toys and mechanised toy trains. It was surprisingly charming – if visited on a quiet day – and almost magical for children. That wet January morning, however, the magic had well and truly faded behind the bright red discount sale signs.

In the garden centre proper we began looking for seed potatoes until a member of staff said we 'were far too early, luv'. Trying not to feel too deflated *again* we turned our attention to peas. Ottie stood in front of a vast wall of seed packets and scanned the images pointing out the flowers and vegetables calling out those she recognised while

I busied myself with keeping Kit in the trolley seat. 'Peas, Mumma! Tomatoes!' Ottie said, handing me a fist full of packets.

Tomatoes were the only seeds I hadn't been given so I picked out two varieties. Tumbling Tom, which, as its name suggests, produces an abundance of small juicy cherry tomatoes throughout the summer and which, most importantly, is easy to grow. I also added Money Maker (one can live in hope) to the trolley. This promised larger fruits and should grow up – if supported – rather than tumble. I gave the large packet of peas to Kit to shake as a rattle. By the time we got home, he had torn it open. I spent the best part of half an hour gathering the seeds into a jar from the crevices of my car which of late had been doubling up as a child's dustbin and second home for the smallest toys.

My first chance to visit the plot coincided with a break in the rain so, with excitement and purpose, I loaded up the trailer J had given me for Christmas with the remaining bags of manure. With a child-free hour or so to play with my plan had been to make a start on marking out the new veg beds and to pick some vegetables for the children's tea and our supper. The fridge had been looking increasingly empty but, in an economy drive, I was refusing to pop to the shops until absolutely necessary.

This had been of great concern to J who'd kept opening and closing the fridge in the hope that something had magically appeared in the intervening seconds.

'We can't have yogurt and spring onions for supper!' he complained.

'We have ham! We have cheese!' I enthused.

'We can't have yogurt, spring onions, cheese and ham then. Is this even edible?' He held out a rather dried-up piece of brie.

I took it from him, broke off a piece (not without some difficulty, truth be told) and tasted. 'It is,' I lied. 'And we can have ham and celeriac gratin. And whatever broccoli the children don't want. And tomorrow I'll do a remoulade. Everyone likes remoulade.'

He had glared at the cheese and then at me and then back at the fridge. Only a few days into a 'no junk food' drive he couldn't even reach for the chocolate digestives.

Pulling the trailer behind me I delighted in the ease with which I was effectively pulling 60 or 70 kilos of poo, one-handed, through the village. No straining to keep the barrow steady, no creaking pram frame tilting dangerously beneath the weight. Just smooth wheels and an axle. The delight was somewhat marred by the vertigo I had been feeling since the end of December and which arched and crashed over me in great waves of nausea and caused me to stagger a little but I was determined to enjoy my solitary hour in the 'flesh air' as Ottilie called it.

The trailer wheels sank in the long, wet grass and soaked ground but cornered onto the paths running between each plot as if on rails. Reaching my plot I dropped the handlebar and surveyed the land, searching each bed as if looking for long-lost friends at the arrivals terminal of an airport.

I frowned. The plot looked different. I mean, it looked exactly the same if you discounted the bucket of pea sticks which had fallen into one of the paths and the tools which were lying akimbo in the long grass (note to self: be more tidy), but the overall feel of the place looked different, as if someone had been moving furniture around.

The broad beans were all right. A few had succumbed to the frosts but they were still there more or less and, anyway, I had a whole new variety to try come the spring.

I looked up to the next bed. Something was terribly amiss. Something was terribly missing. The leafy clumps and ball-heads of broccoli. That was it. The broccoli was . . . gone.

A thousand thoughts ran through my head. The village is close to a county line; were the allotments now somehow part of a massive crime network? I'd read a lot recently about urban allotments being hotbeds of criminal activity including arson and drug dealing. Were local ne'er-do-wells helping themselves to the good stuff while they traded the bad? Deer. I had heard that deer had been spotted in the area recently. Had they found themselves hungry one morning? And badgers? Everyone had warned me about badgers. Nothing added up, however. Why would beasts or baddies single out the broccoli and leave the cabbages? Nothing made sense until I conducted a forensic investigation.

It all smelled very rotten. The corpse of a floret lay slimy in the mud and mire. I picked one stalk and it came away easily. Other plants lay flattened and rotted on the surface of the earth as if melted to it. The problem was obvious. And fatal. It wasn't aphids or heat or me which killed them. It was the frostbite that got them in the end.

Until that moment I had lived with a certain swagger that I – a novice allotmenter – had defied my talent for killing plants on sight and successfully grown broccoli. BROCCOLI, for Christ's sake. The stuff that more experienced gardeners do not even attempt, so prone are they to aphids. 'What a waste,' I said to the rotten mess. 'What a bloody waste of time and energy.'

Crop failure, I reasoned, was a bit like breaking a glass or a mug. It's annoying and could have been prevented but oh well, there is literally nothing you can do about it. Move on. The children could have celeriac gratin as well, I thought, and turned to the rooty orbs.

They were looking curiously yellow and a little bald. Their dark green leaves hung like greasy hair on a pale teenager. I sank the fork into the ground to dig one up and it collapsed, oozing a squelching sort of pus. I tried another and it disintegrated into slime. A third bore no results either, its mandrake tentacles flailing around use-lessly in the butter-soft mud while the orb sank back into yellow pus with a hiss. Rather dramatically, I dropped the fork and began scrabbling at the earth around the remaining six, hoping that I'd chance upon a firm root, but by the ninth my hands were covered in muck and ooze, I was deflated and the smell of decomposing vegetables was horrible.

Rotten. Every. Single. One.

When I think now about the feelings which ran through me it seems incredibly melodramatic but as I sank back on my haunches and surveyed the fresh devastation of rotten vegetables I could not help crying. Silly to be so utterly distraught over a few vegetables – I know that now – but the total and utter disappointment, the anger, the hopelessness and remorse and the nostalgia for a time when they were still alive was a rite of passage for the novice vegetable grower. But it was no less overwhelming.

I'd had something beautiful, taken my eye off the ball – or in this case, balls – and now it was gone. I'd catastrophically miscalculated and underestimated the cold. Quickly entering a state of mourning, I sobbed into my muck-covered hands. The vertigo soared.

Something else soared too. A memory of famine.

I read *Under the Hawthorne Tree* by Marita Conlon-McKenna around the time it was first published. I must have been about ten or eleven and distinctly remember devouring the story. It plots the adventures of three young siblings Eily, Michael and Peggy whose parents disappear during the potato famine in Ireland. They were faced with the prospect of starvation or the workhouse. Disinclined to either, and unsure of their parents' whereabouts, they set out to find their kindly great-aunts on the other side of the country.

The Irish potato famine is perhaps the best-known crop failure of the British Isles. It was a horrific period and one that changed the course of history. Irish tenant farmers, having long existed at subsistence level relying heavily on the nutrient-rich and calorie-dense spud, were destroyed by the spread of a mold known as *phytophthora infestans* amongst their tatties. That year's crop failure was followed by year-on-year failure until the early 1850s. It was the worst famine in Europe in the nineteenth century and caused untold sorrow and hardship as about one million died from starvation, typhus or other famine-related diseases.

The blight led to mass emigration, too, with an estimated two million setting sail for America, Canada or Australia and elsewhere. It is also attributed with boosting nationalism (the relationship between the Irish and the ruling British government was strained to say the least) which ultimately led to Irish independence in 1922.

That's the thing about crop failure. On a massive scale it gets political pretty quickly. Louis XVI, King of France, experienced the ramifications of a crop failure in 1788 and the ensuing bread shortages in France in part contributed to the French Revolution. In more recent years, as a journalist I worked on dozens of stories relating to climate crop failure in Afghanistan and Bangladesh. When life hangs on a thread, a temperature fluctuation or a sudden deluge can be instantly devastating on communities and push them into already overpopulated urban centres to find work. The underbellies of highway bridges of Dhaka are home to destitute farmers who have lost crops and livelihoods and are seeking work in the city while living rough. When the floods came to Bangledesh (which they did with annual regularity), these were the people most vulnerable to waterborne disease. Desertification and crop failure in sub-Saharan Africa continues to contribute to migration, unemployment, poverty and a disenfranchisement of youth who, seeing no alternative, join militant organisations like Boko Haram. Meanwhile Al Shabaab over in Somalia has proved adept at benefiting from climate-induced livelihood loss and food insecurity by attracting fighters with food, protection and money.*

---

* Interestingly Al Shabaab has recently started embracing an environmental agenda by viciously protecting the green belt of trees left in southern Somalia where the group is most active. At the time of writing, anyone caught cutting down a tree will be fined $1,500. Despite adding a ban on plastic bags to their agenda their motivation is largely one of self-interest; they need the trees to provide cover against the all-seeing drones flying overhead.

In 2022, after a particularly bad heatwave, Pakistan was hit with such bad floods that a third of the country was underwater, rendering families homeless and similarly vulnerable to disease. Baluchistan and Sindh, in southern Pakistan, received five times more rain than the thirty-year average and the loss of over half of all cotton, date and rice crops was alarming, not least because Sindh is home to forty-eight million people and contributes about a quarter of the country's agricultural produce.[2] Continued flooding on that scale could over time create forty-eight million climate refugees.

In the opening chapter of *Under the Hawthorne Tree*, Eily watches her mother pulling out rotten potatoes from the ground. 'All around the air heavy with a smell – that smell, rotting, horrible . . . the smell of badness and disease . . . the crop, their crop was gone. All the children stared – eyes large and frightened, for even they knew that now the hunger would come.'

And there I sat, a one-woman crop disaster lurching into a rotten vegetable bed.

The learning curve of vegetable growing is a steep and tiring one and the curveball of severe frosts had just bent the curve by a few more degrees. Advice from books and websites, leaflets and other gardeners is all well and good but the truth is that whatever you do, however lucky or experienced you are, there is one thing you can't help.

The weather.

The vet walked by with his dog and stopped for a brief chat about my losses. He told me he never bothers with winter vegetables because the allotment site was too exposed but focuses instead on digging in manure in January.

When he walked on I slung some manure around and tried to make a start on the new beds but it was all too much.

I'd lost heart, I'd lost faith, I'd lost vegetables. Many, many vegetables.

I suddenly felt very, very hungry.

Not for nothing is Janus the Roman god du jour. New beginnings, old endings, transitions, and doorways. I have always found January to be something of a buffer month. A sort of 'neither here nor there' month. Still full from Christmas and New Year there is a short, sharp kerplunk as we land on 1 January as if dropped from another planet, still half bejewelled and tinselled with Christmas cheer, the 'morning after' the year before.

The days were lengthening minute by minute but the mornings remained dark. So very, very dark. Indeed they seemed to darken as the weeks progressed. Daily, the alarm sounded – rather optimistically – at ten to seven but the indigo skies slipping through the blind made it an implausible hour at which to rise.

For the garden, for the allotment, January is a time of rest. Throughout most of the year, the beating heart of a plant (a healthy one) pulses with the inevitability of what it has to do: grow up, grow down, produce leaves, produce roots, produce flowers, produce seeds (it must be hard work being a plant). In January, however, plants can put their feet up with a well-earned break and rest until the growing season lurches into action, wheels and cogs spinning in the well-oiled machine of nature.

For the grower, it is a time of waiting for the best possible time to start greasing those engine parts and sowing the seeds. My plan was coming on.

J came into the kitchen one evening after the children were in bed to find me at the table which was strewn with seed packets. I was squinting at the small typescript on the back of the tomatoes Ott and I had bought and trying to decipher a growing bar chat. Next to me were two roasting tins, a number of small plastic flower pots and loo roll innards and a bag of unopened compost. The rain smashed at the windows and the wind howled around our feet thanks to a crack in the wall behind the kitchen cabinets.

'Goodness,' he said, taking in the scene. 'Is this a junk modeling school project for Harry? What are you trying to make? Aeroplane? Space rocket?'

I peered up at him sternly. 'Tomatoes,' I said. 'And peas.'

He frowned.

'By the windows. You won't even notice them. Promise,' I said.

'Oh god. Is it that time of year already?' He held his hand to his head recalling last year's 'kitchen garden', and the seed trays made out of various roasting tins and balanced precariously on the windowsills.

The anxiety over when to plant and when to propagate is common to gardeners and vegetable growers. Up and down the country there is a national pause as we listen for the starting gun of nature with a collective held breath, seed packets in one hand, pots of compost in the other. But up and down the country and worldwide, the temperature fluctuates and the weather is different. A spinach grower in Aberdeen is going to have a different start to his or her Cornish counterpart, for example. The question still remains. When on earth do we sow to get the best possible results?

The answer could be in the moon.

The idea is an ancient one. Before those prescriptive, and slightly confusing, multicoloured calendars on the back of seed packets people looked to the skies for a guide.

The basic principle is that if you plant during a particular period of the lunar cycle, your plant's health and harvest will be optimised. During a full moon, for example, the gravitational pull is stronger therefore more water is being drawn to the surface of the earth – like a tide – and thus is available to seeds.

This might sound a little primitive now and scientists have cited Lake Superior, the third largest freshwater lake on the planet, where the tidal influence is only two centimetres as an example of the implausibility of the moon affecting groundwater. But I could not help thinking that perhaps there was something in it. All life form has a circadian rhythm, the effect of the moon on tides *is* irrefutable; even a woman's menstrual cycle is pinned to a twenty-eight-day lunar cycle, not to the Gregorian calendar.

But there is more to lunar gardening than water. The moon's gravity tells roots to grow down not up. We have a 'harvest moon' close to the autumn equinox which traditionally would have enabled farmers to work and harvest crops for longer in the evenings.

Pliny wrote repeatedly about the effects and importance of the moon on the earth. He would only, for example, tackle some garden disease 'when the barley is ripening and at the moon's increase'.[3] Celts, he says, would only harvest mistletoe on the fifth day of a new moon.

More recently, scientists in the United States Department for Agriculture found that certain weed species had a lower germination rate when the soil was tilled during nights with low moonlight.[4]

According to lunar lore, root vegetables should be sown within a two-day window prior to a full moon which ends three days before the following new moon. Anything else can be sown in the window which starts two days before a new moon and ends three days before the following full moon. Then there are the signs of the zodiac to factor in and the elements within which they sit. Sowing and planting should take place in a 'water' sign. JR Gower, the author of *Gwydion's Planting Guide: The definitive moon-planting manual*, gives more detail.[5] His meticulous and complicated charts dictate that tomato sowing should take place between 14 January at 22.04 and 17 January at 08.42, or two days later at 21.22 until 22 January at 09.35.

Looking at these dates and times filled me with even more angst, however. Was I really going to go and shiver in the greenhouse, tomato seeds in one hand, watch in the other waiting for the minute hand to reach five minutes past ten whereupon I could tear open a seed packet?

The answer was no.

In the end I began sowing seeds with Ott on a bright, clear day. From the seed storage tin we pulled out the tomato and pea seeds we had bought.

'Can I eat them?' Ottilie asked, wrinkling her nose at me.

'Not quite yet,' I murmured. 'But maybe in a few months?'

She grinned.

I gave her the task of upending every loo roll innard into a roasting tin which she undertook with great concentration, counting haphaz-ardly. 'One, two, three, eleven, eight, five! Five gold rings,' she sang.

'Excellent,' I said. 'Now we need to fill them and these pots with mud. Got it?'

'Yup,' she said with confidence. 'I need a spoon,' she said, turning to the kitchen drawer and fumbling in among some kitchen knives until she found what she was looking for. Together we filled the loo rolls and then the small pots.

We took the tray outside (in hindsight, we should have been outside all along) to water the soil before sowing. Ottilie clapped her hands when she saw the dry compost wetten. 'It's so beautiful, Mummy! What a lovely mud you've made.'

Squatting down on our haunches we sowed. First the tomatoes. No bigger than a grain of sand, it seemed implausible that they contained all the information needed to become a new plant.

Ottie poked her finger in the packet and when a few seeds stuck, peered at them with interest before putting them in an indentation in the soil I had made with my finger.

The peas were a little easier to handle. They also looked like, well, peas. Ott rolled one between her thumb and forefinger and squeezed it hard. We put two in each loo roll and then scattered compost over them.

It was the packet of beans that made me think of Africa. I was chop-ping them up for supper. Small, rather wizened and, on tasting, not terribly juicy or redolent of beanpoles and sunshine. They were of course imported from Kenya.

Agriculture contributes to 30 per cent of the Kenyan economy and employs half of the country's population. At least it used to. Mirroring what happened in the United Kingdom during the Industrial Revolution in the last decade, more and more Kenyans turned away from mechanised and increasingly chemicalised agriculture to the service and manufacturing industries. The disconnect between food and people was marked. On the various trips I had made to Kenya in the past I was always amazed at the increase in fast-food restaurants in shopping malls and the truly revolting cakes and biscuits sold while, in the street markets, juicy mangoes abounded.

The largest city in east Africa, Nairobi is an intoxicating place. It is old-world *Out of Africa*, with giraffes, elephants and lions living on the city's perimeter. It is new world too with glass and chrome skyscrapers sitting at odds with the vast array of slums and shanty towns and refugee camps. It is bohemian and glamorous, grotty and decrepit. It is traffic-choked and polluted yet green and lush. If J and I were not living in rural England, we would be living there instead. At least that's what I used to tell myself in the depths of winter.

During the pandemic, the disruption in food supply chains in Kenya was not just inconvenient, it was potentially lethal; inadequate access to nutrition weakens immune systems and the SARS-CoV-2 virus just loves a weak immune system. In response to this and to mitigate hunger (another big problem in east Africa), the Kenyan Ministry of Agriculture developed a 'One Million Kitchen Gardens' initiative targeting families in rural and semi-urban places. Part of the launch included a number of model farms across the country where families could learn the principles of kitchen gardening and self-sufficiency.

It was not just food security driving the movement but food toxicity. A third of active ingredients used in Kenyan pesticides are considered to be so toxic that they remain banned in Europe. Through the initiative and thanks to a global conversation about where food comes from, more and more Kenyans were turning their hands green. But unlike in Britain and many western European countries, where gardening and growing is quite an ordinary pastime, in Kenya it is considered to be the preserve of the rural poor and some urban gardeners faced ridicule. Water is also a scarce commodity so the bar to entry remains high; two years after the initiative was launched uptake remained slow.

Space was also a barrier to entry; the most needy live in slums where space is, well, non-existent. The solutions were clever. Micro kitchen gardens were built using plastic buckets with holes in their sides out of which veg could sprout. Car tyres were put to good use too. Filled with earth they were an ideal small planter. Palettes upended could be easily converted into horizontal kitchen gardens. Hydroponic gardening, a system of growing which uses fish waste and less than a quarter of water and space, and which I had last encountered on a rooftop garden in Gaza, was also put to good use.

Globally, the effects of the pandemic and the shock waves of restrictions had a huge impact on people's relationship to food. You could argue that it coincided with a general move to better lifestyle choices and more awareness about food miles but pandemic disruption undoubtedly had an impact.

In China, the epicentre of Covid-19, where the population had endured two long years of systematic lockdowns, food insecurity had become commonplace and in the early days of the pandemic, vegetables became highly prized. So much so that in Wuhan (where the virus is thought to have originated) monks at a thirteen-hundred-year-old Buddhist temple used social media to invite locals to help harvest produce from their garden. They had planted on reclaimed land at the start of the outbreak a few months earlier and now had more produce than they knew what to do with. The uptake was so instant and overwhelming that, in just a few hours, the social media account pleaded for a bit of calm and the monks themselves were reported to be shaking with shock at the surge in demand for their produce.

By 2022 demand for fresh food had not waned and in urban Shanghai, a city of some twenty-five million, many residents started to plant kitchen balconies in an attempt to achieve food self-sufficiency, having spent two years scrabbling for simple necessities.

For others, food freedom also equated to mental health. One novice tomato gardener told the *South China Morning Post*[6] that harvesting her produce gave her a sense of security and another echoed this, adding that her five-metre-square balcony was a stress reliever.

India and Dubai saw a new wave of young first-time urban gardeners switch their weekend visits to the mall for more holistic and 'socially distant' visits to outdoor plant nurseries during the pandemic. One such nursery in a suburb of Chennai reported that the number of customers tripled from seven a day to twenty and fifty at weekends. While in the Gulf, prefabricated, ready-to-install kitchen gardens became all the rage. Not exactly an allotment but in the face of so much uncertainty, nurturing something – however small – could only be a positive thing.

In European countries with an established allotment or urban garden movement, the access to nature and allotments gave people security[7] and comfort in the form of food and certainty and, for some, they were private spaces where Covid and its restrictions didn't exist.[8] But different lockdown rules affected people's interaction with their plots in varying ways. In Poland where the rules were very strict, all green spaces were cordoned off. There was nowhere to go. Except if you had a *działka*: an allotment. Demand for land to cultivate was so high that if one came up for sale (*działkas* are privately owned country gardens, not rented spaces), it would be gone within an hour. Buyers were pushed into unusual auction-like scenarios with even the most decrepit plots inciting bidding wars. Some people were so desperate for green space that they went to extreme measures hunting down the owners of fallow meadows or fields and badgering them into a deal.

The three lockdowns in France were similar to those of the UK but with initial additional travel bans many were unable to even get to their plots despite being allowed to and those who did had strict social distancing rules to follow. In Germany it was business as usual on the five million or so *schrebergartens*. Indeed, echoing our own surge in interest, gardening was one of the most popular lock-down pastimes (along with DIY, hiking and going to drive-through cinemas). The number of visits to the *schrebergarten* increased as did time spent there which meant that while *schrebergartens* were traditionally seen more as private gardens for flower growing and leisure, time-consuming vegetable growing was in while flowers were out. The effect of the pandemic on allotments and self-sufficiency is undeniable but when I looked again at the anaemic packet of beans I sighed.

Those images of nature we saw in the first weeks of lockdown stopped us all in our tracks. Fish swimming in the now clear water-ways of Venice, blue skies next to temporarily shut factories, goats grazing on trees and flower beds in Llandudno, Wales, bottlenose dolphins frolicking in the Bosphorus, wild boar meandering through Haifa, Israel, pink flamingos flourishing in Albanian lagoons, sealife soaring in Thai marine parks, cougars wandering the streets of San-tiago. This, we thought from the confines of our homes with no end in sight, is how the world would exist without humans: very nicely thank you. And we promised to do better.

But long-term, what has changed? We still import fruit and veg-etables we could grow here and choose out-of-season vegetables simply because supermarkets can buy them cheaply from countries who themselves are on the brink of starvation.

It has become part of our DNA to expect to find asparagus and French beans in January and apples in June and it is going to take a long time to alter these habits that we've learned. It is going to take a long time to unlearn a dependence on supply chains and to under-stand our world again, to understand and respect the food we eat and how it grows. And if climate scientists and Sir David Attenborough are to be believed, time is what we don't have.

*

The peculiar warmth of the first week of the year had gone and the mornings became icy and then snowy ones. I took a naïve and childish delight in watching the large flakes tumble to the ground from nowhere. They brought a timeless magic, they always do; cold and clean, falling slowly and silently, landing in cold puddles until they settled and began covering the world, hiding it like a secret and making a new one.

I lifted Ottie up to the windowsill. While not exactly ecstatic she watched the new white world emerge with mild interest. I opened the window and stuck my hand out to catch the flakes and she copied, catching one in her chubby hand and putting it instinctively to her mouth. 'Cold,' she said, before it melted.

We stood at the window watching in silence for some minutes before venturing to other viewpoints. From Ottilie and Harry's room we saw the greenhouse become quickly opaque with snow and in the sky high, high above we watched three birds scurry and flit. With darting movements and wings flapping, they blurred each other. Indeed it looked like they were frolicking.

Downstairs at the glass back door, Ottie stood with Kit, hands pressed against the cold panes, watching the soft silence change the garden before their very eyes. Previously unseen contours and shapes were brought out in sharp relief. They stood there, for minutes, Kit occasionally interjecting with a 'Daaaaah?! Daaaaah.'

The front of the house gave us a view of a white river instead of a road, of our neighbour's beautiful hamstone house which was becoming increasingly Dickensian by the minute. 'Look, Mummy,' Ottie said pointing at the tray of loo roll inners on the windowsill.

'Trees!'

I beamed at her. 'Not trees, Ott. Peas.' For there, snaking into life for the first time, were no less than fifteen first shoots, heads weakly bowed into their necks and wrinkled like a newborn baby but unmistakably there and well and truly on their way to seedling-hood. I entangled myself in that moment. When we eat these peas in the summer, I thought, I would remember this morning with Ottie, watching the world whiten before us, feeling it turn and letting that bubble of excitement rise from the backs of our throats. I did not think about the day when she too would need potting on like these peas would to the plot.

I would remember the uncertain steps she took outside afterwards. Where once there was patchy gravel now lay a thin carpet of white. She stepped gingerly over it, as if balancing and expecting to fall. I would remember that I gathered a fistful of snow into a ball and threw it at her gently and that it half shattered on her coat but she picked up the remains with shy curiosity, pronouncing it to be cold. I would remember, too, the fleeting nature of that snow magic as a few hours later, temperatures rising to a positively balmy 3 degrees, it began to melt with oversized droplets dripping and splodging from leaves and gutters and gates.

I reluctantly slipped – quite literally; the snow had rendered the roads and paths treacherously icy – down to the plot. The sky bled savagely as it does only on wintry afternoons and I tried not to feel too depressed about the broad beans, which I swore I could see shivering as I passed them. Like an ill-equipped army, their future looked precarious. But I had faith. They were a hardy bunch; come spring, all would be well. It had to be.

I never thought vegetables could make me angry but when I walked away from my plot minutes later I felt enraged, blisteringly angry.

What was the point, I thought.

My plan had been to make a hearty wintry soup with cabbage, bacon and potatoes. The green leaf heads I had nurtured through those tough times of August weren't large but, as the cabbages seemed to grow as leaves hugging themselves, I was confident they had survived the cold. When I'd arrived I peered down at the cabbages, aghast. Their leaves had that telltale lacy look of marauding slugs and snails. Nature was waging war and leaving bullet-riddled holes in its wake.

I knelt in the sodden couch grass verge to pick one only to find it even smaller than originally estimated. A small kiwi-sized ball remained and not a very edible-looking one at that. Petrol station vegetables were more appetising at that moment.

It was as if these were children – be they of the vegetable variety – which I had reared through infancy and childhood only to have taken my foot off the pedal when they reached their teens. In those wild years of their adolescence on the allotment I had left them to their own devices and not noticed those slugs or snails, frosts, snow or blight – the plant equivalent, I suppose, of social media, alcohol, drugs, eating disorders and other ne'er-do-wells. I'd left my plants to veer off the rails on a steady road to nowhere and here were the results: crap crops.

Nico and Crystal had admitted to losing all their crops to frost too and this had momentarily cheered me. 'I don't take it personally any more,' Nico had said.

The trouble was, I *did*. I thought about the remaining half of the plot still to dig over and prepare for the summer. What was the point? I had three beds of disappointment. Why double the agony?

In fact, what was the point of the allotment at all? I had taken it on to step off the supermarket conveyor belt, to do something different and raise my children with an appreciation of food and flavour, seasons and sustenance. But right there, in that moment, letting the muddy ground soak through to my knees like tarnish and looking down at the wasted time, energy, hope and crops, I found it hard to stay positive.

I looked at the whole plot through squinted eyes. I was done with the allotment and the planning and digging for my own victory. I was done with reconnecting to nature, to seasons. I was done with the allotment and the allotment was done with me.

February

Orphan peas – A history of potatoes – Signs of life
and a return to our old ways – A cure for insomnia –
A history of the village plots – New allotments –
Heritage seeds – From plot to plate in under a minute –
A plot as the present

I started focusing on the spring.

There had been momentary glimmers of the season to come: clear, crisp days where the light was not quite so anaemic nor the temperatures quite so brutal. But on a cold, flat, grey day in early February, spring felt as near as the dark side of the moon. That's the trouble with February. After the hedonism of December, January is so gloomy and long that when February comes along you have convinced yourself that spring is nigh and that the wait for the starting gun of the growing season is over. The moment the sun shines you're out there in the garden or the greenhouse, lock stock and barrel, trying to bring an end to the horror that is the dark, cold, grey misery of winter.

But then winter has the last laugh, returning again with the sting in its tail. 'Just kidding,' it says as another frost covers the ground or snow flurries gather in the slate skies. 'I'm not going anywhere anytime soon.'

The tomatoes Ottie and I had sowed a few weeks ago had failed to propagate and my mother-in-law had said it would have been due to the cold. 'Nothing would grow in these temperatures,' she'd said. And this only cemented my understanding that try as I might – and I did – I was really not cut out for this allotment way of life. When

315

it came to veg growing, some people had it, some did not. I fell into the latter category and I made my way out to the greenhouse to dispense of the redundant seed compost and to tidy up the whole sorry allotment experiment. I had nothing else 'on the grow'. Time to call it quits and move on to something more manageable like, I don't know, skydiving or learning Hungarian. I would have an awful lot of seeds to give away but no matter, I thought. I knew enough people to . . .

Oh. The peas.

There they were, green tendrils entangled and unruly, searching for light, yearning for support.

I'd forgotten about those peas.

Unlike the tomatoes they were going full throttle and already looked large enough to plant out. Yet with temperatures still close to zero, they'd have no chance of survival on their own. I rummaged around for small stakes, propping up each plant and disentangling tendril knots where possible and then, noticing that the soil was rather dry, reached for Ottie's miniature blue watering can.

There's an irritating honesty to planting, to growing; you can't cheat the season, nor can you cheat the seeds. Sow too early and it is too cold for germination. Sow too late and there is no chance for a plant to reach full maturity. Somewhere in between is what I had in those peas. A bunch of seedlings with nowhere to go.

I sighed. It would be irresponsible to orphan them now.

And then there was spinach I'd overwintered sprouting true leaves in a tray hidden behind the jungle of peas. Unassuming little seedlings waiting patiently for the next phase having diligently done what was asked of them.

If the peas and spinach were up for another whirl on the plot then I supposed I would have to hold up my end.

I wasn't done with the allotment yet.

I returned to my plot plan. Again.

It had been coming along nicely, though I say so myself. Not too bad at all. I'd abandoned a no-dig approach simply because I'd have needed an awful lot of compost and organic matter. Besides, there was something about an allotment which demanded a little extra work, a little bit of elbow grease; a few callouses here and there were a rite of passage. This said, there was half a plot to prepare and the thought of that labour was hardly enticing.

Losing all my produce to frost and slugs had inadvertently done me a favour for, apart from a few dozen rows of leeks and garlic, I now had a cleared blank canvas. Taking inspiration from Frank's potager, I was going to dedicate an entire bed to artichokes – no messing around this time – another to brassicas, but I was going to be armed and dangerous with tunnels and nets and nematodes and, if they were still alive by next winter, fleece. I'd have my carrots in half of one bed – sown every few weeks to ensure a ready supply – and some radishes or beets in the other half. My courgettes would be just next door and, in another bed, I'd have more leeks, more garlic and the three sisters of companion planting: maize, beans and squash. Another bed was going to be given over entirely to broad beans, more runner beans and those precocious peas in the greenhouse. The last bed would be home to potatoes. Lots and lots of potatoes.

*

Often maligned in the last decade or so owing to the popularity of low- or no-carbohydrate diets or low-glycemic index diets, the potato is, without doubt, the most economical fresh vegetable to buy. Last time I checked a fist-sized one was around 11p. But there are something like five thousand varieties of potato – one hundred and twenty or so available in this country: purple ones, long ones, small ones, giant ones, yellow ones . . . quite a departure from the bog-standard bakers, boilers, mashers, chippers or roasters lumped together in huge plastic crates at the end of the vegetable aisles.

Some sources start the domestic cultivation of potatoes in parts of Peru and Bolivia as far back as ten thousand years while others reckon on a more modest four and a half thousand years. Either way, the simple spud has a long lineage.

The conquistadors of Spain and Portugal brought them to Europe from the New World in the sixteenth century but it was Sir Francis Drake and Sir Walter Raleigh who famously presented the potato to Elizabeth I (although this is hotly debated in historical circles).

As with its distant relative, the tomato, the spud was regarded with a good deal of suspicion when it was first introduced to the Old World. A member of the nightshade family, it was considered to be the creation of witches or devils and used as fodder for livestock. Their acceptance as a food was slow, in part due to the fear of poisoning but mostly because gardeners did not know how to grow them and cooks did not know how to cook them.

It was Raleigh who is thought to have introduced the spud to Dorset when he lived at a castle just a few miles from our village, the light soils being ideal ground for growing all those tubers. Not that his gardener knew that at first. Believing that the edible part of the potato was the 'apple' seed which followed on from the flowers he sent these to the kitchen[1] instead. If this is true, it is remarkable that the spud survived as potato berries are rather bitter and can be toxic.

But survive they did, and so well in the Dorset ground that a number of caves for storing Raleigh's potatoes were built in the sunken lanes spidering out of the village.[2] A short walk from our cottage, the caves – now gated, owing to the presence of bats – were a tremendous addition to a muddy walk with the children and, as they were now filled with false widow spiders and some witchy paint markings made years ago, a potentially terrifying one at that.

Culinary errors notwithstanding it did not take long for the spud to become the crop of choice nationwide. It was easy to grow, high-yielding and nutritious. Containing nearly every important vitamin and nutrient, except vitamins A and D, they do more than any other single crop. An acre of land cultivated with potatoes and one milk-producing cow was enough to feed a family of six. Not for nothing were those early allotments of the eighteenth century called potato grounds.

I couldn't help feeling that growing spuds was a sort of rite of passage for an allotment holder; the vegetable equivalent of wearing a cloth cap. 'Experiment with yer cavolo nero and yer aubergines, if you like,' I could hear my allotment saying (my allotment had developed a soft northern accent for some reason), 'but good honest tatties will see you through.'

If the soil around here was good enough for Sir Walter Raleigh, it would be good enough for me. There was just one major elephant

319

in the room. I didn't know how to grow potatoes. And you need to know the basics before you begin.

There's the chitting, the eye separation and the 'curing', the addition of lime, the trench digging, the earthing up. The successional planting of first and second earlies (new potatoes) followed by the main crop not forgetting the problems of blight and potato flies.

Get it right and a single seed spud can produce ten or so potato offspring. Which could add up to a lot of potatoes depending on how many you plant. No wonder Raleigh needed a whole cave to store them.

I had looked online for some recommendations but quickly found myself in a vortex of choice, flitting between different seed suppliers and varieties and, finding myself thus brain-addled, made for the car.

The potato room at the garden centre was dark and gloomy but it smelled earthy. Piles of potatoes of every different size, shape and colour sat in wicker baskets like piles of hoarded treasure in the hold of a creaking ship. There were Roosters, Sarpo Miras and Pentland Javelins. There were Maris Pipers and Maris Bards, Caras and Arran Pilots. I wavered between the baskets occasionally holding a potato in each hand working out the significance of their names and wondering how many I would need.

In the end I left with a modest bag of Maris Bards (first earlies), Charlottes (second earlies) because they sounded friendly and Pink Fir Apples because they didn't look – or sound – like potatoes at all.

I walked back to the car with three paper bags of seed potatoes. As a new-to-me crop, the thick and heavy bags were the clothes-shopping equivalent of a new wardrobe and I felt something of a flutter of exhilaration.

There is a sort of grubbiness to February, a drab muddiness. Entrenched in the middle of winter but with everyone longing for the onset of spring, it is a short, slightly pointless hanger-on month; a boring bridge between two seasons, somewhat invisible but impossible to ignore, the straggler at the party you're stuck talking to way beyond leaving time. With at least three months of inclement weather behind it and fields still empty of crops, it's also the muddiest month. The stuff gets everywhere especially when heartily assisted by the dog. And it is not the good, protozoa-bacteria-nematody mud, it is the cloddy, clayey, soddy mud which clings and sticks and in so doing gives everything a rather drab, desaturated wash. Even the evergreen trees looked muddy.

But, day by day, I searched for the signs of spring. They were there, albeit diluted by mud. The snowdrops dangling their pretty green and white bells in clumps in the woods, the tête-à-tête and gaudy yellow daffs making a break for it along verges and in some of the more sheltered parts of the garden. Budding white blossom shivering on a tree here or there. And then, on one or two gloriously bright days, there was warmth.

It was time to start digging; the perfect half-term activity. After lunch one day, while Ott and Kit slept off the exertions of 'playing' all morning, Harry and I packed my new trailer with spades, a Thermos of tea, two mugs and a handful of biscuits and set off for the plot. Almost a year had passed since we first started digging down there but we slipped back easily to the old ways and picked up our spades, stopping occasionally to examine worms which had wrapped themselves around dandelion roots and spiders scuttling over the uneven terrain. At length, Harry laid down his spade and settled on the upturned bucket, just as he used to, nibbling with consideration at a digestive biscuit and concerning himself with another family of worms at his feet.

When he asked, I told him what we were going to plant and he grinned excitedly when I mentioned potatoes. We examined the pitifully small leeks and garlic leaves and tried to remember which was which and then turned to the remaining four cabbages.

They were still the size of a fist but Harry was unperturbed. 'We should eat them soon,' he said. 'For tea.'

I let the idea lodge. Then as it was warm we took off our coats and continued digging again. Harry to Australia – or so he said – and me from one side of the plot to the other. Having laid tarpaulins over the grass and weeds and sending them into remission, it was surprisingly easy work. I uprooted great clods of thuggish couch grass, turned over the earth – mindful of the worms. I spread manure as I dug, too, breaking the clumps with my bare hands, waiting and hoping for that hit of nature's Prozac. When it came in a surge of energy and vigour I dug again. Un-hemmed in by the four walls of winter, or by sick children or thinking about the next meal, or cleaning up the burned remains of the last one, thinking only of the ground beneath me and what would soon grow with Harry next to me, blond mop of hair falling, as always, into his green-grey eyes, it was happiness entirely that day.

I felt alive, as if the creases and crossness of winter were being ironed out with every spade splice. The light was redolent of the honey gold of summer and generous too, making it feel more like spring, but by four o'clock, when we were at the village play park, the sun was making a hasty retreat in the west. The shadows lengthened and darkened quickly, the temperature plummeted and we shivered like the premature blossom when a 'frosty wind made moan'. Our hands were blue, our ears and eyes stung with cold and our noses were red. Spring was still a long way off; we were still entrenched in the depths of a bleak-ish midwinter.

But this did not depress me as much as I thought it would. Having never been a particularly good sleeper – and despite being habitually deprived of sleep over the last four years – I had refined the ingredients to a good night's sleep. You can wax lyrical about routine, lavender oils and sleep-inducing tinctures but what really makes for decent slumber is good old-fashioned fresh air and physical exertion. And lots of it. Without much of either since the autumn, I found myself often on the edge of an insomniac's insanity during February.

The madness was twofold. Firstly, the sheer exhaustion of not having slept, which anyone used to not sleeping can confirm is enough to send a person into a state of hallucinogenic delusion.

The second madness occurred habitually at around one or two o'clock in the morning. Having lain in darkness trying to sleep for a good couple of hours, by this point in time one's mind is knots and despair. '*When will sleep come? What if it doesn't? I wonder if I should grow spinach now or will it get too leggy? Can you die from not sleeping? Will I be the first to die from lack of sleep? And did I turn off the heater in my garden office? Oh and there was that email I needed to reply to about school uniform. Where was Harry's tie, now you mention it? Must remember to check on the tomatoes propagating. I wonder if it was too early – I mean, they're meant to like warmth aren't they? And milk. Don't forget to buy milk. Maybe I should make a timetable for when to sow seeds. And bread. We're out of bread. Must sleep, must sleep, must sleep. I'm sure I will die if I don't sleep. Can one really die from lack of sleep?'*

And so on. For many years I had taken to removing my mind from the everyday by playing the alphabet game – the sort you might play on a car journey. Choose a theme and alphabetise it. Take countries, for example: Argentina, Bangladesh, Cambodia. Or towns and cities: Aberdeen, Bristol, Cardiff and so on. I was rather well versed in the standard subjects but, the night after I had dug and manured with Harry, I began a new subject to while away the small hours: things we would plant on the allotment. Artichoke, Beans, Carrots . . . whether it was the manure, the air, the exercise or all three, I didn't make it beyond D for Dwarf beans.

I was still curious about the village allotments and whether I was growing vegetables amid the fine company of green-fingered ghosts.

I was not. The site was created in 1978, the barrister told me over a vat of hot tea in her bright and warm kitchen. Indentures dated 1623 and 1637 allocated two parcels of land to help the poor of the village. They weren't allotments per se but the land rent was for the Poor Trust whose responsibility it was to look after the poor.* These

---

* The Poor Law, introduced in 1601, gave parishes across the country sole responsibility for their poor.

became allotments at some point – but no one was sure exactly when. In 1978 the village wanted to build a playing field and under a deed of exchange the two parcels of land were swapped to the current area spanning the allotment site and half the playing field. And although it was the parish council now running the allotments, the land was still owned by the Poor Trust and the income received from rent still helped the poor of the village.

The allotments might not have been as old as I had imagined but I liked the fact that they were still for the benefit of the rural poor some four hundred years later.

I asked the barrister about her own motivations to take an allotment. She had a sizeable garden and with a full-time job and a large family to run surely there was little spare time for cabbages and carrot fly?

'I had an image that my small children would be romping on the playing fields while I tended the plot and I had this ridiculous notion that they'd understand where food came from and that they'd eat it too.'

It all sounded very familiar. Traditionally such a male domain, I wondered if there were mothers like us up and down the country, taking up the allotment challenge and digging with one hand, feeding with the other.

'Every spring I'd feel enthusiastic and begin digging and sowing as much as I could but I may as well have buried fifty pounds instead. The children weren't interested and I was working part-time so it was becoming more of a chore than respite. And you have to be there every day keeping weeds and pests away, especially when the seeds are fresh in the ground. And then come the summer, everything would need harvesting at the same time and we'd be away camping for a week.'

But harbouring hopes that one day her three children *would* be interested and want to be involved, the barrister refused to give it up. 'It was nice to have it in lockdown. We couldn't exactly live off it but we certainly supplemented what we were able to buy and I started to grow broad beans and sprouts quite successfully too.'

With the demands of a now full-time job, time spent on the plot was still a juggle. 'I tend to leave it for days and the days become weeks and then it's too much to do in one go. That said, I am getting more out of it and Sergei gave me a glimmer of how it could be.' But while vegetables could be a burden, needing constant care and attention, it was flowers she really took to on her plot. 'Dahlias and gladioli,' she said. 'Instant gratification when they grow. And Sergei showed me how to look after sunflowers properly too. Who'd have thought we'd have sunflowers in Dorset!'

'Everyone has tried their hands on the allotments,' and she listed half a dozen families in the village, 'but it's really hard work and people tend to give them up after a year or two. Older generations always say that they were able to have a plot and a full-time job at the same time but we use our time differently these days.'

I asked if she would give it up. 'I mean if someone really, really wanted to grow vegetables . . . I would think . . .' She paused. 'Actually, no. I wouldn't. I still aspire to self-sufficiency and I still have this thing about the allotment being a peaceful place that isn't full of the domestic chattels of home. There might always be jobs to do on a plot but you don't mind doing them down there.'

She went on. 'I've had my plot for eight years and am still only consciously incompetent. I'm aiming for conscious competence.'

The vet on the other hand was born with competence. Or rather, he learned 'by osmosis' from his father. One damp February afternoon, he explained that because his father had been a farmer working crushingly long hours seven days a week, he didn't see him that much, but growing vegetables had meant that helping him was a way of spending time together.

What he learned stayed with him. Even when living in Ithaca, upstate New York, and working insanely long hours, the vet still found time to buy a few seeds to grow in a small patch of land next to a converted shed he was living in.

Moving to the village some twenty-six years ago with his wife and a tiny baby, he took up the allotment challenge but when work took over and he began losing the battle with couch grass and bindweed, he gave it up. Ten years later, able to step back from his practices and devote more time to the garden, he snapped up a half plot when one became available. 'It's more manageable and does for the two of us through the summer.'

With a sizeable garden attached to the house I asked him why bother with an allotment? He described the functionality of an allotment and the satisfaction of cultivating and not being bothered if it looks messy or unruly as you might do with your own back garden. 'An allotment is for pleasure. For fun,' said the vet.

He was aiming to get to the point where he could give his spade a rest and let the worms do the work. 'But part of me likes digging, it's rhythmic. And I'd rather do that than go to the gym and there's the added benefit of having something edible at the end.'

But there was something deeper than the first-degree benefits and which appeared to be deep-rooted in everyone I spoke to, myself included. 'I'm a bit of a loner and like just getting on with things,' the vet said. 'It's quiet down there, I can be alone and I can distance myself while doing something constructive. It's a basic instinct to dig, plant something and eat it – part of human nature. I guess I'm tapping into that.' We all valued the peace and quiet of our rural allotment site.

The slate-grey skies hung threateningly but I took comfort in the incrementally elongated hours of daylight as night fell later every day and with less of a thud. It was gently darkening when I made my way through the village one Friday afternoon to meet Terry.

As Terry had lived in the village for his entire life and was a former allotmenter himself, I wanted to find out how the old allotment sites looked and operated.

Terry took me right back to the beginning.

His father, a basket weaver, grew vegetables in their garden when he was a boy and, as such, it was something Terry had been brought up with. 'We had a pig, chickens and ducks which we'd walk down to the stream on a Sunday and my father grew what we ate,' he told me. 'There was no question of not helping. I was put to work digging,' he went on. His father used to put a marker out in the ground, telling him he could go and play once Terry had dug up to the marker. 'It was always dark by the time I'd finished.'

When he married, he and his wife moved into a new house on the edge of the village and he rented an allotment moving to the new – current – site when they were created at the end of the 70s.

'They were lovely back then,' he said. 'We took it in turns to keep it looking neat and tidy, mowing the pathways, keeping the brambles at bay.' He was describing the essence of an allotment community. And when they were under threat from marauding badgers hunting for insects and grubs and which were putting waste to all the produce, the community united and erected an electric fence. There was no combatting the weather, however. 'It's often two or three degrees colder there than in the rest of the village. And losing crops to frost,' he pursed his lips, 'it's soul-destroying.'

I nodded and described the devastation on my own plot. He shook his head in sympathy. 'Soul-destroying.'

'Could you,' I asked, '*did* you live on what you grew?'

'Of course.' He looked at me as if I'd just asked if he knew the difference between a tomato and a banana. 'Having an allotment was just something you did in the country,' he said. 'It was a thing. Everyone had an allotment and everyone knew how to do it because you did back then.'

Terry would go to the plot daily, tend his vegetables and keep on top of the weeds but sometimes he went there to do nothing. 'I would just sit on a bench with a friend chatting until it got dark,' he said.

'Why did you give it up?' I asked.

'Well, it's the work, isn't it? All that digging. I was getting too old for it.'

This was a familiar story. The pub landlord told me a day or two later that he'd taken a plot simply for runner beans. He grew potatoes and shallot onions alongside them but beans were his raison d'être. 'I just love them. Can't get enough of them.' But ultimately the physical work was too much for him too.

Jenny, another village stalwart and former allotment holder I had questioned about the plots prior to meeting Terry, told me that she and her husband gave it up for a number of reasons and not just because of the amount of work – although that was a driving factor when their children left home. 'Seeds were becoming expensive and vegetables were cheap especially in discount supermarkets.'

Terry shrugged when I asked him about the price of seeds. 'I had an old tin of Quality Street full of seeds. Never had to buy any.' But nonetheless, allotment life in the village was winding up in the mid-90s and, one by one, the plots became weed-filled and semi-wild.

I asked him why he thought the allotments had lain unused for so long when the village thrived. 'Times have changed, people have changed. If you live in a house worth a lot of money with a big garden and you can go to the shops all the time, why would you get an allotment?

'I saw them recently,' he went on. 'The allotments. We walked past them. What a bloody mess! Tarpaulin sheets all over the place!'

I recognised the description. 'That's my plot!' I said excitedly and then added with less exuberance, 'They were for the weeds but . . . I don't really know what I'm doing.' I described having contemplated the no-dig method and Terry regarded me with some suspicion.

'Well,' he said with a degree of finality, 'I used to dig and dig and dig. It was the hardest work sometimes but as my father used to say, "Never look behind you, only ahead of you otherwise you'll get demoralised." People garden differently now.'

The old guard had rural roots which ran deep. They were lucky. The vet and Dalius, and even the fictitious Tom Good from *The Good Life* who would have remembered digging for victory as a child, had come full circle in a growing journey beginning and ending with their hands in the earth. As a struggling novice relying on advice from friends or family, books or learning the hard way, I envied this nascent expertise. I don't think my own family had been rural for three generations.

When I was interviewing and photographing civilians trying to survive conflict by gardening for my first book, *War Gardens*, I had imagined that there was something prelapsarian in their approach. War is a man-made thing; gardening was a collective nostalgia and a way of returning to 'Eden' before the fall – 'the fall' of today being ongoing conflicts of our own making. Perhaps that is what we are all doing when we plunge our hands into the soil, plant seeds and look after tender seedlings; perhaps we are all looking to hold on to that clarity, innocence and simplicity of youth before our minds became muddled and our time fragmented.

The twenty-first-century allotment fever certainly echoed this circularity and desire return to another, more simple age. The pandemic removed our civil liberties and reminded us of the importance of the world outside which we had taken for granted. War on the edges of Europe, climate change disruption of supply chains and the cost of living soaring to levels not seen in this country since the 1980s made us see that food security was not a given any more; food was anything but secure and the headline-grabbing tomato crisis of early 2023 was proof of that.

Little wonder then that in 2022, 87 per cent of local authorities reported an increase in demand for allotments.[3] Waiting lists for council-run plots still stood at a hundred and fifty thousand at the time of writing but many of the lists remained closed. With a nationwide need for houses there was simply no real incentive for cash-strapped councils to open new sites. They were certainly not going to take any profit from allotments especially as the 1950 Allotment Act stipulated that councils were not allowed to charge 'an unreasonable rent'.

With land still so highly valued and a housing crisis, the National Allotment Society worked tirelessly not just to protect allotment sites from demolition but also to encourage local councils and planning offices to incorporate sites into new housing developments. They dreamed up the '21st Century Allotments in New Developments' campaign to help developers and planners recognise the benefits of community allotments while fulfilling the planning obligations to provide green space. The campaign was supplemented with training offered to developers and local authorities willing to open new allotment sites.

The shortage of plots inspired others to think laterally.

When Will Gay, a software salesman living in London, tried to get an allotment from Lambeth Council shortly after lockdown he realised that, nationwide, the waiting lists problem was epidemic. He had seen the positive effects veg gardening had had on a friend Ed Morrison, who'd worked a no-dig allotment with his grandmother during lockdown, Will decided to take matters into his own hands.

There was a simple solution. He would start his own site. Renting a meadow from his farmer father near Bath and calling on his twin brother Josh, who was something of an expert in low-tillage, no-dig farming methods, Will, Ed, and another entrepreneur friend Kristian, founded Roots Allotments, the first no-dig allotment site of its size in the world.

Aware of the traditional and a little fusty image of allotments they wanted to remove as many bars to entry as possible. They built ready-to-plant patches (using the do-dig method), which could be planted instantly. No clearing of bindweed or brambles, just decent soil waiting to host plants. Would-be veg growers just had to pick a patch – there are four sizes from 12 square metres, up to 108 square metres – and cough up between £10 to £50 per month. The subscription includes ready-made beds, seed packets, your own trowel and access to shared tools.

The sites are surrounded by wildflower meadows and fruit trees. They also train vegetables to grow up fences – both the general public and plot holders can help themselves. There are bike locks, parking spaces, tools and river views. None of the shanty-town chic of old urban sites where a rusty nail or shard of glass may be your undoing.

Having focused their marketing attention on parents, many of the Roots customers are young families but the majority of their plot holders are novices and, unusually, two thirds are women. Looking at the images of the sites online I can see the attraction. They are open, accessible and look safe; no dark corners or sheds for potential assailants to hide in. I sneakily suspected that the appeal for women is also linked to the total absence of the older, more entrenched version of a plot holder who perhaps might not welcome the presence of women.

The entrepreneurs are clearly on to a good thing; they sold out in Bath within four months and had to open their own waiting lists. But there is something else about Roots, which perhaps unpicks the new need and simmering craze for allotments.

'During the two years of Covid, people had become very disconnected. This is a way for people to come back together,' Ed told BBC *Points West* in late 2022. 'It's lovely to hear laughter and people having a nice time.'

Will expanded on their ethos. 'Many traditional sites run on negativity. You only have to look on Facebook allotment pages to see the bigoted, nasty comments people leave each other. We wanted to create a positive community and to allow members to get to know each other. Ninety per cent of our members have said that having an allotment has had a positive effect on their mental health and so many have said they made a friend. We have three rules on our sites: No Dig, No Chemicals and Good Vibes Only.'

All the former allotment holders in my village had described the site as a halcyon place where people helped each other, and they had united against badgers and deer. They looked out for each other and looked after the site and there was friendship, banter and community. And some terribly good vegetables to boot.

In this age of hyper-connectivity and resulting hyper-loneliness, where the notion of doing anything offline has even been shortened to a text-friendly acronym, IRL (In Real Life), physical community and contact are much-needed commodities and the twenty-first-century post-pandemic allotment movement filled that need for life and nature on every level. As the Romantic poet John Donne wrote, 'No man is an island'. Little wonder then that public and private waiting lists continued to grow and little wonder that more and more people were thinking laterally.

Conor Gallagher, a Londoner originally from Belfast, came across his local allotment site in Brixton a couple of years before the pandemic. He had been growing windowsill herbs and on walking past the site tried to apply for his own plot. He was interested in growing organic food with zero carbon footprint. The problem was that there was little to no information about the application process and, after much digging, (no pun intended), he was told that the waiting list for a plot was closed.

As a former architect Gallagher well understood the constraints of urban living and urban developments. One in eight people in the country have no access to a garden. In London, this is more like one in five. 'A one-bedroomed apartment is supposed to have at least five square metres of outside space,' he said. 'But that can be negotiated or incorporated into a larger communal garden which doesn't necessarily lend itself to growing vegetables. It's an easy cost cut for developers.'

Undeterred by the negative response from his local council, he took to tech and began developing an app where all the waiting lists could be seen in one place between the local authorities. 'But this didn't solve the problem of lack of supply,' he told me over the phone. Nevertheless, he created a web holding page while he worked out where to go with his idea. During those long, isolated days of lockdown he saw a surge in activity on his website. People were desperate for a place to grow and he used furlough to focus on his ideas. When passing an overgrown, unloved garden it occurred to him that there was 'an untapped reservoir of outdoor space in London going unused'.

His online platform, AllotMe, works in a similar way to Hugh Fearnley-Whittingstall's Land Share, linking people who want to grow their own food with people who have small plots of unused land or garden. 'It's an Airbnb for gardeners,' he explained. Moving to a house with its own garden and echoing the home-rental app's founders, Conor was the first 'host', listing his own garden and renting half of it in part to a neighbour and fellow architect, Corrie Rounding. When the platform was formally launched in May 2021 uptake was immediate and within a week there were a thousand people on the waiting list.

With average rents priced between £15 and £30 per month it's more expensive than a typical allotment but by no means a bar to entry. A typical host, anecdotally, is someone too busy with their work or family life to look after a garden or someone much older and unable to tend their patch of greenery. 'Often these hosts would have given their plots away for free, they just want to see their gardens in use,' Conor explained.

When compared to traditional allotment sites, however, the contemporary take has its pitfalls. The numerous Parliamentary Acts scattered through history were passed to protect the allotment holder.

As Phil Gomersall, president of the National Allotment Society said, 'private sites and land-sharing schemes are nothing more than short- term letting agreements. There's no protection. With our suing mentality and in this age of health and safety, if someone hurts themselves, who is to blame? Community gardens and sharing land is a wonderful short-term fix for people wanting to garden but if the people leading it decide to leave, they [the gardens] usually fall apart. No one has any rights.'

Rights aside, demand for unused urban gardens still outstrips supply for users of AllotMe, mirroring that for traditional allotment plots, and with the population of London alone increasing some-where between seventy thousand and a hundred thousand a year,[4] this is unlikely to change in the near future. However, the app is not just confined to the UK and hosts a cluster of plots in the Netherlands and Spain as well as unused gardens as far afield as Argentina and North America. But Gallagher has high hopes and was, at the time of writing, developing an artificial intelligence tool for growing. Forty billion data points, he explained, would give a would-be aubergine grower the exact answer for 'How far apart do I space my plants?'

When he told me this I felt rather queasy. A self-proclaimed Luddite and sceptic when it comes to all things tech, I was not sure how I felt about artificial intelligence alone, let alone its intrusion on the world of natural intelligence. In any case, you only have to look at garden advice from books across the ages to find the answer. I'd rather look things up in Pliny than on an app. But then if tech can inspire people to grow, then perhaps it is a good thing? Perhaps.

The box stood on the table, shiny, neat and blue. It was so full of seed packets the lid did not close and thus open-mouthed it seemed rather impatient, as if saying, 'Well come on then. What are you waiting for?'

It was a few minutes of rifling before I found what I was looking for. The photograph on the packet was of glossy white fruits hanging with abundance from the bush.

'What's that?' Harry asked when I showed him.

'Aubergines,' I said.

'Aubergines are purple though.' He inspected the packet. 'Those are white.'

Many of the seeds I had been given at Christmas were heirloom or heritage varieties, which is just a convoluted way of saying that, with links to ancestral varieties, they were special and a far cry from the bog-standard, uncomplicated, high-yielding hybrid seeds I had been buying hitherto.

Having been on the brink of quitting, jumping in at the deep end with a heritage aubergine when I had zero experience of growing aubergines at all felt a bit like beginning an oil painting having only ever worked with HB pencils or chunky crayons, but this was *my* way of gardening: trial, error, trial, error, trial, error ad nauseum, each time learning a little, each time adding a layer of – if not knowledge, then experience.

In the greenhouse we grabbed handfuls of fine compost that we scattered into two waiting propagation trays and Harry counted out five seeds, pressing each one into the soil before watering.

'Who knows,' I said as we took them inside to a windowsill next to a radiator. 'Maybe we will be picking aubergines on your fifth birthday!'

The pea seedlings needed a bit of righting and, in the spirit of successional growing, we set about sowing another twenty or so. In for a penny, in for a pound, I thought as we dropped a seed or two into each loo roll inner.

'Oooh, I know,' Harry said in a stage whisper as if he were conspiring. 'Let's grow some tomatoes. Big whoppers this high.' He held his arm out above his head. 'Like last summer.'

'You remember them?' I was surprised.

He nodded and held out his hand to indicate the plant's height. I might not be the best grower but at least some of what we were doing was going in.

The tomato seed packets, having already been opened, were easy to find and Harry held out his hands. 'These three in those pots,' I said, indicating the pots already full of seed compost, 'and those three in the other.'

'There's no space.'

I turned to show him but stopped abruptly for there right in front of us were three tiny seed shoots. Just millimetres high but unmistakably there and I was, truth be told, a little dumbfounded.

'Where, Mummy? Where shall I put them?' Harry was impatient. We filled a few more pots, laid the seeds in the compost, watered and then, it being a sunny sort of afternoon, Harry occupied himself in the sandpit, moving toy soldiers through the fungus which had apparently taken a liking to the sodden and quite revolting pit.

I had one more thing to do, however.

When we spoke, Terry had warned against planting the potatoes out until mid-March at the earliest and I had been disappointed. I wanted to get a head start on the year, cross it off the list and reap the starchy rewards a few months later. That initial excitement I had felt at bringing home my first bags of seed spuds – well, I was all dressed up with nowhere to go when he warned me off.

Except I wasn't. I could give the tatties a bit of a head start in life with chitting. Chitting is, in layman's terms, leaving a potato to sprout. It's what I – and probably most people – do by accident. Every few weeks or so a chitted potato or five appear at the bottom of the vegetable basket, dejected and a little shrivelled, covered in tiny – or in some cases, not so tiny – claw-like shoots.

Gardeners – or more specifically, potato growers – up and down the country will debate at length over the need to chit six weeks before planting. Some swear chitting gives an early crop, others say it's not necessary. I was taking no chances and placed the potatoes in old egg boxes before setting them on the windowsill next to the aubergine and wondered if we'd be eating a potato and aubergine gratin at the end of the summer. I hoped so.

Harry was content playing with his soldiers and, blocking out the boy-sounds he was making of an imagined (and really quite brutal) battle, I returned to the seed box and began rifling again, working out what to plant next. I made a mental note of yellow cucumbers and black radishes and wondered if I still had any marigold seeds for some companion planting, looking over to Harry now and then.

He had grown so much in a year and in ways I had not expected. I was oddly moved whenever I looked at his schoolbooks, the wonky-in-the-wrong-place writing, pictures drawn and paints splattered, all of which had nothing to do with me. He was on his own path to deciphering the world and this journey of life. Those pages of gibberish were his thoughts and ideas and a reflection of his tiny world of which I was not part. He had sprouted shoots of inquiry and imagination like a perennial shooting out leaves in spring or a seed potato sprouting roots or like the peas we had just sown would. It had happened naturally and I was so very proud of my first ever seedling.

Inspired by Harry's earlier suggestion, I took the children to the plot one afternoon later in the month for tea. We packed a hamper with a knob of butter, ham and bread and added to that a sharp knife, a chopping board, a heavy frying pan, my portable cooker and some matches. It was a schizophrenic sort of day with clouds gathering and thinning with each passing minute – not exactly picnic weather – and the wind bit at us as we stood to pick the last of the fist-sized cabbages. We pulled away the slug-eaten, bird-pecked outer leaves and I sliced the hearts roughly along with some garlic and ham.

I laid down my jacket as a picnic rug and Harry and Ott huddled under the hoods of their own coats. The wind was unkind and blew out match after match in my red-raw hands but eventually a flame took. I placed the butter in a frying pan over the flame and we watched it fizzle and bubble, dancing around the pan. Harry dropped in the garlic and then we all added a handful each of spring green cabbage and the ham and sat mesmerised as it frazzled and wilted in smoke and steam. Even Kit was hypnotised and ceased his relentless quest to clamber over everything in his line of sight.

We shivered a little in the wind and the children shrugged into their coats but the wait was a short one and I spooned the contents of the pan onto a plate, handed out the forks and waited for the verdict.

'It's really yummy,' Harry said between mouthfuls, butter dripping down his chin. Ottilie said nothing; she and Kit had abandoned the forks and were too engrossed in shoving fistfuls of cabbage into their mouths.

Plot to plate in under a minute. Now that, I thought smugly, was fresh food.

When they'd finished the greens they tore off chunks of bread to dunk in the frying pan, mopping up the juices. Suitably sated, Harry and Ott stood, wiped their hands on each other and ambled over to fiddle about with the mud kitchen while I paced up and down the Somme-scape with Kit on my hip configuring and reconfiguring my plan. I walked between the few brave tulips spearing through the ragged couch grass edges muttering a little madly, 'Leeks and garlic here so potatoes over there, lettuces and carrots . . . no, that wouldn't work. Potatoes and carrots there, lettuces here. Brassicas, three sisters and peas . . . oh and a sweet pea arch . . . yes that could go . . . here and another one there . . .'

I had taken a plot as a novice gardener because I wanted to make a difference to the household budget, to show my children where food came from, to learn how to grow, to eat well and honestly of course, to be bronzed and wear gingham. After the peripatetic life of a rootless freelance photojournalist I needed rootedness and grounding and to find some of Yeats' 'bee-loud glades' or evenings 'full of the linnet's wings'. I needed to find a home.

It hadn't been easy and I had grossly underestimated both the physical labour involved and the absolute desolation of crop failure. I had also underestimated the peace I found on the allotment; the steadying hand it had and the pause it delivered on every visit. When events seemed to spiral beyond comprehension I found a sense of stillness. I tell myself even now that I saved money by growing our own but I doubt the amount spent on seedlings and sticks was more economical than a trip to a supermarket. Nor did we ever wear gingham or get a beehive and the sun burned rather than bronzed us but the fact remains: we grew it. *We* grew it. And I felt proud of this.

Previous allotment holders had listed 'fun' as one of the main motivators for keeping a plot. I'd rather brushed this off as something one says with hindsight over something horrific like childbirth or going for an interminably long and cold run up a mountain. In a blizzard. The body and mind forget the trauma and you convince yourself you can do it again.

But pacing up and down I realised I was looking at my plot and the heirloom and heritage vegetables propagating as something to play with and deciding what should go where *was* a bit of a game. I was one up on the 'me' just starting out a year ago with my overly simplistic plan and naïve understanding of how things grew but I felt armed against the ravages of the forthcoming year – if a little nervous. What would Mother Nature and the weather bring this time?

I shifted Kit onto my other hip and renewed pacing. I would enjoy it more this time, I thought, not worry quite so much over planting out or potting on. I wouldn't agonise over pea supports or second-guess the slugs and nor would I overthink aphids. I had a box of seeds to work through and a greenhouse waiting to be filled with hopeful propagation and a promise of the warmer months to come. But looking at the dandelion seedlings as I paced I realised there was something else.

I used to think that gardening was all about committing to the future – a future made up of Eliot's 'time present and time past'. In the end it was the dandelions which made me appreciate that gardening was more than that. I like to think that they had grown from the fluffy balls of seeds Harry and Ott blew throughout the summer, counting the hours with each breath, letting time drift and spin and contract. Here were those hours and here were the jagged toothed leaves sprouting determinedly, pushing through the earth, the tick-tock march of time: one o'clock, two o'clock, three o'clock, they had laughed as the seeds rose and fell to the ground like memories.

The first digging, the first sowing, the first seedlings, the first peas, the potting on and planting out. The picnic lunches with Harry, the Thermoses of hot chocolate drunk in the miserly spring rain. The conscript potatoes, the pornographic carrots, the lonely wayward peas, the first harvests, the question of badgers, the extreme heat, the extreme cold, the dryness, the wetness, the contrails, the chaos, the reprieve, the release, the snow, the frost. The mud kitchen, the death and resurrection and re-resurrection of the brassicas, the rotten vegetables, the wretched slugs, the success and the failures. The first teeth, the first steps, the first words, the first days of school and the last days of infancy all spinning and whirring and disappearing in an ephemeral year. And it was all there at my feet and all around; the whole greater than the sum of all its parts.

I looked at the children – my own sweet seedlings – at the other end of the plot, filthy and feral already but happy and sated with what we'd grown. This was the past and this was the future, that's what I'd thought at the end of the summer as they blew time away with each puff. And here was the present; the still point of the turning world.

I love you, I love you, I love you.

> *Go, said the bird, for the leaves were full of children,*
> *Hidden excitedly, containing laughter.*
> *Go, go, go, said the bird: human kind*
> *Cannot bear very much reality.*
> *Time past and time future*
> *What might have been and that has been*
> *Point to one end, which is always present*

'Burnt Norton', TS Eliot, 1935

Endnotes

March

1 https://wrap.org.uk/media-centre/press-releases/uk-households-could-get-25-days-year-back-making-most-food-they-buy

2 For more information see Henry Dimbleby, *Ravenous* (Profile Books, 2022).

April

1 For more information see Adam Alexander, *The Seed Detective* (Chelsea Green, 2022).

2 Caroline Foley, *Of Cabbages and Kings*, p.105 (Frances Lincoln Limited Publishers, 2014).

May

1 Susan Campbell, *A History of Kitchen Gardening*, p.115 (Frances Lincoln Limited Publishers, 2005).

2 E. Griffin, 'Diets, Hunger and Living Standards During the

British Industrial Revolution', in Sally Coulthard, *The Barn*, p.66 (Head of Zeus, 2018).

3   Bee Wilson, *First Bite: How We Learn to Eat*, (Fourth Estate, 2015).

4   www.perseus.tufts.edu/hopper/
text?doc=Perseus:abo:phi,0978,001:18:30

5   Adam Alexander, *The Seed Detective*, 'A Broad Bean far from Home' (Chelsea Green, 2022).

June

1   For more information see Adam Alexander, *The Seed Detective*, 'Not Just for Hallowe'en' (Chelsea Green, 2022).

2   For more information see Adam Alexander, *The Seed Detective*, 'The Tale of Two Classy Beans' (Chelsea Green, 2022).

July

1   Adam Alexander, *The Seed Detective*, 'Of Caulis, Krambe and Braske' (Chelsea Green, 2022).

2   *Pliny the Elder, Natural History: A Selection*, p. 225 (Penguin, 2004).

3   Susan Campbell, *A History of Kitchen Gardening*, p.109 (Frances Lincoln Limited Publishers, 2005).

4   For more information see www.metoffice.gov.uk/research/
climate/understanding-climate/uk-and-global-extreme-events-
heatwaves

ENDNOTES

August

1   http://archive.spectator.co.uk/article/23rd-august-1919/7/speed-the-plough

2   Caroline Foley, *Of Cabbages and Kings*, p.167 (Frances Lincoln Limited Publishers, 2014).

3   Ibid, p.170.

September

1   Pliny the Elder, *Natural History: A Selection*, p.225 (Penguin, 2004).

2   www.gettyimages.co.uk/detail/news-photo/gardener-in-the-grounds-of-westminster-cathedral-watering-news-photo/106567894?phrase=the%20plot%20against%20harry&adppopup=true

3   Pliny the Elder, *Natural History: A Selection*, p.225 (Penguin, 2004).

4   https://academic.oup.com/jn/article/131/3/951S/4687053

October

1   For more information see Adam Alexander, *The Seed Detective*, 'Of Caulis, Krambe and Braske' (Chelsea Green, 2022).

2   For more information see Joseph Tainter, *The Collapse of Complex Societies* (Cambridge University Press, 1988).

3   Steve Poole, *The Allotment Chronicles*, p.189 (Silver Link Books, 2006).

4   As quoted in http://moseley-society.org.uk/wp-content/uploads/2016/08/Website-7-The-National-Allotment-Scene-1.pdf

5   www.perseus.tufts.edu/hopper/text?doc=Perseus:text:1999.02.0137:book=17:chapter=6&highlight=manure%2Chuman

November

1   Caroline Foley, *Of Cabbages and Kings*, p.201 ff (Frances Lincoln Limited Publishers, 2014).

December

1   www.nytimes.com/2021/03/12/realestate/gardening-monty-don-pandemic.html

2   https://www.washingtonpost.com/lifestyle/home/britains-gardeners-world-is-the-pandemic-escape-we-didnt-know-we-needed/2021/04/06/e29b66be-8b25-11eb-9423-04079921c915_story.html

3   www.mind.org.uk/news-campaigns/news/over-7-million-have-taken-up-gardening-since-the-pandemic-new-research-shows-spending-more-time-in-nature-has-boosted-nation-s-wellbeing/

January

1   Metoffice.gov.uk

2   www.preventionweb.net/news/floods-after-drought-devastate-
     sindhs-agriculture

3   www.perseus.tufts.edu/hopper/text?doc=Perseus%3A
     text%3A1999.02.0137%3Abook%3D24%3Achapter%3D93

4   https://agresearchmag.ars.usda.gov/1995/dec/tilling

5   https://gardenerspath.com/plants/vegetables/moon-phase-
     gardening/

6   www.scmp.com/news/people-culture/social-welfare/
     article/3173534/balcony-gardens-provide-food-security-and-
     stress

7   https://notesfrompoland.com/2020/06/24/poles-flock-to-
     allotments-during-pandemic-sending-prices-rocketing/

8   https://sciendo.com/pdf/10.2478/fhort-2022-0006

February

1   Susan Campbell, *A History of Kitchen Gardening*, p.114
     (Frances Lincoln Limited Publishers, 2005).

2   Rodney Legge, *Dorset America*, p.97 (Dorset Books, 2006).

3   www.apse.org.uk/apse/index.cfm/training/online-courses/
     managing-allotments/

4   https://worldpopulationreview.com/world-cities/london-
     population

Acknowledgements

The allotment, such that it is, and this book would not have come to fruition without considerable help and support from many, many people. Firstly, thank you to my parents, Sarah and Martin Snow, who provided much manure, a mattock, advice, spare seedlings and RHS magazines, to my brother Jonathan Snow for simultaneously introducing me to Susan Campbell's *Kitchen Gardening* and to bamboo lampshades and thank you to my sister, Minnie Vedral, for being a constant cheerleader and reminding me to 'just get it done'. Thank you to my mother-in-law Sabine Rider for seeds and unfathomable knowledge which she wears lightly.

A big thank you goes to Dr Ashley Jackson who knows a thing or two about vegetables and a little bit more about armed groups, to Crystal and Nico Goodden for guiding and encouraging this simpleton on all things growing and to Ian James for digging out maps and unearthing Victorian treasures. Thank you also to Sophie Mestchersky and Johnnie Wilkinson for introducing me to Frank and to Frank for introducing me to his potager and his potager for inspiring me to 'go long' on artichokes. Philip Norman from the Garden Museum delved into the archives and supplied a plethora of pamphlets and photographs at the drop of a hat while Philip Gomersall and Lauren Lawless from the National Allotment Society answered my endless questions. Thank you.

Thanks also to my perennially enthusiastic agent Roger Field and my inexhaustible editor Richard Milner. And thanks, of course, to Sergei who taught me how to grow leeks, broccoli and carrots and who I hope is now growing sweet peas in his homeland. Nathan Hodge deserves a big thank you for remotely translating when technology failed us.

Thank you to the other allotmenters, past and present, near and far: Mark Newton Clarke, Ellen Hughes, Terry and Sandra Deacon, Jenny and Clive Yendole, Ray Read, Sharon Palmer, Phil Bridger, Dalius Petrauskas, Bob and Pat Mackin, Will Gay and Conor Gallagher. And a further thank you to Tim Harris who knows a fair bit about broad beans.

Thank you to my children for showing me the present and finally to Jon who allowed me to dig with one hand and write with the other, who listened ad nauseum to some longish monologues about vegetable history and Enclosure Acts and who, most importantly, has emerged as an accomplished artist. His illustrations for this book and its cover are more charming and more accurate than any photograph ever could be and his talents seem to know no bounds. I couldn't have asked for a better or more patient artist to work with nor a kinder, more adventurous man with whom to work out this puzzle of life. I arose and went. And I'm so glad you came too.

Selected Bibliography

Akeroyd, Simon, *The RHS Allotment Handbook: The Expert Guide for Every Fruit and Veg Grower*, Mitchel Beazley, 2010

Alexander, Adam, *The Seed Detective: Uncovering the Secret Histories of Remarkable Vegetables*, Chelsea Green, 2022

Campbell, Susan, *A History of Kitchen Gardening*, Francis Lincoln, 2005

Coulthard, Sally, *The Barn: The Lives, Landscape and Lost Ways of an Old Yorkshire Farm*, Head of Zeus, 2021

Crouch, David and Ward, Colin, *The Allotment: Its Landscape and Culture*, Five Leaves Publications, 1997

Eliot, TS, *Four Quartets*, Faber and Faber, 2001

Farley, Paul and Symmons Roberts, Michael, *Edgelands: Journeys into England's True Wilderness*, Jonathan Cape, 2011

Foley, Caroline, *Of Cabbages and Kings: The History of Allotments*, Francis Lincoln, 2014

Fowler, Alys, *The Edible Garden: How to Have Your Garden and Eat It*, BBC Books, 2010

Harrison, John *Dig for Victory; Monthly Growing Guides and Commentary*, Allotment Garden Books, 2020

Hellyer, AGL, *Your Garden Week By Week*, Collingridge Books, 1936

Hodge, Geoff, *RHS Botany for Gardeners: The Art and Science of Gardening Explained & Explored*, Mitchel Beazley, 2013

Leendertz, Lia, *RHS Half Hour Allotment: Timely Tips for the Most Productive Plot Ever*, Francis Lincoln, 2006

Lively, Penelope, *Life in the Garden*, Fig Tree, 2017

Low, Valentine, *One Man and His Dig: Adventures of an Allotment Novice*, Simon & Schuster, 2008

Lowenfels, Jess and Lewis, Wayne, *Teaming with Microbes: The Organic Gardener's Guide to the Soil Food Web*, Timber Press, 2010

Middleton, CH, *Dig On for Victory: Mr. Middleton's All-Year-Round Gardening Guide*, Aurum Press Ltd, 2009

The Oxford Classical Dictionary, 3rd Edition, Oxford University Press, 1996

Pavord, Anna, *The Curious Gardener: A Year in the Garden*, Bloomsbury, 2011

Pliny the Elder, *Natural History: A Selection*, Penguin Classics, 2004

Poole, Steve, *The Allotment Chronicles: A Social History of Allotment Gardening*, Silver Link Books, 2006

Wilson, Bee, *First Bite: How We Learn to Eat*, Fourth Estate, 2015